HONESTY IS NO EXCUSE

THIN LIZZY ON RECORD

MARTIN POPOFF

HONESTY IS NO EXCUSE

THIN LIZZY ON RECORD

MARTIN POPOFF

WP
WYMER
PUBLISHING
Bedford, England

First published in 2024 by Wymer Publishing, Bedford, England
www.wymerpublishing.co.uk Tel: 01234 326691.
Wymer Publishing is a trading name of Wymer (UK) Ltd.

Copyright © 2024 Martin Popoff / Wymer Publishing.

Print edition (fully illustrated): **ISBN: 978-1-915246-52-3**

Edited by Agustin Garcia de Paredes.

The Author hereby asserts his rights to be identified
as the author of this work in accordance with sections
77 to 78 of the Copyright, Designs & Patents Act 1988.

All rights reserved. No part of this publication may be
reproduced or transmitted in any form or by any means,
electronic or mechanical, including photocopying, or any
information storage and retrieval system, without written
permission from the publisher.

This publication is sold subject to the condition that it shall not,
by way of trade or otherwise, be lent, re-sold, hired out or
otherwise circulated without the publisher's prior consent in any
form of binding or cover other than that in which it is published
and without a similar condition including this condition
being imposed on the subsequent purchaser.

Printed and bound in Great Britain by Halstan, Amersham, England.
A catalogue record for this book is available from the British Library.

Typeset/Design by Andy Bishop / Tusseheia Creative.
Cover design by Tusseheia Creative.
Front cover photo © Alan Perry Photography.

TABLE OF CONTENTS

Introduction	7
Thin Lizzy	11
Shades of a Blue Orphanage	31
Vagabonds of the Western World	55
Nightlife	75
Fighting	99
Jailbreak	121
Johnny the Fox	141
Bad Reputation	167
Black Rose	189
Chinatown	209
Renegade	229
Thunder and Lightning	255
Contributor Biographies	281
Special Thanks	285
About the Author	285
Complete Martin Popoff Bibliography	286

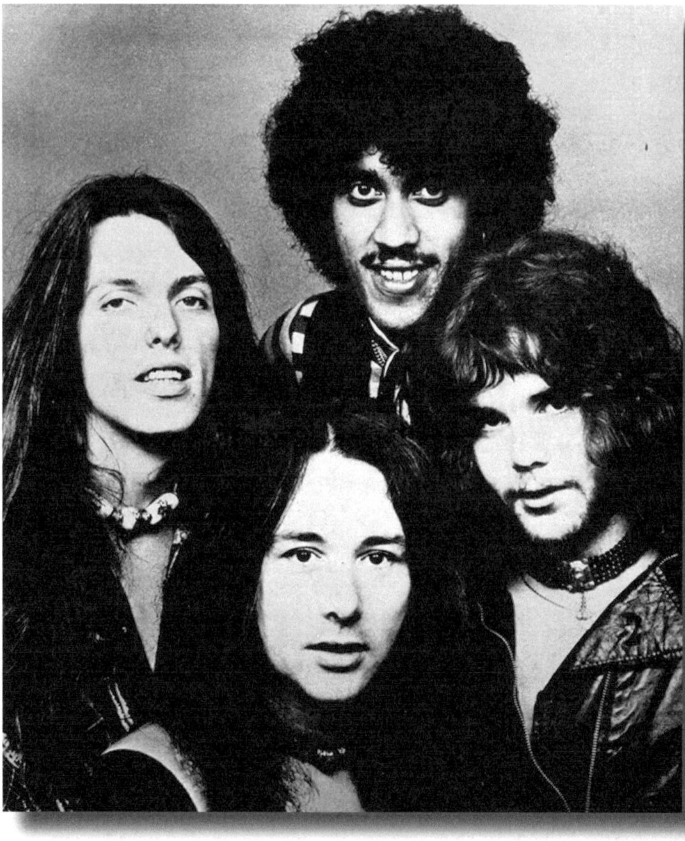

INTRODUCTION

Welcome one and all to another book in the "album by album" series, brought to you by the good folks at Wymer Publishing and of course myself, scribbler about a bunch of (dad) rock bands and actually a healthy little stack on this band, Thin Lizzy.

Not to get too complicated on you, but I had originally written and published a trilogy of books addressing the entire Thin Lizzy story, which then got busted down into two books issued by Wymer. Then we added to that a hardcover coffee table book called *Thin Lizzy: A Visual Biography*. Then the first one got renamed *Emerald*. Anyway, there you have three Thin Lizzy books through Wymer, and now a fourth, with *Honesty Is No Excuse: Thin Lizzy on Record* being completely fresh and utilitarian atop that previous stack. Why is that so? Well, for this present volume we've gathered one of our traditional panels of wise music swamis and talked through the entire studio album catalogue in detail, providing what I think are thorough and vigorous reviews of each album, something that isn't part of *Emerald* (the update and reissue of *From Dublin to Jailbreak*), *The Sun Goes Down* and *A Visual Biography*.

And I gotta tell ya, while listening to the great points my cabal of characters made about the band's classic dozen albums, I found myself constantly marvelling at just how much there was to say about Phil Lynott and this international band. In fact, regularly I found myself thinking, man, I hope that wherever he is, Phil is hearing how much effort is being put into sustaining his memory. I'm sure he would get a kick out of it, as would his dear mother, Philomena, also passed on, and just recently.

I also must add, I never imagined I could get excited about doing another book about Thin Lizzy, but inspired by how much fun it was doing *Dominance and Submission: The Blue Öyster Cult Canon*, it seemed plausible that I could learn new ways to appreciate these albums I know like the back of my hand. As with the BÖC book, fresh insights were in plentiful supply, along with, again, an appreciation for just how beloved this band is, and specifically how Phil Lynott and his character portraits and his flair with vocabulary and vocal phrasing are definitely not forgotten.

As a point of process, I became keenly aware that while these guys were talking in our Zoom calls together, I myself was inspired to come up with new insights that I hadn't known and therefore hadn't prattled on about in my previous Thin Lizzy books. It soon became clear that the natural place to include these new connections made would be right there in my moderator's space, in my question to my awesome interviewees. And soon enough the questions became less brief and perfunctory. They were now marbled with statements and opinions, and suddenly I was part of the conversation rather than just playing the role of interrogator. I feel like there was a fair bit of this already across the previous books in the series, but it is most prevalent here. And if I do any more of these, that might keep increasing.

You'll note as well, so as not to overlap with my other Thin Lizzy titles through Wymer, I've not provided any front matter in the chapters that might include quotes or timeline stuff, the latter of which anchors the coffee table book. Instead, I've gone with detailed album credits, something that in fact isn't a part of the previous three books.

So yeah, consider this a fairly expansive critical review of the catalogue, mostly by my panel but with myself included and chirping in. What I envision happening is that you will read along and be regularly putting a pause on it to go check out the song being discussed because something cool was said about the guitar solo in it or an odd lyric or in the case of "Baby Face," a stark and obvious error! This isn't fantasy, because I've already been told this by readers about previous books in the series, that the album at hand made a perfect soundtrack to the chapter on it, and that because of the dual exercise, they've now been apprised of a bunch of things they hadn't noticed before. And then of course the wider hope is that these guys have made you excited about Thin Lizzy all over again and that you've gained a greater appreciation for these albums you bought a long time ago and are playing them again after letting them lie dormant.

As for my own journey with Thin Lizzy, I honestly can't tell you where it begun; nor are there any fondly nostalgic stories. Something tells me that the first album I was conscious of as a new release was *Jailbreak*, in 1976, when I was 13 years old. I gradually caught up on the old stuff and then from that point forward I was there for every new release, even if there were only eight more years of records to go. I never saw the band live (until the time-warped John Sykes-fronted configuration), never interviewed Phil, but of course I've interviewed all the other guys. The fruits of that labour, again, can be seen in my other Wymer titles.

So to reiterate, what you're about to read is a book of pure and joyous critical review and analysis, and of celebration, really, in honour of these 12 records that endure, each projecting a persona (but a few of them sensibly groupable), and every one of them with unique sub-narratives and generative of just lots to talk about. So let's get yapping, shall we?

Martin Popoff
martinp@inforamp.net; martinpopoff.com

Honesty Is No Excuse: Thin Lizzy on Record

THIN LIZZY

April 30, 1971
Decca SKL 5082
Produced by Scott English
Engineered by Peter Rynston
Recorded at Decca Studios, London, UK
Personnel: Philip Lynott – vocals, bass, acoustic guitar, Eric Bell – lead guitar, 12-string guitar, Brian Downey – percussion, drums etc.

Side 1
1. "The Friendly Ranger at Clontarf Castle (Bell, Lynott) 2:57
2. "Honesty Is No Excuse" (Lynott) 3:34
3. "Diddy Levine (Lynott) 6:52
4. "Ray-Gun" (Bell) 2:58
5. "Look What the Wind Blew In" (Lynott) 3:16

Side 2
1. "Eire" (Lynott) 2:04
2. "Return of the Farmer's Son" (Lynott, Downey) 4:05
3. "Clifton Grange Hotel" (Lynott) 2:22
4. "Saga of the Ageing Orphan" (Lynott) 3:39
5. "Remembering" (Lynott) 5:57

TELEVISION CLUB
New Spotlight presents
TONIGHT ! TONIGHT !
IRELAND'S SHOWBIZ NITE OUT
STATUS QUO
ONLY DUBLIN APPEARANCE OF THIS SENSATIONAL CHART TOPPING ROCK GROUP
FREEDOM
PLUS FAREWELL DUBLIN APPEARANCE
THIN LIZZY
9.30—2
Adm. (Res.) 50p.
Full wine licence.
always Ireland's greatest nightout

Martin talks to John Alapick, Brian Balich and David Gallagher about *Thin Lizzy*.

Martin Popoff: All right, let's get this show on the road. Who is this new band, Thin Lizzy?

David Gallagher: Okay, well, Eric Bell leaves Them with Van Morrison, and we've got schoolfriends Phil and Brian who were in Orphanage, obviously a term that will come back later on. But they very much are a product of the time. You can hear them at the precipice of a new career, a baby band, and I think Thin Lizzy are going to take longer than most bands to establish who they are. And if this was ten years later, they might have been dropped before they had a chance to discover who they were.

Even with a hit single and a couple more minor hits, they couldn't sustain. It would take six albums before "The Boys Are Back in Town" would give them a run of things. So it's very much a band looking for a sound. They know what they like, they know they're a power trio. Well, they were a power quartet, if you will, at the very, very start, for one single. But we know that they've got their heavy rock influences, their very folky influences and that they've got a very unusual lineup.

One thing that's often mentioned about Thin Lizzy that I don't think is a big deal, is the racial thing with Phil. More important in Ireland, especially in 1971 is the divide of north and south. And Thin Lizzy smashed that. It didn't matter if you were Catholic or Protestant. It didn't matter if you were from the north or the south, you could be in the band. And that's much more important in 1971 in Ireland; that's the year of Bloody Sunday. That's when the British army were opening fire on innocent people in Belfast. So that's much more pertinent than Phil's racial identity. And I think that's why his Irish roots are much more important than his Afro-Caribbean roots would be to him lyrically.

Martin: Before we get to the debut album, what can you tell me about the single?

David: So the single is "The Farmer." And Phil starts off doing a very over-the-top US accent on "The Farmer." But it's nice to see that it starts off the whole Thin Lizzy catalogue with a little bit of spoken word, something that would stick with them, a very Phil Lynott thing to do. It's literally a rarity of a release because people kind of forget about these two songs. And they forget about these albums from the early years in general, or they're not bothered about them. People think they start with the twin guitar lineup. But something like 400 copies of the single were sold, so it's a rarity in every sense. And rare because it's the only recorded output of the band as a four-piece with a keyboard player.

It does sound like a lot of music from this very specific period, very early '70s, like they've stumbled under the spell of The Band, specifically, rootsy, Americana-influenced and not particularly establishing of their own identity. Clapton is probably the best example of this, namely someone who has ditched rock 'n' roll stardom and guitar hero syndrome for a rootsy sound. That very much feels like the environment they were stepping into.

"I Need You" on the B-side is a very strange track for Thin Lizzy. It's written by the producer John D'Ardis. It's a pure soul track, a kind of dance stomper. But even for 1970 when the single comes out, it sounds dated. It's bizarre. It doesn't seem like it should be a contemporary track for 1970; it sounds like 1963 or 1964. So it's a bit of a throwback idea. But it's interesting that as early as their debut single before they recorded an album, before they've got a deal with EMI, they are doing soul. And so maybe *Nightlife* isn't quite the outlier that people think it is, because it's part of their identity on this single, actually, more than rock is.

Brian Balich: Which continues on into the album. I don't think they quite know what they want to do. They'll go from folk to attempts at harder rock. It's a mixed bag, a band putting together an album that is perhaps too diverse. It feels like they were experimenting to see what stuck and if one style stuck, maybe in the future they would follow that path. If another style stuck, they'd do that. It's all over the place. There's a wide difference between these years, these first three records, and then *Nightlife* and then what came after. It's interesting, I never think to grab *Thin Lizzy* off the shelf all that often, but when I do, I'm like, "Why don't I listen to this more often?" (laughs).

Martin: John, what would be your general survey of the situation?

John Alapick: Well, as David alluded to, this was recorded at a time when your record companies would actually work with the artists and let them grow, let them mature, let them find their sound. And what results is that a lot of these bands' first few albums are a little adventurous, a little different than what would bring them success. And these early records can sometimes be more interesting than when a band has found their sound but then they don't grow, where the songwriting ability wanes. So Thin Lizzy are trying to find themselves. You've got Phil Lynott on bass guitar, acoustic guitar and vocals. You've got Brian Downey on drums and percussion and you've got Eric Bell on the guitar. Eric Bell would play on the first three albums, this one, *Shades of a Blue Orphanage* and *Vagabonds of the Western World* and these were all released originally on Decca.

Now I've read that *Thin Lizzy* was recorded on a shoestring budget, but from the CD copy I have, with bonus tracks, I'd say that it was very well-recorded. The mastering must have gone well because you can hear all the instruments on here very distinctly, which isn't always the case going forward. So yeah, it's 1971 and we get their most Irish-sounding album, I would think because Phil was writing about things that he had experienced in his life at this time. He's talking a lot about Ireland, a lot about family and what he was going through.

Martin: Is the sum total of the thing a little behind the times for 1971? To me it sounds like a 1969 album. Deep Purple *In Rock* is out. Sabbath's got two records out. This is like a folk boom album mixed with a blues boom album.

John: Yeah, I can agree with that, because by that point Hendrix was already gone and Eric Clapton had already left Cream. He was in *Derek and the Dominos* at this point. He made a Blind Faith album a little bit earlier than that. So he was already going for a more earthy sound. He was sounding more like The Band than the guitar god that he was in Cream, or even the bluesier stuff, like John Mayall's Bluesbreakers. But yes, I feel like Eric Bell was more old-school.

Martin: All right, let's dive into the tracks. If anything, the album starts off psychedelic.

John: Yes, our first song is "The Friendly Ranger at Clontarf Castle." Now when I first heard this, there's the bongos going in the background, you have two guitars so far back in the mix and Phil's doing the spoken word thing. You're thinking, "Where's he gonna go here?!" He's gone Gil Scott Heron on us, like The Last Poets. But then you're thinking, well, he's not angry. He's really whimsical. The things he's talking about, you're not going to get a "Home Is Where the Hatred Is" out of Lynott because Phil Lynott loves where he came from. But you're right, it's psychedelic, mixed with folk rock.

David: First of all, there's no concession made to commerciality with that unwieldy title. This will be a recurring theme with Thin Lizzy as well. We will not disguise any Irishness. We'll not do what a band like, say, U2 would do and say, "No, we're just citizens of the world." No, we're proud to be Irish. So we're getting a name like Clontarf Castle, which is not the catchiest thing to put on a single or a poster, and then with "Friendly Ranger" to boot, which is what most people call it.

We open with wah-wah-styled guitar pedals—Eric's guitar owes a lot to Peter Green—but with Irish drums and again, more spoken word from Phil. So it does set some of the scene for what would come from Lizzy. Phil's voice is on point from the outset. It's been said that in his earlier bands, Phil was always told, "You always sing out of key; you can't sing in tune" blah, blah blah. I don't think you hear that on any of these songs. Phil absolutely nails it from day one here.

There's a lovely lyric. There's going to be a lot of lovely lyrics throughout the catalogue, but there's a particularly funny lyric, I think, which is very Phil, very funny, where he says, "All the people's faces turned strawberry blonde," instead of saying red. And that's almost an in-joke for anybody in Ireland or Scotland, any of the Celtic countries, where they're almost ashamed of being redheads. So they don't refer to themselves as redheads—they're strawberry blonde, thank you very much. So your face turned strawberry blonde. I've never heard that anywhere else. But it's a fun little turn of phrase. That's always stood out to me. From the outset though, this track sets a tone of being rock but again informed by their own national identity. So that's very much what I take from "Friendly Ranger."

Martin: Next is "Honesty Is No Excuse," pretty much my favourite track here, and sort of a fully-formed Thin Lizzy ballad.

Brian: Yes, and if "The Friendly Ranger at Clontarf Castle" is unusual and unique and a little bit on the R&B side, "Honesty Is No Excuse" is more of a straight-up folk ballad kind of thing and I love it. Including the sonic space it's in. The production is pretty good. It's clear, with bits of orchestration. Sounds-wise, everything's in its place where you can hear it. Phil's vocals are nice and loud in the mix. It's not the production of the later records. It's definitely a first album kind of thing. You can tell they didn't spend as much time in the studio. Very clean electric guitar.

It's interesting, especially when someone like me goes back. Which is probably like a lot of people actually, especially in the United States, who experience these early albums after knowing the classic Thin Lizzy sound. It's a shock going from the heavier electric guitars to this record where it's quite clean-sounding. They get a little down and dirty on "Ray-Gun" and "Return of the Farmer's Son," but otherwise even the electric is utilised in a folky way. So it's interesting as a fan of the band to retroactively discover these records.

John: When I listen to this, I'm thinking Phil was listening to a lot of another great Irish songwriter named Van Morrison, specifically *Astral Weeks*. Now, this has Mellotron on it and *Astral Weeks* did not—it had real strings, real horns. But the way he's singing so expressively, it reminds me a lot of Van Morrison, who sang a lot about Ireland as well, not to mention love and sunshine and all that (laughs). Anyway, that's the vibe I get from this.

David: It wouldn't be 1971 if someone didn't find a Mellotron somewhere, would it? So we get a Mellotron added here. And retrospectively it does sound a bit like what you'd expect a 1971 track by a rock band to sound like. It's not particularly unique. It feels a bit like talent searching in vain for identity at this point. We know they'll find it, but they are almost "waiting to become." There's not a lot of dynamics going on here. It's not very up and down and loud and quiet. It's very much a vibe, one continual sound that goes right through it.

But Phil's voice is fantastic. It's got that aching and yearning quality. Brian's doing some frenetic drumming and there are lovely parts from Eric. The major difference in this three-piece here as opposed to later on is separation, standout parts, where it's like, "Right, you do your part now; you do your part next." Whereas we know Thin Lizzy will become synonymous with a wall-of-sound approach later on, where everybody's playing in tandem and there's twin guitar leads etc. This feels very much like the power trio approach of, "It's your turn, it's your turn, then it's my turn" kind of thing. The fade-out, because, again, being so one-note, meanders a little bit. I don't think you can find a climax to this song. You just need to fade it out somewhere. There's no dynamism to it. But it's got some vocal vamping from Phil where he's just making scatty noises. It must have reminded Eric of being in a band with Van Morrison, because that's pure Van Morrison there.

Martin: With "Diddy Levine," I feel like we're back in the sort of psychedelic jam band space of the opening track.

John: Yes, and this time it's a seven-minute epic, and similar to the kind of early epics you'd get from Rush back on the first album or Scorpions on *Lonesome Crow* or Judas Priest on *Rocka Rolla*, so all first albums, actually. It's like they're putting remnants of songs together; it's not fully cohesive. So while it's interesting, it starts out folk and then it goes into this main riff, which is pretty cool. It's a decent song. It's something that's fun to revisit as a longtime fan. But if you're just getting into Thin Lizzy, this isn't where you go. You go to the more universal albums like *Jailbreak*. But if you're in a contemplative Lizzy mood (laughs), you listen to this and you're like, oh, this is different. Yeah, it's not an anthem, that's for sure. They are still trying to find their sound.

Anyway, good playing, interesting parts, and in particular, I'd say that Brian Downey was already shining like the sun as a drummer, right from the first album—he was already great at this point. Now Eric Bell, when you have a trio, your guitar player has to have a very expressive sound; he really has to have his stuff down. He has to be a showstopper, so to speak. Eric Bell wasn't that guy, although he sure loves his wah-wah pedal. Plus he's down in the mix compared to Phil and Brian. I don't think that he ever found that distinctive sound, even after three albums, although he became a better player. Sure, there's some good guitar work on this album, but there's not solos that you remember.

David: "Diddy Levine" is the longest track by far on the record, and this is probably the first real instance of Phil trying to illustrate the poetic side, the storyteller, the man who's kissed the Blarney Stone, the Irish talker who you'd meet in a pub and can just sit and ramble all night long and tell you these old stories that may or may not have happened, but you don't really care because they're interesting anyway. But they do add some Americana in here, which I think is interesting. For example, one of the characters joins the US Marines later on in these lyrics. Whereas if he's trying to be Irish, they should be joining something like the Garda, the Irish police. So even as early as this, there's kind of one foot in each camp, which I like; it's this historical approach.

At the music end, there are heavy parts, so there's a dynamic quality to it, which, at seven minutes long, you'd hope so; you'd absolutely hope so. It was trimmed on some copies of the record earlier on and I think I can see why. I'm not sure the idea quite made it to seven minutes. But there's a lovely storytelling quality here, even if it's quite meandering. So you need to be in tune with that more meandering spirit. Because there isn't a brevity of lyric or music here. There is strong playing by everyone, but it's very jam-heavy. We don't think of Lizzy as a jam band. But early on, sure, sort of like Cream or Taste or insert power trio name here, jam was the sound. So it doesn't have the structure that we know they would find later on. But despite quibbles, pick out any thirty seconds of this and I'm going to enjoy it, and at seven minutes long, I don't want to be the guy who tells you what parts to take out, because I'm enjoying the whole ride.

Martin: Next is "Ray-Gun," where we get more of that wah-wah you were talking about, John.

John: Yes, this sounds like a song that was recorded for the Jimi Hendrix Experience's *Electric Ladyland* but didn't make the cut. Yeah, it's good for what it is, namely three minutes of Jimi Hendrix, but it's not really much of a song.

Brian: It's no surprise that Eric Bell wrote it. It's got that Hendrix kind of funk; Eric is a straight-up '60s guy, bluesy and funky like Clapton and Hendrix. His work in Thin Lizzy is pretty much blues rock, although quite regularly at the inventive end of blues rock.

David: In 1971, Hendrix has only been dead for a year. We're going to be seeing a lot of acts trying to take on Jimi's mantle. Robin Trower's the most obvious, but Robin Trower's guitar sound was closer to Hendrix than Eric Bell's. And you had Jimmy Dewar, who was a better singer, or a more pure singer for that style than Phil would be. I can't imagine Thin Lizzy being a pure Hendrix-like power trio, but this is definitely a track where they are. There's a very derivative wah-wah sound. It sounds like they're jamming on top of a Hendrix backing track.

We get a lyrical part here where Phil's inserting the question of a relationship with God, and that will be a thing he returns to occasionally. So again, there's lots of little crumbs along the journey here. We're seeing things that will be developed later on. So although Phil himself and the band aren't quite in a place where they know what they are—they probably couldn't have told you themselves—it's in there somewhere. They just need to focus; they need to reshuffle a little bit. But all the ideas are in embryo form here somewhere. There's a part where Phil screeches. Every so often he's doing these high screeches, which... was Prince listening to this? I don't know, but it's kind of bizarre to hear Phil doing some screeching rather than just hollering.

Martin: With "Look What the Wind Blew In," the main thing I'm think is, there's some talent here. It's a novel song construct.

John: Absolutely; that is like the first fully developed track on the album, and I'm like, okay, this is good. It's got a very good riff and the guitar playing really fits the song. Although it's not fully wired that way, this is closer to the Thin Lizzy we know and love starting with the *Fighting* album. It's more in that vein. It's the first very good song.

Brian: Yes, and it's where you find them on a bit more of a hard rock footing, and like John says, alluding a little bit to what comes later. I always liked that song. It's a dramatic, short piece, and complex, although I don't want to call it progressive.

David: I love the chorus on it—Phil's voice is fantastic on the chorus. But I also love the guitar interplay between the words in the chorus, that "Run, boy, run in your skin/Look what the wind just blew in" bit. It's the first time we hear the Lizzy sound. In the middle of the chorus, each time, that's the first time we get a fleeting moment of that dual guitar sound, which was done as overdubs here. But it's the first time we can hear that somebody has decided to do two guitar sounds but both playing the same melody at the same time. So that's another embryo, another brick in the wall, to jump into another band you've done multiple books on (laughs). So it's a solid rocker, fantastic playing from Eric and Brian, and like I say, Phil's voice is gorgeous on the chorus. All the tracks, really, they're very accomplished despite the fact that the guys are so young. But this track in particular is a blueprint for where this lineup could have gone if they had stayed together and decided to be a power trio.

Martin: I feel like there's a frantic, fearless Skid Row influence here as well.

David: Very much so. We know that a certain member of Skid Row was in and out and about the band and would always be in and about the band. So there again, it's power trio 101. They're not breaking any new ground here. They're just doing what they're doing and doing it particularly well. To be rather blunt, it's just good music.

Martin: With "Eire," we're back to the psychedelic; it's almost a Doors sound.

John: Yeah, it's brief, 2:07, and very moody and mellow. Doors is a good comparative, but I'm also hearing early Black Sabbath, like "Solitude" and "Planet Caravan." So it's psychedelic, but more in the dark "Solitude" vein. It's okay for what it is, but again they're still searching.

David: "Eire" is obviously a purely Celtic title, and its somewhat Celtic folk. This to me is the fork in the road. Thin Lizzy could have doubled down on the power trio thing and stuck with that. Here's one of the other directions that they could have taken. They could have been a folk-rock band. They could have been the Irish version of Strawbs, who were having massive hit success at this point. So it wouldn't have been a bad commercial idea. Some of Phil's best early lyrics are about as Celtic as you get. He's literally saying the name Ireland in Gaelic as the title, which is fantastic. As a Scot myself, and with an Irish father, it rings true. It doesn't feel like anybody's trying to fake it. It very much feels authentic. He's proud of his roots, and Northern roots more importantly. It's another good one, and it shows that Phil can do an epic without a seven-minute runtime—it's two minutes and change and that's all he needs. The guitars are nicely set back in the mix but Eric's lines are still very evocative, which gives you that bit of space and room to breathe.

Martin: "Return of the Farmer's Son" is both complicated and heavy, or it would be heavy with a different approach to the arrangement and production, I guess.

Brian: Yes, I'd say "Return of the Farmer's Son" is the heaviest track and my favourite on the record. That's the one where you could tell, even as early as this song, where the band would head. There's a direct lineage to "Emerald" and songs like that. It's got the big Celtic riffs and although it only has one guitar, it's got an implied double guitar kind of vibe to it because of the riff. I always loved that one. We had actually planned on doing a Thin Lizzy tribute album at some point, and although it never came together, this was one of the songs on my list. I'm surprised that no one's covered it yet. Definitely a heavier track with lots of potential in terms of making it sound modern.

John: This is a great track. Lyrically, it's all about family and steeped in Irish tradition. The vocals are very expressive, and I love Phil's ad-libs. That shows his growing confidence. Plus, Brian's playing some tremendous fills, and even the beat is sort of relentlessly busy and energetic. So yeah, the lyrics are Irish folk, but the music is riveting and heavy. And I agree with you guys: this could have been polished up and put on *Fighting* or *Jailbreak*.

David: "Return of the Farmer's Son." Farms. What's going on with farms? We start with "The Farmer," we've got "The Return of the Farmer's Son" and we're going to have a farmer on the EP. There's a lot of farming going on. So yeah, I'd say there's this rustic quality in early Thin Lizzy. The part where he's singing, "My father is a farmer," it's the exact vocal line of "Whiskey in the Jar." "First produced his pistol, then produced…" It's the exact vocal line. It's bizarre. It's so well-played, written well, it's evocative, it's sung powerfully.

But we know this is very much DNA and not the full body. But it does have some of Brian's coolest drumming. I think Brian comes out fully formed. I don't think he needs to become anything. Brian's already an absolute beast. And Eric as well and Phil as a bass player, but to lesser extent. Phil never thought he was a good bass player. And I think from day one, Phil was a good bass player, and this is his first album or first recording sessions as a bass player; he was a guitar player before. Also, I think this song is one of Eric's best showcases. Rhythmically and mood-wise, as Brian has pointed out, it points in the direction of "Emerald." So, I think with "Emerald," they're finding something stored in the back of their minds and saying, "We did something a bit like that once before. Let's now try and do it better."
Martin: What are your thoughts on "Clifton Grange Hotel?" Short

one, seems to utilise all the same obscure textures as some of the other full-volume songs.

John: I feel like the next couple of songs are not fully realised. "Clifton Grange Hotel" starts out like funky meets progressive, and then it gets laid-back. It sounds like something you'd listen to at two o'clock in the morning at a low volume while you're chilling out after a long night out. You don't want to play it too loud. But for chilling out, it's pretty decent (laughs).

Brian: I feel like Phil is still finding himself in a lot of ways. I enjoy this whole record and some of the songs are really unique. It's a good starting point. Songs like "Clifton Grange Hotel" and also "Remembering Part 1" are unusual. But it's a record of its time. Some of the songs have that rockin', bluesy kind of vibe and then some just lean towards a folky thing and "Clifton Grange Hotel" is more like quiet prog rock. Phil could have easily had a career doing folk. He's channelling Van Morrison, who's obviously a big influence on him, with the way he phrases things and in the tone of his voice. So, I think it's a good start. If you're a Thin Lizzy fan going into songs like this expecting to hear "The Boys Are Back in Town" or "Jailbreak" or "Emerald," you might be disappointed. But yeah, I think it's a record that over time holds up for what it is. And keep in mind it's a different band. This three-piece band is a totally different creature than what came later, although Downey and Lynott are obvious through-lines. Phil's voice carries through, but the style certainly changed quickly over the next few years.

David: "Clifton Grange Hotel" is the name of Phil's mother's—Philomena's—hotel, and it's very much a little slice of life about the place the band knew well because they crashed there and Philo would look after them every time they were in town. And it's a great example of Phil eulogizing his mother without being sappy. Because it doesn't go into too much of why he's eulogizing this hotel. If you didn't know it was Philomena's hotel, there's not much here that would tip his hand. But he's singing about "this refuge of mercy," so he's telling you how kind and decent his mother is, even though the place itself is a little strange. He's telling you about the oddball characters. He's doing a very Bruce Springsteen thing, showing you all these street characters. It's street poetry more than anything else.

Musically it's fine; there's some cool playing. But I think the biggest takeaway is that yeah, there's glorification of his mother, which is very Irish, very Celtic. Because Paul McCartney, from Irish stock of course, he does it himself with so many songs, about his mother. Bono does it in a million and one U2 songs about his mother. So it's very much a Celtic thing, to not be ashamed of being a mommy's boy, if you will.

Martin: There's blues in it, there's prog in it, there's even a bit of reggae in it.

David: Yes, but I think it's much more of a lyrical track than it is a musical track. And I think that's the dichotomy of Phil Lynott in general. There's the poet and the rocker—which one am I? It doesn't matter. I'm both. It doesn't matter and I'm never going to just be one or the other.

Martin: "Saga of the Ageing Orphan" is pretty much the most sober and conservatively folky song on the album, right?

Brian: Sure, but it's cool, the whole album is good. But you're right; this one is most relentlessly mellow. There's none of Eric's fiery guitar lines. It's all acoustic, and it sounds like Brian is playing with brushes.

John: Phil's singing is so quiet and personal. Like you say, this one is mellow the whole time. I don't think it fully develops. It's decent but I sense that Phil was still trying to find his way as a songwriter. This album has a little bit of, let's throw everything at the wall and see what sticks. Some of it sticks, but the folk stuff, it's not quite his thing. They pull it off, but he wasn't going to find tremendous success with it; put it that way.

David: "The Saga of the Ageing Orphan" is interesting because it sounds closer to traditional folk rock from the UK or America from that period. You can hear Cat Stevens "Father and Son" in some of it or elements of Laurel Canyon. Phil could have ditched anything Celtic about his identity and just doubled down on the troubadour nature. He could have tried his hand at being the tender vagabond, with a guitar slung over his shoulder, the wandering minstrel Donovan type. He's certainly got the velveteen, mournful tender voice for it, and there's a melancholic feel to what he does in this song. I think it's lovely and placed on the album intentionally so. Like John says, they're throwing everything at the wall and seeing what sticks. And even on this album, it's a new, unusual style.

Martin: All right, *Thin Lizzy* closes with another busy art rocker, using all the electric textures heard on the heaviest songs so far, right?

John: Yes, the last track, "Remembering"—sometimes it's called "Remembering Part 1"—this is a long, reflective epic with soft verses and then these louder choruses. The main theme really rocks hard. And again, Eric loves his wah-wah and he sounds really good stomping it. I love the counter bass lines that Phil is playing behind Eric's solo—I'm a big fan of that. I don't like when they just play a main theme the whole time; I want to hear something that's countering it. There's some nice jamming at the end. It's a good, boisterous, noisy song to end the album.

David: "Remembering" is probably the most consistently heavy track on the album, but it's still not heavy, heavy. And it's still not the Lizzy that people would traditionally think of, if they're more casual fans. It's solid, there's tasty solos, tempo changes about halfway through. It becomes a bit heavier again, which I think is needed because it's a six-minute runtime and I'm not sure it quite justifies all of that. But if the tempo didn't change, it really wouldn't. But they deliver another early piece of the puzzle. Lyrically it's a heartfelt reminiscence of a long-lost first love. You get to hear Phil the poet, but not being precious about tender emotions. He's being aware of, I'm a rocker. I can't do that kind of thing. It adds to that dichotomy of a breakup. Why is this being played in a more up-tempo way when the lyrics, if you just read them, would suggest that this should be a sad folk song? Well, some breakups go that way. You get angry. So, it's a more frenetic approach to what could have been a rather saccharin ballad.

Martin: Yeah, it's another one on here that's kind of written heavy but not recorded heavy. The guitars across this album are ever-present and squealing and squalling away but there's no sort of unadulterated distortion pedal to it.

David: Yeah, I think they've got all the elements here. It's like they've got a power trio but they're maybe recognizing that they can't quite incorporate what they want into that format so they dilute themselves. They're on record saying they weren't happy with the production. They weren't happy with how it was recorded. Being a young band, they didn't have the pull to be able to do anything much about it. So, I agree. I think there's a heavier album in here, but as it is, I like the outlier nature of it. Being so Celtic, it's very much up my alley. It's an album that you can imagine bands like Big Country listening to and being influenced by. It's very seminal in a completely underground way. Because it's Celtic rock that would go on to influence The Waterboys even, I believe. But it's not the Thin Lizzy who would influence 99% of the bands that they would actually influence. So, it's influential to a very niche audience.

Martin: All right, how about a few words on the interim *New Day* EP? For those who don't know, this is a four-song seven-inch that came out just two months after *Thin Lizzy*.

John: Yes, and it's been added to the copy of the debut album that I own, and it's on many of the reissues. It begins with "Dublin," which is folky and very personal in terms of Phil's lyric and vocal, which is very emotional. You've got those sparse, dreamy keyboard notes in there—on the one beat I believe—that give it a different feel.

David: The EP is literally just, "That didn't work guys; didn't really sell. Can you try and have a hit for us, please?" Back in the days when you were allowed these kinds of indulgences, it's like, "Okay, we'll give you an EP." What's going to be on it? More of the same, governor. So, we started side two of album one with "Eire" and now we're gonna start with "Dublin" itself. There's this quite haunting opening reverb guitar, but with a lovely acoustic being played as well. If Paul Simon was Irish, this is the kind of thing he'd have been doing.

But it does have a little bit of "America" by Simon and Garfunkel going through it. It's reminiscent of "Saga of the Ageing Orphan" on the album itself. And then there's the guitar being mixed down and Phil with the velvet throat and whatnot. But it's a love letter to the city. Lyrically it's obviously, I love the city, the city is sometimes bad for me, it keeps me, and I love it and it loves me but it lets me indulge in my worst excesses. And anybody who comes from an old ancient city like Dublin, like Glasgow, like London, like Paris, can identify with that notion. It feels ancient; people have been living here for a thousand years plus. And it keeps you and provides for you and you love it. You fall in love with your city. And "Dublin" is very much that. I just don't think this is what the record company would have been hoping for in terms of, "We did ask you for something a little bit different, guys." They're not really giving them anything different.

Martin: Okay, next is "Remembering Part II (New Day)" and actually this has a different sort of melodic framing to anything we've heard thus far, although it's the same frantic drumming and general performance and arrangement vibe.

John: Yes, cool tune. It's only two chords during the verses and then they add the extra chord in the chorus. The chorus is pretty cool, almost anthemic, and the soloing by Eric is quite lyrical. The song's a bit long for something that simple. If they'd cut it down to three minutes instead of 5:05, it might have worked better, because, again, it's only two chords and you add another chord in the chorus. I don't think you have to go on five minutes for that.

David: "Remembering Part II" I really like because it's pretty frenetic from start to finish. I like the "remembering" aspect to it because it could have just been called "New Day." Because they don't literally say remembering on either "Remembering" or "Remembering Part II." But I like that it's very much a different side of the relationship. So, the first one was the breakup; we're down in the dumps feeling sorry, feeling sad. This is very much, but there's always a tomorrow. So, it's very much literally a part two, a call to pick yourself up, dust yourself down and keep going. Very R&B vocal from Phil, or very Frankie Miller vocal from Phil, oddly enough, given that Frankie shows up on *Nightlife*.

Martin: The chorus bears a similarity to "Remembering" but the verse has this kind of interesting ragga riff to it, almost.

David: Yeah, musically, and lyrically it's telling a different story from the same starting point, which I think is quite an interesting way to do a part one and a part two. It's not just a reprise. It's very much the same situation, two different approaches.

Martin: Well, if the label asked for different, they certainly got it with

"Old Moon Madness," which is almost like Lizzy doing Mothers of Invention or Captain Beefheart. Or keeping it local, you might say the chaos aspect of it recalls Skid Row.

John: Yes, lots of music, but then the lyric borders on spoken word. You've got another good solo in here from Eric and very busy bass lines from Phil, which was really interesting to hear. This proves how underrated he was as a bass player.

David: "Old Moon Madness" is power trio 101 kind of stuff. I like Phil doing the rather over-the-top howls. Before Warren Zevon even met the werewolves of London, Phil is going "Ooohhhh," doing that stuff. Some lovely bass playing from Phil. I think you can hear on "Old Moon Madness" while even though Phil thought he was never adept on the bass; Ritchie Blackmore of all people wanted him to be in a new power trio with him. We all would love to have heard that, but we all know that would not have lasted more than an album or two before they probably tried to kill each other. But I think Phil underrates his own abilities. The bass playing here is tremendous. It's a little bit of a novelty song in terms of the howls and the actual story itself, but nobody phones it in. Nobody says that this is just a silly throwaway track for an EP so we'll make it a bit more fun because people like that kind of thing on an EP and it might just crossover if it's strange enough.

Martin: Okay, last track, and I guess performance-wise, it's more of this energetic, frantic playing that is becoming a trademark of the band.

John: Yes, and I would have put "Things Ain't Working Out Down on the Farm" as the last song on the first album. If you think about it, they're already growing as a band because between the time that the first album came out and this EP, you already see more cohesion. And again, they don't really sound like demos. The EP is recorded quite well. This song would have brought the first album up a half star for me because it's the first song that you can listen to and sing along to the chorus. It's like an anthem, a really cool track, and it has that same Irish theme to it. It might be the catchiest song from the first album cycle.

David: Yeah, and because there's this kind of West Coast USA vibe to it, it doesn't sound like anything else on the album or this EP. And Phil does more spoken word parts that then would lead into some more singing. Again, they're throwing stuff against the wall. Does it stick? No, because they would never do anything like it again. But at the same time, I'm glad they did. We're back to the farm, and it turns out things ain't workin' out down at the farm this time. And the playing here, phenomenal stuff. Downey is just a beast.

But when I think of this track, I think of one thing and one thing only. And that is Phil's bizarre pronunciation that no one in Ireland has ever used. He says things ain't working "oueeettt." Nobody has ever pronounced the word "out" like that: "Things ain't working oueeettt down at the farm." No, he's doing this bizarre thing, almost just to add a little fun in the middle of a strange track, this strange pronunciation. And he's really drawing attention to it by holding it for so long as well.

It should be a fun sing-along and a fun rocker, and it is, but lyrically it's very dark. There's a whole section where it appears to be about male rape, where he's at the farm and he's being molested and he's having to pretend that he's enjoying it. It's not the kind of thing you would imagine if you'd just heard the musical backing track, that that's what the song would be about at all.

Again, it's just another song thrown against the wall—will it stick? No. But I do love that an old Irish folk song is what would ultimately break them when they're trying everything bizarre and new and odd. Ultimately, they'd have to reach back into their own country's past to find where the future lies. That's very Thin Lizzy.

It shows how little influence that the band would have that they would be able to go on to Funky Junction where Thin Lizzy become Deep Purple impersonators. Now Elton John started his career doing covers of American music, but nobody knew who Elton John was at that point, so that was fine. And he was doing a compilation album. I don't know if you had this thing over there. But a compilation album would be say £4. But you can get the £3 version where it would just have sound-alikes. It was a bizarre phenomenon. And Elton John was one of the musicians that started out recording that way.

And then Lizzy were able to do that, even though they'd already been Thin Lizzy and already recorded an album and an EP. They're given the chance to become one of those low-budget recording acts, doing a Deep Purple tribute album. They were allowed to do it as a complete band. Phil didn't think he could replicate Ian Gillan's vocals and that's the only reason he's not singing on it. So, it's not like they were trying to disguise their involvement. He just didn't think he could do the vocals. So that *Thin Lizzy* album and the EP had such little influence and sold so little that they could be a Deep Purple tribute band for a while, and nobody would have noticed.

But yeah, *New Day* is a lovely little EP. I think it's terrific stuff. I like the album. I like the EP. I can see why people want to skip them. I can see why they're treated like Deep Purple Mk 1. But I think wrongly, because Phil, Eric and Brian, they've got some fantastic stuff here. Yeah, it's not the interplay that we're gonna get later, but I still think it's good music. And I think the lists that predictably put the first two albums rock bottom… no, I don't really see that myself. It's almost become shared wisdom that that's the case, but no, I'm not really having that, to be honest.

SHADES OF A BLUE ORPHANAGE

March 10, 1972
Decca TXS 108
Produced by Nick Tauber
Engineered by Louie Austin
Recorded at De Lane Lea Music Centre, Wembley, London, UK
Personnel: Philip Lynott – bass, acoustic guitars, vocals, Eric Bell – lead guitar, acoustic guitar, Brian Downey – drums, percussion
Key additional personnel: Clodagh Simonds – harpsichord, Mellotron

Side 1
1. "The Rise and Dear Demise of the Funky Nomadic Tribes" (Lynott, Bell, Downey) 6:52
2. "Buffalo Gal" (Lynott) 5:19
3. "I Don't Want to Forget How to Jive" (Lynott) 1:43
4. "Sarah" (Lynott) 2:51
5. "Brought Down" (Lynott) 4:08

Honesty Is No Excuse: Thin Lizzy on Record

Side 2
1. "Baby Face" (Lynott) 3:18
2. "Chatting Today" (Lynott) 4:08
3. "Call the Police" (Lynott) 3:28
4. "Shades of a Blue Orphanage" 6:47

Honesty Is No Excuse: Thin Lizzy on Record

Martin talks to Brian Balich, Tim Durling, Peter Jones and Steven Reid about *Shades of a Blue Orphanage*.

Martin Popoff: How has Thin Lizzy changed for their second album?

Brian Balich: Well, *Shades of a Blue Orphanage* is considered part of a pair with the debut, even though there are three with Eric Bell, right? Even though it's my least favourite Thin Lizzy record, it's still something I like better than a lot of other records that I have and love. There's some really weird stuff where it's like, I don't know what they were thinking. Talk about being all over the map. They really don't know where they fit in the rock landscape. Hard rock, folk—where do they fit? I don't think you would have heard any of that stuff on AM radio back in the day—it's too Irish-sounding to make it on American radio. Maybe if "Borderline" was that old, they might have competed with The Eagles, but I don't see anything like that on those old records. I'm not surprised that "Whiskey in the Jar," even though it's a cover, wasn't a big hit over here. And in addition to these records being all over the map, it's a case of who are you appealing to? You're not going to appeal to the soft rock fans, but you're not gonna appeal to the Sabbath and Deep Purple fans either, although you might appeal to Zeppelin fans. It falls in between too many cracks and it just sounds of its time. Nor does the production hold up very well.

Steven Reid: It certainly follows on from the debut. The style is similar; we're still looking more at folk and blues than hard rock. Production-wise, raw would be a kind way of putting it. I wouldn't suggest that it's particularly tidy around the edges; it almost feels like a band kind of captured live, warts and all, and maybe a little too much in places. But you do wonder sometimes if it had been a really powerful, big, shining production on this, I'm not convinced that would have worked either. It's an intimate album that calls for an intimate feel. It's melancholy, which occurs regularly nearly all the way through the Lizzy catalogue; that's a word that I would use on a regular basis. Even sometimes when they've been heavy, this band is melancholy.

Martin: In a general sense, before we get into the songs, it almost seems like they make their first album and they don't learn any lessons from it. They almost double down and get even more obscure in a way, right? It's a bit like Rush moving from *Fly by Night* into *Caress of Steel*. It's like, well, you're actually getting *less* commercial here.

Steven: Yes, and it's maybe also an element of its time, because I think that once we moved into the mid-'70s, especially into the '80s, not just for Lizzy, but in general, bands had a plan, or a producer had a plan. We're going to make an album that sounds like *this*. In fact, as we move onto the third album, Lizzy were also somewhat doing that, so they weren't immune.

Tim Durling: I have no idea what kind of band they were trying to be, Martin, and I don't know who this album was made for. It's a puzzler. It's so varied. And I don't hear anything on this that's overtly commercial or that radio might have latched onto. But it's a fascinating listen, and I have to say that going back into this catalogue, when you go way back into the early '70s, you're always thinking, is this just going to sound completely out of date? Frozen in time like a late '60s holdover? And for the most part, I don't think so. For the most part, it sounds like Thin Lizzy minus the quote unquote heaviness.

Peter Jones: Yeah, I agree with Tim. It's got some elements here. This is a band in its infancy, Martin. Unlike some of the other bands we've talked about, they didn't come out of the gate almost fully developed, like a Boston or Van Halen or Guns N' Roses. They took a while to find the sound that became them and their true stylistic delivery. But *Shades of a Blue Orphanage* is important as a step of maturation. Like I say, it's got a lot of elements but across a wide range, and some of them work, some of them don't work. And it's important not only to discover what does work, but what doesn't, and some of the things become elements that you take with you, and the other ones, you kind of drop them off and maybe don't revisit them again over your career.

Look, it's 1972, so the album sounds like 1972. It's got very dry and non-resonant drums when it comes to the toms. They sound very muddy a lot of times, so no resonance to the heads and things like that. And they're still a trio at this point, which contributes to a thinner sound than what we would be used to on later records. This is also because Eric Bell predominantly was a Stratocaster player. Strats are glorious instruments, but in a trio setting, if they're not heavily distorted or enhanced with that kind of sound, the band can sound a little thin. So that's part of the tone here. Eric Bell's a very solid player, and I think he gets overlooked for his contributions, but I see him more in the style of a Nile Rodgers than I do a Gorham or Robertson, a more chordal type of guy, not that flashy. Some good riffs, but it's much more of the chicka-chicka kind of thing than it is riff-playing, the heavy stuff.

There's some tight unison moments that we can go over as we look at each song here, and that is an element that they hold onto. Downey firmly establishes himself as one of the era's great drummers. And like I say, many of the ingredients that make up their golden period are present in little bits and pieces, but they just haven't found the right recipe yet to put it all together. It's not cohesive from top to bottom.

Martin: What does the album cover do for you?

Tim: Well, I'm assuming it's supposed to represent the band, because they've got the corresponding band shot on the back of it. By the way, my copy is a 2007 reissue, which has as many bonus songs as are on the album proper. I also would like to say that to this day, *Shades* is quite obscure, because as someone that collects various formats of my favourite albums, if I go on our old trusty Discogs, there are no cassettes listed. There are no eight-tracks listed. So there can't be too many of those floating around. There's no reason to think that it wouldn't have existed in most formats. But that just speaks to the relative obscurity of this album, even after all these years. All you see are different vinyl versions and a lot of CD reissues. So I'm gonna guess this album didn't exactly set any charts on fire in 1972.

Peter: The cover is interesting but kind of bland. The logo is okay. I guess the title gives a nod to a couple pre-Thin Lizzy bands but it's awkward.

Steven: I always looked at this album cover and thought, I don't like that. It was the last Thin Lizzy album I ever bought, purely and simply because it looks dowdy. You don't look at it and go, do you know what? I'm in for a fun time tonight! I know that there's a riff on previous band names and that's brought together here, so there's a nice idea. But then when you put that title with the three poor little lads on the front, that couldn't look any less happy if their lives depended on it. It's a bit on-the-nose, isn't it? It's just like, I was hoping for a nice Friday night. Yeah, I'm not sure this album is going to deliver a nice Friday night. It's a better album than that, but already it's on the backfoot even before you would have put the slab of vinyl on your record deck. Already you're going, oh, this is depressing stuff.

Martin: Well, let's see how that plays out. What do you guys think of the opening track, "The Rise and Dear Demise of the Funky Nomadic Tribes?"

Brian: I really like it. Long-winded title, poetic, and it's proggy and busy like some of the first album. Don't forget, Phil is into actual poetry as well.

Tim: Yeah, right away we're getting a song title that you can't confuse with any other band. Right off, the album is starting out uncompromisingly, with a long title and a long song, at 7:09. The drumbeat at the beginning immediately gets your attention. Seems like there's an odd timing to the riff. I'm not sure it's outside of four/four or if it's just that the riff is playing against the drums. It's extremely rhythmic but it sounds like Thin Lizzy. And they do that riff in different keys throughout the song. It's fascinating. It's kind of impenetrable as far as what the lyric is actually about, but it's a fun listen because you get the idea that these guys were doing exactly what they wanted to do and no A&R person was breathing down their necks saying we need a hit single to kick this album off. Because this is not it.

Martin: What '60s influences might you be hearing?

Tim: Given the fact that they are a trio at this point, probably Cream. I don't necessarily hear The Beatles, which is odd, because you usually do. I don't really hear any Stones. Possibly The Who, due to the lack or at least paucity of rhythm guitar. You've basically got bass, drums, vocals and guitar, but Eric plays licks as much has he holds down the fort with proper rhythm or riffs. And the thing about this band is I'm sure that there are influences that someone like me, who grew up and lives in Canada, are never going to identify because they're so intrinsically Irish.

Peter: With "Rise and Dear Demise," right at the beginning we have a tribal drum intro from Brian, which is something that's revisited over their next few albums. It's got a nice, solid riff from Eric Bell and strong bass work from Phil. It's got a lot of call-and-response, which is a traditional songwriting style, here between the band and the drums. It's funky, which is also in the title. But Phil has always had a lot of that element in him. And Brian's playing lends itself to that kind of writing. He delivers a tight, quick 16th note high-hat groove. As Phil says, "Got to keep a' movin on," so there's an appropriately propulsive feel. It's got a lot of individual lines but then they use this ascending line. That's a trademark they would hold onto; that's something you hear in the section right before the solos in "Jailbreak." It's something they started here, because I don't hear it on the debut. So it's an interesting track, but kind of long for an opener.

Martin: Peter, could you explain a little more what you meant when you said non-resonant tom heads?

Peter: A lot of times the bottom heads weren't even on the toms, or if they were, they were heavily taped or muted. The running joke was that they always had tampons and duct tape on them. You'd hit it and you could easily put a microphone on a table and get almost the same sound. But the snare and bass drum, even back in the early '70s, and even the '60s seemed to come out okay, if you recorded them properly. But toms were always hit or miss.

Steven: "The Rise and Dear Demise of the Funky Nomadic Tribes"—isn't that a great song title? It's absolutely brilliant. Tells you nothing about what to expect. And that in itself is the message, I feel, across the whole album. But the opening track is a great example of just picking ideas and putting them together and let's see if it works. Do you think all these ideas stick together, do they work, do they flow? Not really, not always. It's bluesy, there's some drum thunder and bits of Cream. You get that kind of proto-rock riffing.

Martin: Skid Row as well, right?

Steven: Yeah, absolutely. Which makes a lot of sense, to be fair. But there are also little nods at this stage toward what's going to come. This is one of maybe two songs on the album where you get that classic, rhythmical Lynott vocal. "Got to keep a' movin'/Got to keep a' movin' on." That's a signpost of, "I've got an idea. This is maybe a better way to present myself." Unfortunately, we don't necessarily get that right across the whole album.

Martin: I feel like "Buffalo Gal" is the first one of the band's fully-formed cowboy ballads.

Steven: It's got a real charm; I think that's fair to suggest. Phil's already telling really nice stories. You've got characters, there's little snapshots of kind of life and opportunities lost, love squandered, frittering away things that offer some hope. It's very Phil, isn't it? I like a lot of Eric Bell's guitar. There's a lot of crying guitar work here. And I've got a lot of admiration for Brian Downey; he's one of my favourite drummers. He's not spoken about enough as a great drummer, because he plays for the song. He's busy here, but he doesn't seem to intrude on what is a really gentle groove, a melancholy mood. He's able to add little flicks and other restrained drum ideas that don't detract. He supports Phil's sense of longing and loss, even though he's busy.

I'm not sold on that repeated bit of "Buffalo buffalo buffalo buffalo." It seems to offer a path that the song resists going down. It feels like an idea that isn't really fleshed-out and doesn't necessarily belong to the rest of it. But it's there most of the time on and off throughout that song and I find it a distraction. It starts up again and it's like, hmm, don't do that. Please don't do that. You could have trimmed the song a bit, but for something that is quite restrained, it's still edgy.

Tim: "Buffalo Gal" is strangely hooky, but mostly because it's got the "Buffalo buffalo buffalo" that gets in your head whether you want it to or not. Yeah, I have no idea exactly what kind of parallels Phil was trying to draw with this song. I did notice that there's a reference to The Friendly Ranger, who we get on the first song of the first album. His publishing company was Pippin The Friendly Ranger, and Pippin was his cat. But the lyric is inscrutable.

Peter: It's an unsettled song. The riff doesn't seem to sit well. It's not proggy, but it just doesn't feel like it's where it's supposed to be, like it's missing a section. Once the chorus comes in, it sits better. But each time it returns to the main riff in the verse section, it just feels unsettled. There's good background playing from Eric, but it's buried in the mix. One of the inconsistencies with this record is how from track to track the instruments are laid out and bounced between themselves. We see that on a lot of records, where track to track it's not consistent. There's something missing that is needed there to hold this song together. And then it lingers on a bit and it kind of doesn't go anywhere compositionally, at least to my ears.

Martin: Next is "I Don't Want to Forget How to Jive," which is in a style not remotely addressed on the first album or EP.

Brian: Yes, it's a straight-up Elvis-style rockabilly, nothing like we've heard on the first record or anything after, although we know Phil pays tribute to Elvis here and there, including "King's Call" on *Solo in Soho*. Plus there's Elvis in Phil's vocal.

Martin: Of course there's parallels to "Crazy Little Thing Called Love" by Queen. And when you bring up rockabilly in a British context, you also have to mention skiffle.

Brian: For sure. It seems out of place, especially where it is on the record, track three. It's such a weird diversion in the middle of side one—right there. Again, this is a case of throwing things against the wall and seeing what sticks.

Steven: It's just an Elvis-inspired rock 'n' roll standard, isn't it? To me, it feels longer than the sub-two minutes that it is. You listen to it and you go, it has to be longer than that. But there's nothing really going on. There's no real kind of adventure about it or pushing the boundaries. Even the lyrics. Phil wants to keep his woman, but he doesn't want to be tied to his woman. And the jive is used as a pretty obvious way of expressing that. Considering what a poet Phil could be, ultimately, it's a song that didn't really need to be there. It doesn't add much. For an album that lacks flow or cohesion, it's a throwaway moment. A rockabilly song feels a bit disingenuous.

Tim: Like Brian says, this is Phil's love of Elvis and it's even in the echoed treatment on the vocal. It's a fun exercise. It's a short little song, about right at 1:56. Because a lot of those early '50s rock 'n' roll songs tapped out before you hit two minutes. Phil was such a big Elvis Presley fan. This was just a chance to put a little echo on that vocal mic and have some fun.

Peter: Clearly, we hear about Elvis later on *Black Rose*, especially on the fade-out, which is a lovely little tribute that sometimes people don't stick around long enough to hear. But yeah, nice riff, nice chord changes, plus some old-school piano. It might have been positioned better as a closer, almost an afterthought. But as a standalone composition, I don't really see that it contributes much. And this was a style that they didn't revisit.

Martin: Speaking of piano, that's actually central to "Sarah."

Peter: Yes, and not to be confused with the "Sarah" on *Black Rose*, which is actually called "My Sarah" on early US pressings of it. It's a gentle piano ballad, with good sympathetic vocals. Phil is sometimes not given the credit for being able to vocalise these non-heavy songs. He's got an emotive voice and can deliver an emotional lyric, an emotional sentiment. It's just a quiet track and one of the real gems here. The accompaniment that Eric provides underneath is very subtle. There's no distortion or anything like that and his playing really suits the track. It's a good listen; I don't have a problem with it.

Steven: A beautiful ode to Phil's grandmother. It's a case of beautiful intentions, but it's maybe a little overt in its execution. I wouldn't say it's twee—that would be unkind. It's much more balanced than that. But it's maybe a bit too on-the-nose, a little too heartfelt in actual fact, although that's undoubtedly the intention. Like I say, "I Don't Want to Forget How to Jive" feels disingenuous to me. "Sarah," on the other hand, feels too genuine. It's almost too *not* raw. It's just, "This is who I am; this is how I feel." And it's odd going from one to the next. It's a jarring combination, between the two, a bit of a struggle.

Tim: So this is a quiet piano ballad but it's not overtly commercial. Again, it's funny that Decca would be hearing this and keep on giving Thin Lizzy a chance to make more records that aren't particularly appealing to anyone. At the time, you don't know they're going to put out *Jailbreak* and have hits for years hence. But I admire the fact that they're just so uncompromising and doing what they want to do, even if they don't know what they want to do at this point.

Martin: As far as I'm concerned, "Brought Down" is another early-days, fully-matured, desperado ballad from the band, and my favourite song on the album.

Brian: Yes, we go from "Sarah," which is a cool ballad, touchingly written for his grandmother, to "Brought Down" which is even better. It's another one of those that they would revive and give some overdubs years later. And from that rendition you can see how it could have potentially fit with the newer material. And I like the Spanish kind of flamenco guitar thing you get with both "Chatting Today" and "Brought Down." It'd be interesting to hear some boots of these songs, what they'd sound like ramped-up in concert, because I think it would play differently.

Tim: I like the way this one builds in intensity, in volume. It's in a kind of bizarre waltz time, with parts that go beyond three/four as well, specifically that break and also the chorus, for that matter. That break, which starts at 2:05, actually reminds me of ZZ Top's "Master of Sparks." And I gotta say, even on what is a type of pop ballad, Brian Downey's drumming keeps things at an interesting level, because his patterns are more complicated than they sound and yet they're hooky within whatever song they're in. You just kind of latch onto them. And I think that's the strength of the group. I agree with that sort of common belief that he was the best musician in the band from the beginning. I think he was just a naturally gifted drummer.

Peter: Acoustic guitar with Phil singing, kind of folky. Some of these elements of his are not necessarily Celtic. Soon the band comes in and the intensity picks up and we get this nice, driving chorus. Brian is playing a strong and driving beat with lots of snare fills and tom fills. He's actually quite busy for a song like this. And that's the fun thing about Brian. He can find his spots where you would think it wouldn't fit or be too much, but it always seems to work.

To me, this is one of the first songs where you really hear some of the key elements that would solidify in their classic material. There's even some solid double guitar tracking plus more distortion, although in this case it's probably more overdrive, because guys weren't using as much distortion back then, just more overdrive. It almost has an early Queen vibe to it. So yeah, the elements are there but it's still not entirely working. You've tasted the sauce, but it's not there yet. But you listen to that heavy riff, and I imagine that with two guitars and a little more power and distortion, this track could easily have been something from the more classic era.

Steven: There's a little bit of Cream in "Brought Down," I would suggest, certainly in the instrumental sections. It's a nice ballad but it doesn't rest on its laurels. There's some real rock guitar in there and some great drum rolls too. I like the way that those sections create tension. It actually makes the more mellow sections much more intense. Phil, to me, he's kind of put himself in the shoes of an older character here, torn by previous girlfriends and an unwanted pregnancy, it would appear, and those events now touch on everything that comes after. That's life shaped by one event, realistically, and I suppose there's a semi-autobiographical element in that, although it's removed from his circumstance. There are parallels to be drawn.

But what I like more about it is that Phil is only in his early 20s here, and he seems able to put himself into these situations and give you these kinds of stories and almost become the character—you just believe him. You're there for every word that he's saying. There are such desperate situations across some of these albums, from really aggressive stuff to really heartfelt stuff, and for the most part you listen to it and think, yeah, he means every word of this. And that's quite a rare skill, and one of the reasons he's so endearing.

Martin: How much Van Morrison is there in early Thin Lizzy?

Steven: In the early days? I think there's enough to merit the accusations; maybe not quite accusations, but certainly to merit the similarities that are highlighted there. It's natural at this stage for them to be influenced, and especially by an influence that's so close to home. You do hear it, but there's enough else going on across the first two albums especially, and maybe even into albums three and four, to make you wonder if it's really just a band pulling from a variety of influences, not sure of where to go and how to turn. And they do maybe rely a bit too closely on some of those.

Martin: And any perceived Van Morrison influence isn't particularly more pronounced on the formative albums. It's just lightly sprinkled throughout.

Steven: Yeah, I find, especially at this stage, it's maybe a guitar line here and there. It's not like the whole melody line through a song. I've never listened to a single Thin Lizzy song and thought, Van Morrison should be singing this. But you do definitely think, oh, maybe I hear him on that. At this stage, it's more in the odd song structure than it is actually lifting this section and putting it there. Also in the way the guitars talk to the bass. But I'm okay with it. It's an influence, and young bands are going to do that kind of thing.

Martin: "Baby Face" is yet another in a long line of heavier songs by the band that are fussy, kinda tricky. And it's another heavy one with a non-heavy title!

Tim: Yeah (laughs), and it's probably the heaviest song on the album, and for 1972 the lyrics are kind of suggestive. Phil was one of those musicians that used the studio as an instrument, with the repeated lines, the echoed lines. There's a lot of that here and he would do that in the future. This album was recorded at De Lane Lea Studios, which is where Queen did some of their first album. So I think that he was very aware of the fact that you can do these things in the studio. Not trickery per sé, but just things to catch the ear. He would do that a lot in Thin Lizzy and this is an early example of that. Surprisingly heavy for 1972, and given a heavier production, "Baby Face" would stand toe-to-toe with the heaviest of the era. You kind of wish that you could reach over to Eric Bell's amp and turn that gain up a little bit.

Brian: Without being on the inside there, it feels like there would have to have been some push and pull between Phil and Eric, even though Phil was the main writer, just in terms of where the band was going musically, between the heavier things and the folky singer-songwriter stuff. I love Phil's voice on this record. Even early on, his voice is well-developed and has a lot of the things that we like about it. And lyrically he's got his storytelling vibe in place over the first couple records.

But *Shades of a Blue Orphanage* is a step back from the first one in some ways. In fact some of those tracks that didn't make the record, like "Black Boys on the Corner" would have made the album stronger.

That's one of their heaviest songs from back then too, heavier than "Baby Face." As it stands, people wouldn't know what to make of this record, what they're reaching for. It's diverse, but in a different way than a Led Zeppelin record is diverse and would feel more cohesive. This feels all over the map. I hate to keep coming back to it, but it feels like a band still trying to decide where they're gonna go. I guess I'm implying Eric would want to be heavier but maybe also bluesier and funkier. "Call the Police" isn't necessarily funky, but it still has a good groove to it, as does "Baby Face." Over the first couple of records, there are places where it reminds me of Funkadelic, when Funkadelic would dip its toes into rock.

Martin: That Ritchie Blackmore, Ian Paice and Phil Lynott power trio we talked about… that was going to be called Babyface.

Steven: Yeah, and it would be lovely if there was a link to this song, but as far as I know, that was a one-off jam. But yes, it seems to have gone by the name Babyface. The romantic part of me would love to listen to this song and hear that, or have some sort of link to it. It's just not there. Really, my main issue with the song is when you're really sitting down to listen, I'm not 100% convinced that the bass is in tune all the way through. It's just the odd moment, because most of time it's locked-in and I think it's quite tidy. But there are a few bass lines where it comes to the front, and you're just like, "Ooh, I'm not feeling convinced that's exactly what was intended there." And it's a shame because now, with hindsight, it catches my ear every time. It's kind of removed me from the song.

Plus this is really quite amusing. There's what sounds like a pretty big mistake at the 2:20 mark. They come back in with that kind of main chorus riff and it doesn't feel like everyone's quite in sync. It's a complete botch, to be fair. It stutters back in. And I can't help but think, why would you have left that in? Wouldn't you have re-done that? But it's part of the character now; it's part of the charm. But it maybe highlights how seat-of-the-pants things were at this point. However, it's still a powerful rocker and it's still really good. I like it a lot. But it seems to highlight both elements at the same time, that we're kind of making it up as we go along, but we also still really know what we're doing, and we can meet somewhere in the middle.

Martin: And how are you feeling about these guys individually at this point as players?

Steven: To be fair, I feel like Eric is really quite versatile on this album because he brings Clapton and Hendrix and there's some areas where he sounds like he could be playing with Van Morrison still. And there's other points where he really is just a folk guitarist. Plus there's straight-up blues in there as well. He's an unsung hero here. Phil's vocals are great too.

But Brian Downey is the one that strikes me as nearly the real deal. He sounds like he's ready. He would go on to be a phenomenal drummer, but those bare bones are there. He's on his game already while the other two show it in flashes. It's there but then it kind of goes. But there are moments in songs where you think, well, if they can hold this and capture that, the sky's the limit. It's a shame that this lineup never really quite did that, I would suggest. And Phil, he became a phenomenal bass player. He became almost the leader of the pack with the way that he played bass. But at this stage there are points where you feel like he's more trying to keep up. It's interesting listening to that growth as they go through the albums.

Peter: "Baby Face" is the first one that really makes me think of typical Thin Lizzy. It's a great riff. Ironically, though, Phil is playing a different style of bass than he would later play. He's not doing the driving that I always envisioned him with, that right hand kind of thundering along with his pick. There's more great drumming. This one would be very easy to imagine live with Robertson and Gorham, with Phil thundering underneath. It's my favourite track on the album so far. It's just something that sounds familiar. If you are listening to the album sequentially, it would feel heavier and kind of an outlier versus some of the earlier tracks.

Martin: "Chatting Today" is another gorgeous sort of ballad, with Phil channelling his inner Woody Guthrie or Bob Dylan.

Tim: Yes, I get a folksy vibe to this. It's very working-class Irish. Working on the railroad. He's rhyming union with communion. "The railway, there's no better way." I don't know if all of these songs were conceived at a similar time, but it wouldn't surprise me to find out that this was the oldest of the batch.

Peter: Kind of a Spanish flamenco track. It's something that they just felt was moving them (laughs). It really doesn't go anywhere or do anything. I don't see any elements of this that carry on into their mainstream stuff moving forward. It's just kind of there.

Steven: "Chatting Today" is one of the ones where I think, okay, I can hear the Van Morrison. There's a mood and a vibe and there's the little lead lines that overlap the strumming acoustic. It's subtle and it's suggestive. But Phil's vocals are quite gravelly here, which adds character and colour. He's talking about a homeless guy who's sleeping on the railways, and he can't hold a job down, much though he's tried.

It's funny, you go find and read the lyrics online, and I keep reading that the line is, "And I'd like to thank someone for mascara and good things that I've done." And you read the rest of the song and think that makes no sense. I always thought that he was saying Miss Carol. He was thinking of a woman who would hear his story and take him at face value. No matter what the public would think of this guy. I suppose to use a Scottish term, you would class him as a bit of a waster. Someone that isn't holding anything down and can't keep it together.

I really like the closing lines in this song, that, "I don't know no better way than just lyin' back and drifting away. I can hear it. I can hear it." Are we hearing the train coming to finish the job? Is that where Phil's taking us here? It's quite powerful stuff. And we would get more of this going forward. He isn't frightened to suggest to you that a lot of these characters don't make it out the other side in the way we'd like them to. These are not heroes he's creating. And that itself is quite rare in an awful lot of rock music. A lot of the characters that we're sold win the day. Not many of Phil's win the day. There were a few, but not many.

Martin: "Call the Police" begins with a buffalo burger of a riff, but then it gets a little herky-jerky once Phil starts singing.

Brian: Yeah, this is another one of their Hendrix-inspired songs and one of the quote unquote heavier songs on the record. If you're going into this record looking for the harder-rocking stuff, you might not get too much of it. But "Call the Police" is a cool, upbeat song.

Tim: Yes, relatively heavy, or actually partly heavy. It's hard to measure heaviness at this point, because it's very politely recorded. But you have to listen to what the guitars are actually doing and think if there was distortion on that. It's not just a boogie woogie type of riff. There's a heavy riff there but it just doesn't sound like it. This one has some slide guitar in it, which you don't often think of with Thin Lizzy.

Steven: Those sirens that close the track, that's almost completely just lifted and stuck on "Jailbreak" a few years down the line. It's pretty overt in that sense. And I like the fact that the band name is just about in the lyrics, but not quite there. Phil sings, "Thin Miss Lizzy was kept very busy." I like that; it's a nice little touch. But the attitude is here. The song rocks, it has real intent and there's some degree of groove. In Lizzy, up to a certain point, there's always groove at the centre of the song; it's what really is bringing it all along. And obviously, we've got one guitarist in the band at this stage, but this is maybe the one song on that album where you kind of go, I can hear the two guitars here. Hindsight is a wonderful thing, but I can hear the two guitars. I can feel Phil leaning against two guitar players that are not quite there. You almost create them because you know what's going to come. "Call the Police" is another song that you could lift and stick it further down the line. You wouldn't question it at all. But it almost sticks out on the album because of that.

Peter: Yes, solid track. Phil is underscoring the riff. It's not the twin guitar attack. It's actually a trio. In songs like "Emerald," they're going to take those riffs and all three of them will play them in unison. The heavy intro riff to this song is one of the first places where you get that syncopation, which will definitely carry over into other songs moving forward. Great, solid drumming, but here the drums sound better to me than elsewhere. The snare sounds crisper, a little tighter, not as tubby, and it's a better overall mix, to my ears. Great playing from Eric and a lot of wordplay from Phil, where lyrically he's producing a lot of words in the verses, which is something he's really good at. But "Call the police" repeats too many times. But that's a compositional thing, trying to get the hook going. But there are some solid moments in here and like I say, some good lessons on where they're going to go.

Martin: Okay, the guys close the album with the title track, which is surprisingly quite murky and psychedelic, not a leader among songs that title tracks tend to be.

Tim: Yes, you look at the album cover, and this song certainly matches it. It's depressing, seven minutes long, it's got Mellotron, and it sounds utterly like late '60s rock coming out of the UK and it's not even progressive. This one didn't do anything for me. I certainly don't think it needed to be this long. I'm really not sure what the lyrics are trying to say. He's proposing all these comparisons and parallels. It's the only song that has the lyrics printed, so obviously they looked at it as a centrepiece of sorts.

Peter: Right off the bat, Martin, I'm struck by how poorly this song is recorded. It sounds muted and muffled and the mix is weak and recessed. It's got a Celtic and kind of folky feel to it but it lacks a presence. There's some nice harpsichord in it and some good elements from Eric, but it kind of just lays there compositionally. There's nothing to really to grab onto. I think it's the weakest track. It's an inconsistent album, but that shouldn't diminish its importance. But the sonics from track to track are off. Plus, Phil really hasn't found his voice on bass yet, even though his vocals are good. But there are some great moments here that serve as seeds for ideas on future albums, so it's an important stepping stone, an important album. Because they weren't fully matured, they had to test things out.

Steven: I don't know. I think it's a fine way to close the album out. It digs deep into your emotions. The album is bookended, really, by its two epics, both seven minutes long. One is kind of rabble-rousing and tribal and giving you the spirit of its name through big drums. At this end, we're more about poetic lyrics. There's a meandering style that's a bit like blues, or maybe more like blues balladeering.

"Shades of a Blue Orphanage" is pure melancholy, really. There are also some aggressive moments and experimental things, but I think it's quite brave to end the album on such a down moment. It would have been easy to put the title track and "Call the Police" the other way around. Let's close on the one that knocks you out. I quite like the fact that there's nothing that follows "Shades of a Blue Orphanage." You're just left with silence if you let it play and stop. There's a real kind of heft about the song in that sense. And same again, Phil's talking about a character, and he even gives him a name—Dan. Obviously it starts in his childhood and then he brings it into Dan's present day. And then we look at his future, and you just know that his future is going to be kind of unfulfilled and unrealised. Phil was laying it out early on here. If you're looking for happy stories, I'm not necessarily your man. And he's not frightened to leave the album on that note. You think, oh, my God really? (laughs).

Martin: Any comment on the bonus tracks? They are of the period and important to the story.

Tim: Yeah, well, first off, I've got two versions of "Whiskey in the Jar." Obviously that was their breakthrough hit and it's one of those songs that doesn't really belong to any album. "Black Boys on the Corner" is an interesting song, kind of heavy, and I've got two versions of that too. One is the 1977 overdubbed and remixed version. Plus, I've got an early version of "Suicide" that sounds like Status Quo with Manny Charlton playing slide (laughs). Other than that, there are versions of songs that are on the album like "Buffalo Gal," "Sarah" and "Brought Down."

Martin: What do you think of "Whiskey in the Jar?"

Tim: I've heard that Metallica version so many times I can't get it out of my head. It's never been one of my Lizzy favourites. But it's interesting how Thin Lizzy took this old traditional song and had a hit single with it, at least in the UK. The guitar is very interesting in it. If you didn't know it was an old traditional Irish song, just getting into this band, you might have thought Phil had written it. It just shows you how he follows on from that Irish storytelling tradition.

Steven: I know they were resistant to "Whiskey in the Jar" and I understand why. You could argue that forcing that out as a single was the correct move, because it put them out there. You could argue that maybe it wasn't. It was a great interpretation of a traditional piece of music but it's not a great song. But they made it into a great song. And yeah, it was viewed as a millstone. The B-side, "Black Boys on the Corner," certainly would have helped the album. You do wonder if it's a little on-the-nose lyrically for people to be comfortable with back in the day. Do we really want to put that on the album? That's maybe the question. But musically and attitude-wise it belongs on the album. "Whiskey in the Jar," not so much.

Martin: Yeah, it's funny; "Whiskey in the Jar" sounds like it could have been the band's first single from a year earlier, and "Black Boys on the Corner" is almost too professional for *Shades of a Blue Orphanage*.

Steven: Yeah, it's a good stepping stone toward *Vagabonds*. As I say "Call the Police" is the one for me where I'm thinking I can see where we're going. Add another rocker and we've changed the album. Then you'd have three or four and you'd be thinking you see a clear direction. So yeah, would I add it to the album? I probably would, because I like it enough that it deserves to be better known than it is.

Martin: All right, any closing remarks?

Brian: Well, I'll add that *Shades of a Blue Orphanage* definitely suffers from that old-style production. And stylistically, they're still confused. Arty is not the right word. Maybe they're quirky, and too quirky to have stood the test of time beyond the Thin Lizzy fan base. I don't know who outside the base you would play these records for. I still think Phil's a good songwriter and I love his voice and the playing is good. I don't think you can argue with the musicianship of these guys. But I don't know who these records are made for, let alone now, in terms of holding up.

Martin: It's almost a situation like Jethro Tull with that first outlier album, or Yes with two outlier albums to start, or Genesis with their poppy debut. It's that space between psych and prog for those guys, and here it's that space between psych and hard rock. Like a poor-selling Vertigo Records band or something.

Brian: Yeah, and it's interesting you mention those records. None of those are really the records people who know those bands reach for. So, taking it a step further, who outside of the fan base of those bands really cares about those records? Not too many people are talking about *Time and a Word*, let alone Yes fans. I like those records, but they don't hold up as well. And I think part of it is that when a band is confused in their identity, there's a difference between being diverse in your record and being confused in your direction.

Martin: You might drag Deep Purple Mark I into this as well.

Brian: Yeah, those records are spit-balling in a way too, like throwing darts at a dartboard. Let's try this and see what sticks. Whereas by the time we get to *In Rock* and *Machine Head* and *Jailbreak* and *Johnny the Fox*, there's identity and confidence and intention. And at that point, when they did more diverse material, it still sounded like them and it still fit with what they were doing. Whereas when they were diverse earlier, it sounds like maybe three different bands on the same record.

Martin: To telegraph forward for a second, how would they change for *Vagabonds*?

Brian: *Vagabonds* is in a similar vein, but I think the songwriting is tighter, which you see on the title track. It's definitely a more modern Thin Lizzy song. You get "The Rocker," which is where we first started hearing that more upbeat hard rock vibe that you get from '74 onwards. When they rocked hard on the previous two records, it was more of that heavy blues and Hendrix and funk vibe, whereas with "The Rocker," it's more the rock star kind of thing, more straightforward, hitting you across the head. But there are wonky things like "The Hero and the Madman" too, with those unusual vocals layered into the chorus. But the first two are the truly transitional records.

Honesty Is No Excuse: Thin Lizzy on Record

VAGABONDS OF THE WESTERN WORLD

September 21, 1973
Decca SKL 5170
Produced by Nick Tauber; associate producer: Philip Lynott
Engineered by Alan Harris and Kevin Fuller
Recorded at AIR Studios, London, UK and Decca 4, Tollington Park, London, UK
Personnel: Philip Lynott – bass guitar, vocals, Eric Bell – guitars, vocal, Brian Downey – percussion

Side 1
1. "Mama Nature Said" (Lynott) 4:52
2. "The Hero and the Madman" (Lynott) 6:08
3. "Slow Blues" (Lynott, Downey) 5:14
4. "The Rocker" (Lynott, Downey, Bell) 5:12

Honesty Is No Excuse: Thin Lizzy on Record

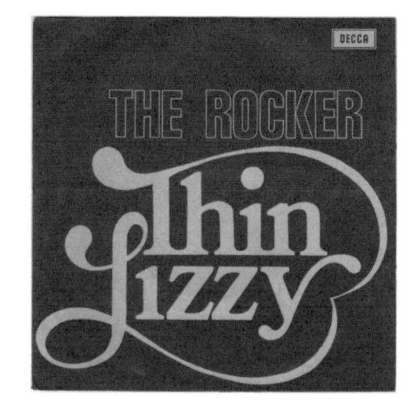

Side 2
1. "Vagabond of the Western World" (Lynott) 4:44
2. "Little Girl in Bloom" (Lynott) 5:12
3. "Gonna Creep Up on You" (Lynott, Bell) 3:27
4. "A Song for While I'm Away" (Lynott) 5:10

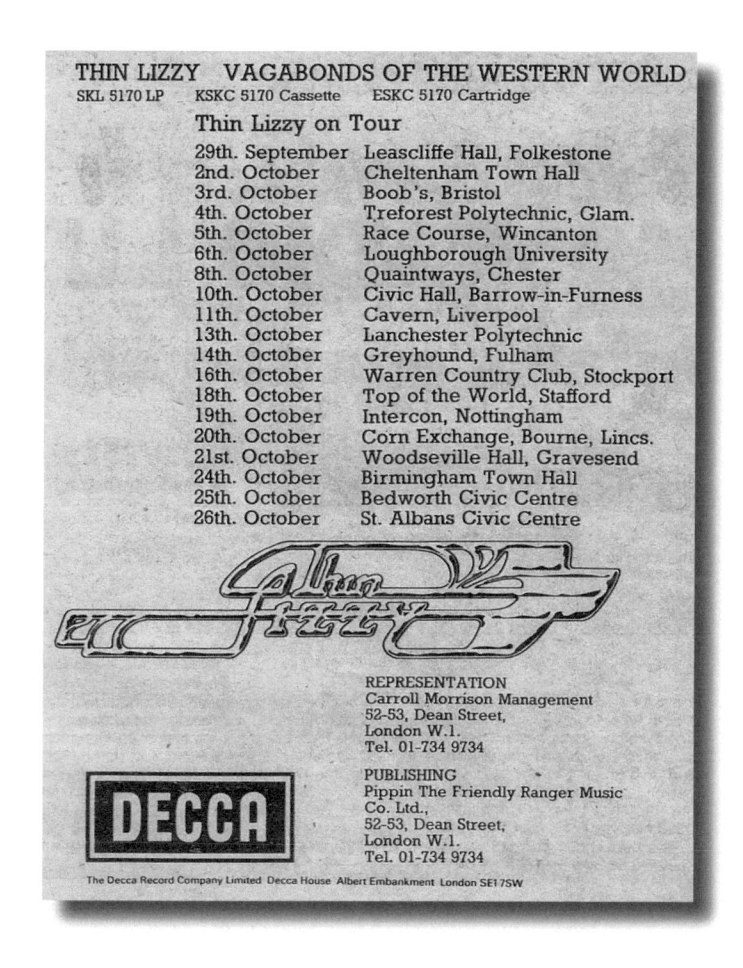

THIN LIZZY   VAGABONDS OF THE WESTERN WORLD
SKL 5170 LP   KSKC 5170 Cassette   ESKC 5170 Cartridge

Thin Lizzy on Tour

29th. September	Leascliffe Hall, Folkestone
2nd. October	Cheltenham Town Hall
3rd. October	Boob's, Bristol
4th. October	Treforest Polytechnic, Glam.
5th. October	Race Course, Wincanton
6th. October	Loughborough University
8th. October	Quaintways, Chester
10th. October	Civic Hall, Barrow-in-Furness
11th. October	Cavern, Liverpool
13th. October	Lanchester Polytechnic
14th. October	Greyhound, Fulham
16th. October	Warren Country Club, Stockport
18th. October	Top of the World, Stafford
19th. October	Intercon, Nottingham
20th. October	Corn Exchange, Bourne, Lincs.
21st. October	Woodseville Hall, Gravesend
24th. October	Birmingham Town Hall
25th. October	Bedworth Civic Centre
26th. October	St. Albans Civic Centre

REPRESENTATION
Carroll Morrison Management
52-53, Dean Street,
London W.1.
Tel. 01-734 9734

PUBLISHING
Pippin The Friendly Ranger Music Co. Ltd.,
52-53, Dean Street,
London W.1.
Tel. 01-734 9734

DECCA
The Decca Record Company Limited Decca House Albert Embankment London SE1 7SW

Honesty Is No Excuse: Thin Lizzy on Record

Martin talks to Rich Davenport, John Gaffney and Peter Kerr about *Vagabonds of the Western World*.

Martin Popoff: I feel like *Vagabonds of the Western World* is the Eric Bell era in colour. What are your thoughts on the third and last with Bell on guitar?

Rich Davenport: I'd say it's the definitive statement of the original three-piece lineup. Everything comes together in a big leap forward from the previous album. The sound is much more coherent and cohesive and the diversity of Phil's songwriting has been channelled into a more defined band identity. The diversity is still there, but on the first couple of albums it kind of jumps quite severely between different styles. Sure, you get the Celtic feel, the blues feel, a bit of funk and quite a bit of hard rock, but it's more tied together centrally. There's less of a sense of radical shifts in style.

John Gaffney: Previously they'd been confused, unfocussed, not finding their sound. For me, really, this is the first album that sounds like Thin Lizzy. But like I said, those first two albums are sort of folky and searching and the production isn't that great; the performances aren't captured that well. I see them as anomalies in the catalogue much like Mick Bolton-era UFO or Mark I-era Deep Purple.

But with *Vagabonds*, they're hinting at things to come. They are coming into focus, with everybody stepping it up a few notches in the playing, singing and songwriting departments. The production by Nick Tauber and Phil is also headed in the right direction. Although it's simple and dry, it does manage to capture the energy of the band. They had the standalone single that preceded the album. "Whiskey in the Jar" could be seen as a good thing or a bad thing, good because it charted and brought more fans and attention to the band, but bad because those fans who bought *Vagabonds* expecting more rocked-out traditional Irish songs, they were going to be disappointed.

But they still have one foot in the blues here. They haven't completely moved away from that. The production is kind of boxy and dry, which also makes it sound dated. You can hear that they're still wearing their influences on their sleeves. Phil is coming into his own but hasn't completely found his songwriting voice yet. It's really *Nightlife* that moves them out of that late '60s kind of sound, even if it's an outlier for different reasons. But on *Vagabonds* I'm still hearing that connection to Hendrix and Cream.

Peter Kerr: Agreed. They're still very much a power trio in the Jimi Hendrix mode. Phil was a huge Hendrix fan, so he's wearing a lot of these influences on his sleeve. Vocally, it's quite interesting. There's a different vocal inflection from Phil, sort of a couple of degrees of separation from Rod Stewart. I'm thinking early Rod solo might have been an influence, maybe a bit of Faces. But it's still completely different to the Thin Lizzy that you and I are very familiar with, with the dual guitar attack. It's very stripped-back, three guys working very much within the confines of the power trio genre. I almost hear a very proto version of stoner rock (laughs).

Martin: And your thoughts on the production?

Peter: I think it's actually sparkly for that era, with good separation between the instruments. It really brings out the space between the instruments as a power trio. I don't have a problem with it. It's actually livelier than some of the later ones, which can be a bit overblown.

Martin: And how are they doing for 1973?

Peter: Well, what was out in 1973? You had glam, you had like, Heep, Zeppelin, Purple and Sabbath and there's lots of progressive rock. I've read comments from you that you thought it was a bit behind the times for 1973. I still think there was an appetite for this sort of music. There were enough bands of this type who would be doing *The Old Grey Whistle Test*. But it's still a starting point; Phil was evolving, and *Vagabonds* is a progression. Like the first two albums, it's got sort of pastoral, acoustic passages and they're still psychedelic, although maybe a couple of degrees of separation from that. Phil's still just finding his feet. But yeah, I'm not quite sure that it was dated, because there were quite a few bands still swimming in that stream.

Rich: I agree with Peter on the production. It's sparse but you really hear the dynamic of the three-piece. There are overdubs when needed; well, on most of the tracks, actually. But the bass is quite prominent. There are places where Eric is playing a riff or chords, but sometimes it's just slide, like on "Mama Nature Said," and it leaves that space in there. There are a couple of places where it sounds like the vocal might have gone slightly into the red and distorting, but overall, I think it works for the album.

Martin: What do you think of that album cover?

Rich: Oh, fantastic; yeah, much better. The fact that it's by Jim Fitzpatrick points to the significance of the album. It's the first Jim Fitzpatrick painting and it's quite a spectacular one. And I'm really glad that the original lineup got one of those, because he's more associated with later and more popular albums, *Jailbreak* and things like that. So I'm really glad he did one for this lineup, because I feel they deserve it. Especially with this album. Yeah, it's a striking, evocative portrait of the band.

John: It's very kind of comic book, Marvel Comics, if you will, and spacey, with the spaceships and the moon and everything. And the boys on the front look maybe not like vagabonds of the western world but vagabonds of the universe. It's a cool, colourful cover. Jim's *Jailbreak* cover also has a comic book superhero-type vibe to it. But bottom line, this stands head and shoulders above the covers for the first two records, again reaffirming this idea that Thin Lizzy are finally coming into their own. But yeah, trippy, psychedelic vibe with the moon and the flashy colour scheme. I'm a comic book fan, so I like it for that reason.

Peter: It looks like something from a space rock album. It's lurid and cartoon-ish. I also like the connection to what Jim did on the back cover of *Black Rose*, where once again he illustrates the band. That's actually something he did a number of times along the way, a little bit on *Jailbreak* but on some compilations as well.

Martin: Okay, into the contents, and we get "Mama Nature Said," which reminds me of Nazareth, given the energy and all that slide guitar.

Rich: Yeah, yeah, and also some very assured, very capable bass playing from Phil. I don't think he was schooled in theory or anything like that, from what I've read, but considering he only started playing bass at the start of Thin Lizzy, he's come a long way. That's something that struck me when I interviewed Brian Downey for the *Rock Legends* box set a few years ago. I think part of his sort of golden handshake for leaving or getting the boot from Skid Row when they figured out they didn't need a singer was that Brush Shiels gave him some bass lessons. And Phil's first gig playing bass was with Thin Lizzy.

And I asked Brian how he made such amazing progress, and he said he really was putting a huge amount of effort in. He would call 'round to see Phil at his grandmother's house, and he'd ask where Phil was. "Oh, he's upstairs practicing." He was putting in like four or five hours a day to learn the bass. And that's reflected on "Mama Nature Said," with the sort of syncopation between the bass and the drums. Also Phil's vocals are much more confident. And even though it's a boogie-type track, the chords point to Phil's songwriting prowess. Even at this stage, the chord changes aren't sort of cookie-cutter blues changes. He's putting some quite sophisticated changes in the songs.

John: I like how the song opens up with bluesy slide guitar, and then Phil's chugging bass locks in with the shuffle feel on the drums. Like Rich says, although it's blues-based in structure, this is more sophisticated blues, with lots of chromatic movement between the chords. So it's a blues that breaks from standard structures, the way Jimi Hendrix might have approached the blues, with interesting twists and turns. Phil's lyrics about Mother Earth give it a grounded earthy feel; He goes "It's murder what you've done," which emphasises the point that man is to blame for not respecting Mother Nature. Phil also has some nice walking bass under the guitar solo.

Peter: Yeah, Phil does a lyric here that is going down a socially conscious path. As we go through Phil's career, there's all these different personas he presents. You've got the socially conscious Phil; you've got the boasting Phil and you've got the sensitive Phil. And it's interesting that on the first track on this album, he's lamenting about the environmental woes of the world. It's an interesting, topical kick-off to the album, so to speak.

The first thing that hits you is the tasty slide guitar of Eric Bell. Eric doesn't get a lot of recognition because the later guitarists—Robertson, Moore—get more of the spotlight. But in the context of a power trio, he was really good, and he delivers lots of slide guitar all over this track. Vocally, Lynott's a bit raspy, a bit gritty, which, again, is a couple of shades left of Rod Stewart. It's not fully into Rod Stewart mode, but it evokes him for me. His bass just thumps along on the song and Brian Downey, I guess maybe because he's in a power trio, he comes to the fore as quite a sublime drummer. It reminds me of the Jimi Hendrix trio with Buddy Miles, very much in that mode. So, it's a great opening track, both thematically and sonically.

Martin. Next is "The Hero and the Madman," an intriguing, psychedelic journey of a track.

Rich: Yes, and the narrator on this is Radio Luxembourg's David "Kid" Jensen, who was pretty much the first DJ to pick up on Thin Lizzy. He's Canadian, originally, and I think he's still on Radio One here on the BBC. So, he's doing the narrative, and I believe they brought him in as a thank you, from what I understand, for the support he'd given the band, as the first DJ of note to give them airplay.

Very accomplished bass licks from Phil, and, again, some great chord changes. It's not exactly psychedelic, but it's a strange, quirky track and it works. And Brian Downey, he's that rare breed of drummer, so underrated. He plays with a lot of power. He can lay down a solid drum pattern or beat, but he can let rip with Keith Moon-style wildness as well. Phil's lyric is poetic, fantasy-based, and Eric is heavy on the Hendrix, with the wah-wah.

John: I'd call this a slightly progressive number, something we don't usually associate with Thin Lizzy. It starts with an ominous-sounding bass line underneath a spoken word part from Kid Jensen. Kid's delivery is overly dramatic in a '60s campy detective show kind of way. There are these crowd chants of "Go higher!" and a strange helium-sounding voice high up in the range in the chorus that gives the song a surreal, bad acid trip-like feel. Phil uses a storytelling delivery, something he's always great at. It's some sort of hero fantasy tale, experimental, and not really something Thin Lizzy would ever really return to. But it's interesting and engaging. Eric Bell's biting guitar solo makes me think of Uli John Roth if Uli used a different guitar sound.

Peter: "The Hero and the Madman" is a bit of a mixed bag. It's jazzy, funky, it's got a little prog, and again, Lynott's bass is very much to the fore—he's just propelling things, all the way through. It's about a horseman traveling the desert to rescue a woman. So, Phil's in mythmaking mode, perfect in his guise as an olden days-type storyteller.

Martin: Next is "Slow Blues," which this song isn't.

Rich: No, it's quite funky, which is something the band would later revisit with things like "Showdown" and at other points on *Nightlife*. Phil and Brian form quite an intuitive rhythm section, perfect for the quite clipped, funky chords from Eric, whose solo uses a sort of Peter Green-style minimalism, with this fast lick at the end. And the lyrics are quite poetic; there's a nice line about "Let loose this lover's ship to sail." The macho side comes storming in with the next track, "The Rocker," but this one shows perhaps the more whimsical and sensitive side that was prevalent on the first two albums.

John: Yeah, it's a rather boring, uninspired song title, "Slow Blues" (laughs). The song begins with a traditional blues wail from Phil doubled by the guitar. The timpani in the background gives it a dramatic effect that lifts it above stock blues. Luckily though, they quickly move off this pulled-back, old-school blues thing and open up into a funkier feel. Phil's vocal is soulful and nicely laid-back and behind the beat. Phil's a master at doing this and it would become a trademark for him. So yeah, it's a blues mood or vibe, but with some twists. They would perfect this style later on with the song "Still in Love with You."

Peter: That opening bit where Phil sings along with Eric's guitar, that's another thing Hendrix would do quite regularly. But then the song takes a left turn and gets groovy and that sort of pace remains for the rest of the song. Bell does these little tasty licks, and it becomes more self-contained sonically within the song, although there's a good couple of minutes at the end that you might call a breakdown or extended wind-up. But yeah, there's a fair bit of funk and groove on this album, and a little bit of wah-wah. For somebody that's accustomed to the classic Lizzy sound, it's a bit of a shock. But once you become accustomed to it, it yields some rewards.

Martin: Side one of the original vinyl closes with the album's sort of career-sustaining hit, "The Rocker."

Rich: Yes, and brilliant track. I think it shows what a strong track it was because the band were still playing it years later. It also was on the original version of *Live and Dangerous* and they definitely kept playing it for years to come; the new lineup kept that one in the set. And this is Phil's macho Johnny Cool persona that he regularly returns to, even on "The Boys Are Back in Town" and all those sort of tough guy characters that Phil would sing about.

I believe Eric wrote that riff, and again, the song shows how criminally underrated Brian Downey is, precise and wild by turns, which you can hear in the pattern under the verse. Also, something that really arrives here is Phil's skill as a vocalist and not just a singer. The scanning of the lyrics and the meter is all over the place, but it fits. It's that soft-spoken near rap that he does. Not like hip-hop rap, but '70s rap, like rapping about what's going on, having a conversation about this tough guy business that's going on. And he will do that in a more precise way later on, famously with lines that go over the number of beats in the bar. And then you'd also get multiple rhymes in the same line. So yes, classic track with a fantastic solo.

Peter: "The Rocker" has lots of bravado and energy and it's right in the domain of the power trio. Again, it's like Phil's paying tribute to Jimi, with his conversational delivery. I often say that Phil sometimes puts aside singing for having a conversation with the audience. His delivery is more of a conversation than just a vocalist singing lyrics. And then underneath it, Downey's playing is very busy with all these tasty licks, once again reminding me of Buddy Miles. He's possibly the most valuable player on this album; he really shines.

John: Things get kicked up a few notches with this one. Eric Bell sort of starts the engines with a biting single-coil bridge pickup sound, while playing an aggressive blues rock riff. Phil ditches any semblance of crooning for a more aggressive delivery, showing us his tough side, telling a lady, "Got my cycle outside; you wanna try?" There's this sort of young man swagger you also got from Bon Scott, who was another lover and fighter we lost too soon. Eric takes a cool, extended, Chuck Berry-on-speed solo that also slips into wild Hendrix wah-wah turf. Sadly, the solo is almost completely removed from the single version, because this is maybe his finest moment with the band. There's a line where Phil says, "Down at the juke joint, me and the boys are stompin'." I hear that and it makes me wonder if this is part of the same story we get with "The Boys Are Back in Town."

Martin: I've always kind of had it in for this song. Despite loving heavy music and only heavy music when I was hearing this pretty much in real time in maybe 1975 as a 12-year-old, it always sounded dated to me. And I remember getting *Fighting* as a new release and thinking the same thing about "Rosalie."

John: Yeah, I see what you mean. If you think about it though, it's sort of a Teddy Boy lyric, which is a close sort of cousin to the official idea of "rocker" too, right? There's the motorcycle in it too and he says "bippin' and boppin'" and even actually Teddy Boy at the end. So he's referencing the '50s, the birth of rock 'n' roll. So for me, it's kind of like a tribute song, if you will, a nod to late '50s rock.

Again, Eric Bell's solo for me is very Chuck Berry, over-the-top Chuck Berry, even a tip of the hat I think to Hendrix, with the wah-wah pedal and everything. So yeah, it does have this old-timey rock 'n' roll feel to it. But I dig it in kind of an AC/DC, the song "Rocker" kind of way, with Bon Scott even singing the same thing, "I'm a rocker" and about blue suede shoes and stuff like that. It's essentially a nod to Chuck Berry and Buddy Holly and the classics of rock. So, I think it's fun and there's a lot of energy on it.

Martin: And John, as a bassist yourself, how about a bit more about Phil and his bass-playing?

John: Man, Phil is both understated and underrated. He never overplays and he always serves the song. He has a lot of little creative and interesting parts, at times reminding me of someone like Paul McCartney, who's also a bass player who never flashes but is always keeping the song in mind. Specifically on *Vagabonds*, I would say that his bass is loud and clear. It's maybe the loudest we hear Phil's bass on any Thin Lizzy record. So, it does really jump out on this particular album. Another thing, he definitely plays with a pick and his right arm is almost always kind of moving, keeping the rhythm, so it's very rhythmic and driving. But again, it's not in a flashy "Look at me" kind of way, but more in a song-serving type of function.

Martin: And even though the parts might not be hard, they get harder when you think about him and his complicated vocal phrasing, cramming in lots of words, and then often going over the end of the bar.

John: Oh yeah, absolutely. Phil is fantastic at singing behind the beat and singing over the bar line, if you will, to use a musical expression. And very conversational, never really locked into any kind of firm beats or anything. He just sort of floats around with his melody lines and is always relaxed, which, as you mentioned, makes it all the more impressive that he's able to play bass and keep the steady, regimented rhythms while he's doing this very relaxed, free-flowing line over the top. Whenever I hear Phil's vocals, I always think he's taking influence from say Elvis or Frank Sinatra more so than your typical rock wailers like Plant or Gillan. With that baritone and range and style of singing, he leans more towards a '50s crooner than he does a typical modern '70s screamer, if you will.

Martin: One more thing that people have said about Phil—and this is maybe more so later on—do you know anything about this idea of him putting a lot of phaser on his bass?

John: Oh, yeah, I'm gonna be bringing that up a few times later on. That's almost a signature of Phil's, where he would have this flanger sound on his bass. You especially hear it on *Black Rose* and it's all over *Bad Reputation*. You really hear it when Phil does this sort of thing where he's playing dead notes on the bass, where he's muting the strings and his right hand is going, so you get this sort of rhythmic effect. It's almost a Phil Lynott trademark.

Martin: While we're at it, Rich, as a guitarist yourself, how about a few more words on Eric? Since this is the last time we're going to see him.

Rich: Sure, well, he's fantastic. I think he's so far ahead of his time. I interviewed Eric in 2017 or 2018, for *Record Collector*. And, again, he just doesn't get the credit, really. The very first track on the first Lizzy album has a harmony lead, a twin guitar lead, and it's Eric overdubbing. And obviously, that's all over "Whiskey in the Jar" and it's on some of the tracks on this album. Which, by the way, there's this famous story that Eric's told quite a few times where they were just jamming something, almost like a mocking the song. And the manager came into the room and said, "What was that you were just playing?" And when I interviewed him, he said they couldn't think of the song. And he's like, "No, it wasn't that one." And then Phil realised what it was. "Oh, for fuck's sake, it was 'Whiskey in the Jar.'" If I remember correctly, Eric told me that they moved away from Ireland in part to get away from that kind of music (laughs).

Anyway, Eric was exploring this idea of twin leads. It tends to be... I did an interview with Scott where he talked about how he and Brian hit on the twin leads later on and put their own slant on it. But Eric was doing that on his own earlier on. And I actually asked him where that came from. He cited Randy California because he used to do that with Spirit, overdubbing, and the other guy was Harvey Mandel. There was an album of his that Eric mentioned where he does something along those lines. So, as I say, it tends to be the later lineup that gets the credit, but Eric was already putting the twin leads in. And he does some quite fast, jazzy runs, which are uncommonly fast for that era, really, outside of jazz. And he told me he was influenced by people like Django Reinhardt and Wes Montgomery and Hank Marvin.

The other key thing he told me was that although there's a big blues element to Eric's playing, everybody else in Belfast where he grew up was copying the John Mayall album, *Blues Breakers with Eric Clapton*, and he made a point of not doing that. So, I think as a result of that, he's a very individual player. This album is just a showcase for some amazing playing, right from the slide lick on "Mama Nature Said." And then when he plays in a more Hendrix-influenced style with the wah-wah, again, he doesn't sound like a Hendrix clone.

I really like that sort of long freakout solo on "The Rocker." It showcases Eric's skill as a player, really, that he can sustain it for that long and hold your interest. And when he plays on "Slow Blues," I suppose this points to the Mayall thing, where it's clean-sounding and Peter Green-like but not rote. It's not typical, clichéd blues licks that he's putting in. The harmonies in "Little Girl in Bloom" are just fantastic. That's one of my all-time favourites. He's fading the feedback in and layering it to make harmonies. That's quite ahead of its time, And there's a Celtic feel to the playing as well.
So yeah, *Vagabonds* is a real testament to what an amazing guitarist Eric was.

Martin: Nice, okay, over to side two, we get the approximate title track, which marks a nice advancement in the band's writing and arranging. It's sort of the next in line of the band's complicated heavy metal songs.

John: Yes, and like you say, it's not exactly a title track because it's plural for the album title and singular for the song title. Here we get the centrepiece of the album, kicked off with some traditional Irish tribal drums and Phil singing, "Too-Ra-Loo-Ra-Loo-Ra," which is Irish for "Goodbye; I'll be seeing you later." I guess it gives those new fans from "Whiskey in the Jar" a quick Irish wink and smile. Then a nasty verse groove takes over, with Phil telling the story of a roving vagabond, who on his travels falls for a blue-eyed lady. The way I see it, Phil's always perfectly at home telling tales of cowboys and renegades and vagabonds, maybe seeing himself as one of them lonely vagabonds and lonely travellers. I like how there's added menace and heaviness when we get to the chorus. That just shows off his knack for creative songwriting. Favourite song on the album for me as well as an all-time favourite Thin Lizzy song.

Rich: Yes, for sure, and there's that Celtic influence again, foreshadowing things like "Emerald." It's also a demonstration of the precision of Brian Downey's playing. There's sort of crushing power chords, but also a melancholic, Celtic, minor key feel in some of it, underscored by Phil's almost scat vocal, the "Too-Ra-Loo-Ra-Loo-Ra" bit. And that verse is carried by an almost bluesy heavy metal riff. Still, there's a lot of energy in it. The bass and the guitar lock in with sort of counter-harmonies at one point, which is interesting, and there's another fantastic solo from Eric. Phil's charisma, his persona, is so much more confident and assured on this album. This is a theme or persona Phil would revisit quite a lot, like with "Wild One," for example.

Peter: Fans generally cite this as the best track on the album. I like how Phil uses a completely different singing voice for the verse as opposed to the chorus. He gives us a lyric about a gypsy who travels the country searching for fortune and fame, breaking hearts of the maidens. He says, "No lady ever got to know his name." So, he's basically creating the myth and mythology behind being the lady-killer, the vagabond, the rogue. I think he's really just talking about himself and what he would like to be. And it goes into the category of the bravado Phil. Music-wise, it's got that wonderful little Downey drum fill, folksy little vocal touchstones and for the verse, this sort of deep stoner rock groove, again, propelled by Phil's bass. It's classic power trio playing. I agree with consensus that it's the standout track on the album.

Martin: It's funny, "Little Girl in Bloom" might be my favourite song on the album, but I don't like the arrangement. I don't like the parts—any of them!—especially the drums, which sound clunky.

Rich: I can understand that, yeah. It's sort of heavy and edgy but dreamy at the same time. There's the feedback and the swelling in with the volume right at the beginning too. I don't know if people still call it that, but in the '80s that used to be known as violining, where you sort of pull the volume right the way down on the guitar, fret it up and then turn the volume up. You can do it with the volume pedal as well. It's like a violin effect. The beat's really sparse. Brian is displacing the beat quite cleverly, though. It's quite a hypnotic beat but I can see how you would call it clunky. Phil's vocal phrasing is amazing. The solo from Eric is fantastic and the way he phrases the notes is also quite unique. It almost sounds like he's playing backwards, but he isn't.

I've read different accounts pertaining to the lyrics. One is that Phil's singing about his own mother, Philomena, when she was pregnant with him. But there's stuff that's come to light subsequently about Phil and one of his girlfriends who had a child, a boy. His name is Macdaragh Lambe. And he's been acknowledged by Philomena and the Lynott family as Phil's son. But they were both very young at the time and he was adopted. So I've read somewhere that the song might be alluding to that situation as well.

John: We take a mellow turn here with this one, with Phil telling the tale of a young girl conceiving a child out of wedlock, whatever the specifics may be. It's all about Phil's gentle, sympathetic vocal delivery, with the music taking an almost backseat/backdrop position. Essentially it's a familiar topic, that of the outcast and marginalised. Brian Downey adds some tasteful fills to move things along in the chorus. The vocal harmonies are very Beatles-like to my ears. The Beatles are an unavoidable inspiration for anyone growing up in that era.

Peter: I like this one. It's a very sweet song. Like Rich explains, it was inspired either by his mum, who fell pregnant quite early, or by a girlfriend of his who fell pregnant at the age of 19, or both. There's a bite to it. When you look at the lyrics, it talks about a blushing bride who loves a blushing groom, and who carries a secret because she has his child. But there's a touch of menace. It says, "Don't tell him"—her father—"'til alone/When your daddy comes back, go tell him the facts/Just relax and see how he's gonna react." So there's a little bit of edge. On one hand it's a very sweet song, but there's this edge, this warning that there could be some trouble. And that's the thing about Lynott. Some of the lyrics, you think they're kind of simple, but there's more depth to them than meets the eye.

Martin: All right, next is "Gonna Creep Up on You," yet another venture into heavy rock that is more complex than block power chords.

Rich: Yeah, and also quite funky. I like *Nightlife*, but this song, as well as "Black Boys on the Corner," represent a slightly heavier version of the kind of funk feel that they would explore on that, and then recapture with some of the subsequent albums. Memorable riff, a lot of dynamics in Phil's vocals, some odd timing in the riff as well. On the verse riff, Eric's using the wah-wah percussively for effect in between vocal lines. So yeah, I really like that one; quite a propulsive, slinky track.

John: As a bassist, I love the throaty bass that starts this one off (laughs). Then we're into a nasty groove, with wah-wah guitar adding to the unsettling vibe. Phil's maybe playing the role of a creepy stalker or a dangerous person of the night, starting the song with the chorus gets everything right to the point. Brian Downey has an awesome, note-dense drum fill in the middle of the song. The guitar solo section gets busy in a jamming sort of way. Let's take a moment to talk about Brian Downey; the guy is never mentioned enough among the percussion greats, in my opinion. He's slightly jazzy and swinging like a Bill Ward but with a bit more chops. In fact, he's got crazy chops all over the kit like Keith Moon, but he's way more controlled. I can actually imagine Moon the Loon playing this chorus. It's a shame, but where is Brian's "Toad" or "Rat Salad" or "Moby Dick?" I suppose the closest we get is "Bad Reputation."

Martin: He's celebrated for his finesse, his light touch, as well, right? He's compared to Ian Paice a fair bit.

John: Yeah, he's very sort of jazzy. He's nowhere near as heavy a hitter as Ginger Baker or John Bonham. He rolls all over the kit, but again, it's not in that sort of uncontrolled, crazy kitchen sink Keith Moon style. For me, he combines elements of Buddy Rich and John Bonham, if you want a weird comparison. I think he's extremely underrated. I'm not quite sure why he doesn't get mentioned when people talk about the great heavy rock drummers of the '70s.

Martin: It might be because his parts are so well integrated into the songs. In other words, they're so musical that they don't distract.

They don't break the fourth wall. You get to the end of the song and unless you're a drummer, you just know that you've heard a great song. All right, Peter, any thoughts on this one?

Peter: Someone once described "Gonna Creep Up on You" as Red Hot Chili Peppers, ten years ahead of time. I have to agree—it's got a lot of attitude, it's got swagger, with the bass basically plays the riff. It reminds me of what Flea would be doing. And I'm talking about early Red Hot Chili Peppers, not that nonsense in the middle section onwards. Bell plays this proggy guitar riff and then it goes almost improvisational, from like the middle of the song to the end. But yeah, it's definitely got a funky groove. I'd describe this as more of a feel song.

Martin: Nice. Man, I never would have thought about it that way. Okay, we close with a ballad in three-four time, waltz time.

Rich: Yeah, I feel like "A Song for While I'm Away" would have made sense on the first album. Plus, it points to later tracks like "Sarah." There's a nice high-octave bass riff from Phil. It's quite old-fashioned, really, this one, in terms of the writing and the lyrics as well. You can almost imagine someone like Nat King Cole or Tony Bennett singing this.

John: This one is contemplative and very melodic in a Beatles way. The George Martin-like strings add to the Beatles vibe and give it a dreamy, ornate sort of tone. Phil's vocal is gentle and he's expressing remorse: "You are my life, my everything, you're all I have." It's Phil, the hopeless romantic, closing out the album with a beautiful love letter. Don't worry, lads. He'll soon be back tearing up the town with the boys (laughs).

Peter: Yeah, that's Phil baring his soul. There's always going to be a vulnerable song on every album that plucks at the heartstrings. He's singing in a different vocal register, a little lower. It's not pitch-perfect, but being not pitch-perfect, it gives the listener a sense that he's being more vulnerable—he kind of wins the listener over. And you've got that string quartet backing straight from the Tony Visconti school of string quartets. Melodically it's not as interesting or compelling as some of Phil's later ballads, but it's a nice little song.

Martin: All right, in closing, I want to ask, why do you think *Vagabonds of the Western World* is markedly heavier than either of the first two albums? Any takers?

Rich: That's a good question. I wonder if it's come from gigging and from playing live and working out what works live. Because I read in your book that they had a really difficult tour early on supporting Slade, with Suzi Quatro on the bill as well. I know that Slade's manager, Chas Chandler, kind of reprimanded the band or reprimanded Phil for not being a forceful enough frontman. And I suppose in a situation like that, they've got to really project musically. Maybe the new sense of edge came from what they had to learn quickly about winning over a surly mob of Slade fans (laughs).

Honesty Is No Excuse: Thin Lizzy on Record

NIGHTLIFE

November 8, 1974
Vertigo 6360 116
Produced by Ron Nevison and Phil Lynott
Engineered by Ron Nevison and Ted Sharp ("Recorded by")
Recorded at Saturn Studio, Worthing, UK, Trident Studios, Soho, London, UK and Olympic Studios, Barnes, London, UK
Personnel: Phil Lynott – bass, vocals, guitar, Scott Gorham – guitar, vocals, Brian Robertson – guitar, Brian Downey – drums, percussion
Key additional personnel: Gary Moore – guitar solo on "Still in Love with You," Frankie Miller – vocals on "Still in Love with You," Jean Roussell – keyboards on "Frankie Carroll," "Showdown" and "Dear Heart," Jimmy Horrowitz – string arrangements on "She Knows," "Frankie Carroll" and "Dear Heart"

Side 1
1. "She Knows" (Lynott, Gorham) 5:13
2. "Night Life" (Lynott) 3:55
3. "It's Only Money" (Lynott) 2:47
4. "Still in Love with You" (Lynott) 5:40
5. "Frankie Carroll" (Lynott) 2:02

THIN LIZZY
FIRST VERTIGO ALBUM
NIGHT LIFE
ON TOUR
21 December Stadium DUBLIN
26 December Kelly's PORTRUSH
27 December St. Johns LIMERICK
28 December GALWAY
29 December DERRY
31 December Horans TRALEE
3 January Flamingo BALLYMINA
First Vertigo Single
Out Now – PHILOMENA
marketed by phonogram

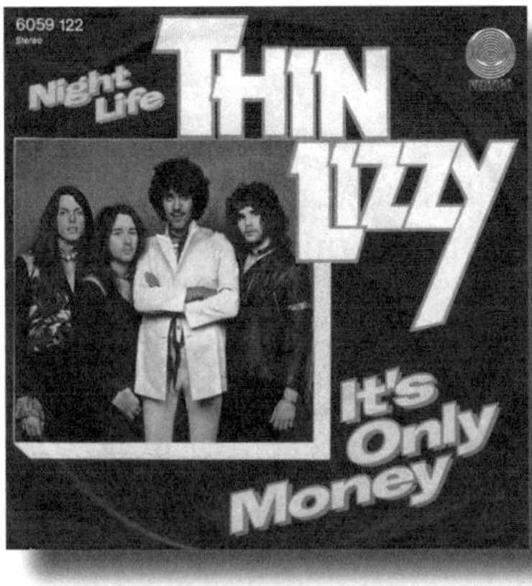
6059 122
Night Life
THIN LIZZY
It's Only Money

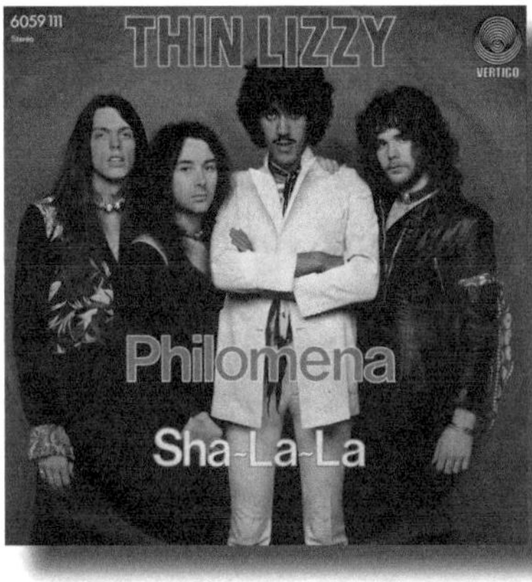
6059 111
THIN LIZZY
VERTIGO
Philomena
Sha-La-La

Side 2
1. "Showdown" (Lynott) 4:30
2. "Banshee" (Lynott) 1:25
3. "Philomena" (Lynott) 3:47
4. "Sha-La-La" (Lynott, Downey) 3:25
5. "Dear Heart" (Lynott) 4:50

Honesty Is No Excuse: Thin Lizzy on Record

PHIL LYNOTT (THIN LIZZY)

Thin Lizzy
Gary Moore   Phil Lynott   Brian Downey

Martin talks to Rich Davenport, David Gallagher and Peter Jones about *Nightlife*.

Martin Popoff: Fresh start for our heroes with *Nightlife*. How do they respond?

Peter Jones: Yes, this is the first of a new era. Obviously, we've got the famous lineup with the addition of Robertson and Gorham. And they're now on Vertigo Records and produced by Ron Nevison. As for what Nevison does, it's still dry. There's not a lot of ambience to it. But in Ron's defence, for a band like Thin Lizzy that is guitar-driven, the guitar tones on this are good.

Drum recording in general really doesn't get better until later. We've talked before how drums are the most complicated thing to record. Microphones are so unforgiving. If the drums are not tuned well, if the player is not focused on that kind of thing, it's easy to just say, "Oh, sorry, something's ringing or buzzing or vibrating—just put a piece of tape on and that'll kill it." We used to joke about duct-taping our wallets on the snare head, kind of thing. And if you've got a bigger kit, that's even more complicated because the more drums there are, the more they cross-talk with each other. There are so many variables.

So, they deaden them up and I think that became standard fare until drummers started going, "Hey, wait a second. They're supposed to ring." Which is why Bonham was such an anomaly. He did everything opposite: heads on both sides, huge drums, wide open, no muffling, no nothing. But he was fortunate enough that he had engineers who would trust what he was doing and use really old-school, minimal miking techniques in good rooms. Which is why those records sound different from everyone else's.

Rich Davenport: Yeah, concerning Nevison, in one of your books, Robbo's a lot kinder on that one than he previous was. He's perhaps mellowed with age. I know he basically said that Nevison got in the way, getting involved with the amplifier settings and things like that. And I read somewhere that he made him play through a tiny little Fender amp, which neutered the guitar tone a bit. And I think it's in your first Thin Lizzy book that Nevison mentions that he's listened back to it and thinks he'd kind of dropped the ball a little bit on *Nightlife*. From all the accounts I've read, they kind of went along with him because he'd engineered these big albums with like Bad

Company and The Who. And I can see why they would get a producer like that. But I know that they were definitely at odds with him. And I think that's why Phil produced the next album. Because they didn't consider this a particularly positive experience.

Martin: It reminds me a bit of Rush's *Caress of Steel*, where it's very correct and meticulous but lacking in bottom end. As well, both albums are a bit of a misstep.

Rich: Yeah, absolutely; that's a good comparison. On the heavier tracks it doesn't quite have the punch. There's a lot of clean tones on this album. You wonder whether that was down to Nevison perhaps smoothing things out. Whereas if things would have had more edge, as they did on *Fighting*, it might have come out better. But I like the album. Unfortunately, for me, they've lost the cohesion that they had with *Vagabonds*. In some ways, it's a nice problem to have because it shows the diversity that Phil's capable of as a writer. But it's gone back to that disparate spread of styles without so much of a central link, which, like we were saying about the heaviness on *Vagabonds*, it anchored all those influences in a slightly heavier sound that was more uniform throughout the album. And it's understandable given the massive lineup change. I read that they even thought about changing the name of the band. It's effectively a new band. There's a lot of good songs, but it's all over the place.

Looking at the personnel, by this stage, Phil, and Brian Downey were kind of the old hands, because this is album number four from them, so it's not their first rodeo. Plus they've put in a lot of roadwork. Whereas for Scott and Brian Robertson, they'd only been playing maybe a couple of years at this point. Scott had been a bass player in one of his early bands and I know that he was given a guitar when a friend of his passed away from the band he was in. And Robbo was very young; I don't think he had much experience in terms of recording. So again, the diversity of what they come up with is vast. As I listen to it retrospectively, I can see why it didn't do much for their career at this point. It's hard to get handle on the band. I'm glad it's there as part of the canon, but it's confusing.

David Gallagher: I always think it's fascinating that people talk about the inherent Irish nature of them—Lizzy and their twin guitar leads—as if they're synonymous. When the twin guitar leads are by a Glaswegian and an American. They're about as Irish as you are.

It's bizarre. So, we've got Robbo joining the band and we've got Scott Gorham. Scott's from L.A. and Rob was from here—he's from Glasgow. And Rob was 18 years old, which, when I think about what I was doing at 18, it breaks my heart. But it's difficult to call *Nightlife* an outlier, because they still hadn't quite discovered who they were, even though we were now onto album four.

Martin: What do you think about Ron Nevison's production?

David: I think it's very suitable for the album. I don't think it's particularly suitable for the guitar sounds overall, but I think it's suitable for the general approach to the R&B, to the blues, to the soul; I think he's perfect for that. I don't think it's very copacetic with the guitar parts that we're hearing, or for the drum sounds for that matter. But as an overall feel, I think it works. There's never any moment where it feels like they just said, "Let's do Stax; let's do Motown." It's very much filtered through the Lizzy prism. Another producer would have, I think, taken over and turned it into something different featuring Thin Lizzy. A pure soul album or a pure Stax album featuring Thin Lizzy. Fortunately that doesn't happens here. Good stuff.

Martin: And how about that album cover?

Rich: Jim Fitzpatrick again and very striking. It's sort of a nighttime planet scene like *Vagabonds* but this is more modern. I could imagine the *Vagabonds* cover on anything from like 1968 onward. *Nightlife* has a *Marvel* comic feel to it. And I've read that the panther is an allusion to the Black Panthers.

Peter: It's of course by their friend Jim Fitzpatrick, and I think it's really cool. It's certainly striking and catches your eye right off the bat.

Martin: Okay, so first track on the album is "She Knows," bright, airy, unexpected, especially for an opener. Not that Thin Lizzy are known for predictable sequencing.

David: Yes, "She Knows" tells you we're getting something very different from this new lineup. We're getting R&B and funk and vibe and feel. There's a laid-back warmth to "She Knows." I think you can hear that they've been listening to Van Morrison, especially I think in terms of how to mix the inherent Irishness with accessibility. They're thinking, maybe this can work for us. Maybe it will work if we're sort of more Celtic rock or Celtic soul than Celtic folk. "She Knows" had, I think, hit single potential, if it had been pushed the right way and if they had already cultivated an audience. But they hadn't, so this wasn't going to be the album that broke them anyway. It certainly has an appeal. I think it's a lovely, lovely opener. And just from a historical point of view, for that to be the first thing that we hear from Robbo and Scott, that's a little bit of history in its own way.

Rich: Yeah, I really like "She Knows." It reminds me of Tom Johnston-era Doobie Brothers, that first run before Michael McDonald, which I love. There's almost a funk feel to it. Great beat from Brian Downey, quite driving. It's not exactly like The Allman Brothers, but it reminds me of some of their tracks as well, the more mid-paced tracks. There's a hint of a twin lead guitar in there. It revisits the layering of acoustic and electric guitars that they had on "Whiskey in the Jar." I wonder if that was conscious or not. And there's some great twin lead work towards the end. Lyrically, there's a hint of religious imagery, which Phil will touch on quite a lot throughout his career. He speaks about Mother Mary and things like that. But I think it's a good opening track. Not as full-blooded as it might have been. Perhaps a rock track might have been a better opener, but it's certainly a very good song; I do like it.

Peter: With "She Knows," you get a big acoustic intro with 16th notes and instantly, you sense a fuller production. It's got a much broader sound and the power chords are nice. And while it's not as heavy and aggressive as they would later become, the dual sound of the guitars is instantly recognizable, and the drums are still really dry. But this is a tight and solid drumming performance from Brian, with very tasty high-hat work. I think one of his strongest suits is how he opens and closes his high-hat and uses those nuances to kind of push or move the verses and choruses along, almost like a big band drummer, where he'll find that syncopation in the riff or a vocal line and he'll just slightly accent it or enhance it or support it. Those things instantly catch my ear.

   The whole band sounds strong now. Phil's bass line is driving and it's helping fill out that low end. I also get that Allman Brothers feel, but from the chorus mostly. But you can clearly distinguish the two different guitar tones between Scott and Brian versus Eric, and to me that conjures up Duane and Dickie. And that's not surprising from both a sonic standpoint and an instrumentation standpoint, because we've now moved from a single guitarist with a Strat to two guitarists who, for the most part, were playing Les Pauls through Marshalls. So, the sonics there are going to be different. And of course that's what Duane and Dickie were famous for, their Les Pauls, and a stronger tone. But the Les Paul sound to me becomes the sound of Thin Lizzy, an important element. The song goes on a bit too long, but that's personal taste. Otherwise, it's strong opener.

Martin: Well, if you didn't like the sequencing of "She Knows" at track one, welcome to track two, "Night Life."

Rich: Yeah, exactly (laughs). This is an odd running order. It's a good blues track. Again, the chord changes are quite intelligent. It's not a standard blues progression; it leans perhaps towards "Stormy Monday" by T-Bone Walker, that kind of thing. Phil's confidence is still there from the previous album, but it's a bit downbeat for the second track on an album. It gets funky as it goes along, which is good, but it's still quite laid-back. And then we get into light strings and a bit of a jazzy solo, which I assume is Robbo, and some flute. We're already getting into a different feel from the first track, but it's like, oh, where is this gonna go?

David: It's "Night Life," right? I like that it's two words and the album title is one word. I don't know if that was intentional or if it was just somebody writing things down differently. But I like the separation, because nightlife and night life are two separate things. The song itself takes the chorus from Willie Nelson's "Night Life," but Willie was probably too stoned to get his lawyers on it. So, they were lucky about that. Otherwise, they might never have seen a royalty cheque again. Still, it's a bit cheeky to steal Willie's work.

But it comes off like a track by Bobby Blue Bland or James Carr; a little bit of a throwback. Bluesy soul, very American, very laid-back. But then Robbo's solo is his first moment of genius, I think. Robbo, even though it's laid-back, gives us a gorgeous solo. Scott, I think, takes a bit longer to get there. But Robbo was an 18-year-old prodigy. Because they are synonymous as a two-fer, I think people are reticent to put one above the other, or perhaps didn't know which one's which sometimes. But Robbo was by far the best player—always was, always will be—and he comes out swinging with this album.

Phil's bass playing is also wonderful here. It's got a lovely tempo to it. It's got a lovely R&B blues filter, but his bass playing tells you they've also been listening to funk. I don't think there's any funk on this album in terms of pure funk. You're not going to mistake it for James Brown or Sly Stone but they've certainly been listening to it and it's in the bass playing. It sounds like Larry Graham's bass, for example. I could do without the string section. That's my one complaint about "Night Life." I don't think it adds anything to the track.

Peter: Much more of a traditional blues song, although they do change it up a little bit. It's got some '70s orchestration in it. I hear The Spinners or some of the more Motown things. It's similar to the pop songs of the day. When I listen to the guitar solo, it's really hard for me not to hear Mark Knopfler and that Dire Straits sound. It's not remotely the heavy and fiery sound that they presented at least a little bit on the first track. They're obviously moving forward, but it's a product of its time, and maybe not as relatable. Still, it's a classic song in a sense. But we've got two very different compositions so far as their first two tracks, a more straightforward rocker at the beginning and now a more pop-oriented song with orchestration.

Martin: Next is "It's Only Money," a heavy one that's actually been covered a few times.

Rich: Yeah, I love this track. Great riff, great arrangement, and it's a highlight for me. And just as "The Rocker" on *Vagabonds* was a template for what came later, this is kind of the closest thing to later, classic Lizzy here. With a bit more punch in the production, a bit more grit, it would have made it a stronger track but it's still great. Inventive drumming from Brian, with the displacement of the beat and the bass drum work. It's another one with some religious imagery, with Phil talking about selling your soul to Satan and "You don't believe in Jesus" and worshipping money. There's a great riff in the middle as well. It breaks down into another riff which is quite complex in the way it's phrased. The beats don't land where you expect them to. Brian Robertson actually later reprised this on *Diamonds and Dirt*, his solo album from 2011.

Martin: Amusingly, this is another example of the band writing fairly complex when they enter the heavy metal space. The riff reminds me a bit of "Black Boys on the Corner."

Rich: Yeah, true. I actually really like "Black Boys on the Corner." Fiery, funky riff plus a slide solo. That's one of Phil's first statements about being a person of colour, about being a black man, which he will pick up on later. Although he was dual heritage, he did refer to himself as black quite frequently. There's an interview that I read where he said words to the effect that it was an important track. He was making a statement about being black. He had wanted that for the A-side and they put it on the B-side instead. He'd touch on that again on tracks like "Ode to a Black Man" and, although it's not an appropriate term to use, "Half Caste." That's another one where he sings about his own racial heritage and the discrimination he's experienced.

Scott Gorham has said that he felt if Phil was alive today, he'd be very supportive of Black Lives Matter and things like that. When I interviewed him just before Christmas, he told me that Phil didn't bring it up often, but when he did, he made some very eloquent statements about it. But yes, it's got a similar complicated rhythm and riff to "It's Only Money." There's quite a bit of that throughout the career, where they bring those almost prog-level chops, but use them sparingly and tastefully.

David: "It's Only Money" features these funky drums from Brian, on a song that is squarely heavy rock. *Nightlife* has two tracks, this and "Sha La la," where non-*Nightlife* fans will still say, "Oh, but I do like those." We won't name names, but we both know Thin Lizzy fans who will just not be able to deal with this kind of period of Thin Lizzy at all. But they could easily handle "It's Only Money" if it was on the next album, *Fighting*, or the album after. They could have handled it no problem if you took this one track out and gave it to them. It's probably where people imagine the Thin Lizzy sound comes from. This is the first time it kind of kicks right off, "It's Only Money," with Brian's drums holding it all together. So, this very much is the first time chronologically where you can hear twin guitar and the tight rhythm section—the Thin Lizzy sound. Even though it's on an album which people don't think of as the Thin Lizzy sound at all. This is the embryo of what we'd come to know and love.

Peter: Absolutely. Powerful riff and powerful drumming too, featuring one of the elements that Brian is really strong at, snare on the one and the three. He's just pushing every quarter note. It's not just the two and four backbeat but this very tasty groove. I love the isolated vocal section with just the drums, which is followed by a response. Again, it's a kind of traditional trope from the blues. You think of the early Peter Green stuff, where they'll break it down or give a vocal part and then the band will respond. After the second chorus, there's a super-tight unison section, and the band is really in sync and it's got a very cohesive feel to it. This track easily could have fit on *Johnny the Fox* or any of those other ones. It's got a great cohesive sound to it. And like David says, it really starts to foreshadow what we'll hear a couple albums down the road.

And I like that thing you've pointed out about how these early hard rock songs are not just power chords. You're right, they're almost all at a higher level of complication, aren't they? Some of these riffs are not just your run-of-the-mill kind of patterns there. I hate to say progressive, because it's overly used, and also because it's not really progressive. Because unlike much prog, you can hum a lot of these riffs, which is unusual. It's a component of theirs, especially once Scott and Brian started writing and contributing. Because right now Phil is still pretty much driving things compositionally. But those riffs become really prominent. And I think part of that is how the doors open when you have two guitars, much like Maiden.

Martin: Now we arrive at "Still in Love with You," which is in a blues ballad space I've never cottoned onto. Frankly, not much of a fan of this song, which I know, is blasphemy.

Peter: Yeah, well, this is *the* big ballad of the band, right? It's something that's been a staple in their live shows ever since this came out. This version, however, feels a bit rushed. Not sure it's played too quickly, but somehow, it's just not sitting right. Later in their live versions, Brian finds the pocket and it really ends up sitting where it's supposed to. Of course, we've got Gary Moore coming in to set the template for the song. And if you'd only heard the live one— and I'm not diminishing what Brian Robertson was able to do with it, because it's one of his signature solos—but these elements are presented first by Gary.

And Brian is very respectful of those elements. He reproduces a lot of those riffs note for note, and then expounds and improvises on top of that. But Gary set the terms. As it gets to the later part of the song, there's a huge feel change from an eighth note to a 16th note pattern, and more really great syncopation and open high-hat work. At this point the backing track feels like it's moving forward; it's got some propulsion to it. And the solo at the end from Gary has got a Carlos Santana vibe to it, with the ringing and the amount of sustain. And let's not forget, it's got a really passionate, strong vocal from Phil.

Rich: I know that "Still in Love with You" was key to the band landing the deal with Vertigo Records. Gary Moore said in an interview that he co-wrote this. It was basically almost a mash-up of a song of his called "I'll Help You See It Through" with a song of Phil's and he put the two together. And although Gary's not credited on it, Gary said that Phil gave him some money for it later on. And it's Gary solo on the album. There's quite a long solo on the faster part of the song where you can tell it's Gary's phrasing. And this was apparently something that they played to Vertigo and it was integral to them getting the deal.

Like Peter says, this is a faster version than the classic version. I'd say the classic, definitive version of the track is on *Live and Dangerous*. So this is a bit faster, although the arrangement's kind of in the same place; it follows the same format. Frankie Miller is duetting with Phil on this and harmonizing with him. I think it's testament to Phil's vocals that Phil kind of holds his own next to a vocalist as incredible as Frankie Miller. Phil doesn't pale in comparison. It shows Phil's capability as a vocalist. The song fits the mood of this album, quite laid-back, although ironically this one is a faster version. And there's some great syncopation on the bass and drums towards the end of the track, which was kept on the slower version as well. So, the running order of the album, we've had a mid-paced track, a ballad, then an upbeat track and then another ballad. So, it's a bit strange.

David: "Still in Love with You" stands as one in a long line of songs and periods where Phil and Gary Moore would become intertwined, going right up to Phil's death and the duets and they did "Out in the Fields" and "Military Man." Plus they did "Parisienne Walkways," and this is a sort of proto-"Parisienne Walkways." So, we've got Gary Moore in the band here. This was recorded before Robbo joined, but Gary Moore said, "You don't need to credit me; it's okay." Gary didn't want to join permanently because he and Phil both recognised that we're good friends but as two strong personalities in a band together permanently, we might not be friends anymore so let's not do that (laughs). So there's the long relationship where Gary Moore comes in, sprinkles some magic and then leaves again. And that will happen so often throughout the Thin Lizzy and Phil story in general.

It's bizarre to me when people say, "Oh, Robbo sounds great on that." Because that is so obviously Gary Moore. If you even slightly know Gary Moore, this is just signature Gary Moore. Unlike Thin Lizzy, he sounded like Gary Moore from the very, very early days. Distinctive as hell. Robbo couldn't play this. Well, he could and does, but Robbo wouldn't have come up with this as a default. This is pure Gary Moore.

I would love to have heard what that lineup could have done. But that band was Robbo and Scott. No, I think things worked out well for all concerned. Gary would obviously go into Colosseum II; that's where he would end up next. But yeah, I think this is probably one of the best examples of a Thin Lizzy ballad, because it doesn't go into saccharin at all.

Frankie Miller joins to do some co-lead. I love Frankie Miller; he's one of my favourite singers. I think he's a better classical soul singer than Phil would be, and I think he's more adept at it. That's Frankie Miller's raison d'etre, this kind of soul music. I almost think that if Frankie was the lead singer of this band, and maybe they called it something else or did it as a side-project, it could have worked out even better. Frankie had to sub once for Brinsley Schwarz and they did Van Morrison's "Wild Night" and it's just phenomenal. So, Frankie Miller is perfect for this. I do think, though, that him and Phil are too similar vocally for them both to be doing it at the same time. There are parts where they're doing a to-and-fro and I think either/or would have been fine. We don't need both, but I'm glad that it happened, as somebody who loves both. But I don't think there's enough of a musical gap between their vocals for it to be particularly interesting. In fact, some people even think that that's just Phil and they've done something to his voice in production.

Martin: We close side one of the original vinyl with "Frankie Carroll," a piano ballad, which I'm actually more on board for versus "Still in Love with You."

Rich: Yeah, again it speaks to the album being all over the place. But it shows what an accomplished writer Phil was and how he could turn it on for these different styles. Lyrically, it's another of Phil's character studies, which have been there since the first album with tracks like "Diddy Levine." He's very good at painting quite a vivid portrait of a character, where you almost feel you know the person by the end of the song. I don't dislike the track, but it kind of comes and goes quite indistinctly, really; it's quite sparse.

David: it's definitely an odd one. A dark piano ballad with big orchestration. On the face of it, if someone asked you what Irish act this is from the 1970s, you'd be more inclined to think Gilbert and Sullivan rather than Thin Lizzy. But again we're seeing DNA toward something like "Didn't I" from *Chinatown*. Phil was much more than just the rocker and just this and just that. So, if he decided we're going to have a piano-and-strings ballad and I'm going to sing my heart out and it's going to be a bit sappy and saccharine but the lyrics are going to be dark, then that's what they would do.

Still, Phil's greatness in terms of the wandering nature of his personality and musical inclinations were probably a detriment in this period in terms of them finding an audience. It would take that dual guitar lineup for them to really find their space musically. It's only then that people would discover Phil's genius. But I don't think they would have got there just with this approach of Phil as an eternal wanderer looking for something. Sometimes you need to cultivate an audience by sticking to one thing and battering that home.

Peter: While this is played on piano, it's very similar to the opening that we would hear on "Cowboy Song." It's got that kind of feel to it, although there's also the orchestration. The rhythmic pattern of the chord progression and everything's got an "Eleanor Rigby" kind of feel to it, to my ears. It's a simple, gentle song, and really short, barely two minutes in length. It's a nice palate-cleanser. It probably has more sentiment than I'm aware of, in that vocal delivery and who Frankie Carroll is or was. But it was important enough for them to put it on.

Martin: How much connection do you feel Thin Lizzy has to Van Morrison?

Peter: I feel like Van Morrison's compositions are sometimes not recognised. Clearly Bob Seger was a fan of Morrison's writing. Lizzy does "Rosalie" and they've got songs that work like that, because even though there's a hard edge to Thin Lizzy, Phil's base root is in songs. He's a songwriter, so yes, there's an element of Van Morrison.

Yes, it's got the dual guitars and the heavier riffing, but Phil's a songsmith and he likes melody. I also think he likes good harmony, and Van Morrison was really great at that. So, I think it's a natural thing with Phil, but I think also he was influenced, by Van, but also a wider range of people.

Martin: Complex vocal phrasing too, right?

Peter: Very much so, and I will say this: I've been a singing drummer ever since junior high, but there's one band that I cannot drum and sing along to at the same time, and that's Thin Lizzy. Because Phil sings in one feel and plays his bass in a different feel. Yeah, I can latch onto his bass playing, but his vocal phrasing can carry over bar lines and it drives me nuts as a singer on drums trying to do it. So I don't try. It's too hard. Yeah, it's a very unique thing for him, and very few singers can do that.

Martin: Over to side two, and we get the first of two squarely funk tracks in "Showdown."

Rich: Yeah, and I like the track. Great bass playing from Phil. I think it's nodding towards what they do on "Johnny the Fox Meets Jimmy the Weed." There's a lot of atmosphere to the track. The guitars are clean, but with a touch of wah-wah. There's a jazzy feel to the chorus, but not much punch; it's a bit indistinct. But there's a rise in energy towards the end, and some nice bass licks from Phil that mirror one of the licks from the guitar solo. But again, the song adds to the vagueness of the album.

David: "Showdown" is quite jazzy, with some pedal work that wouldn't be out of place on some of Stevie Wonder's '70s peak-years records. There's some really tasty guitar licks and fills—pardon the pun—about halfway through, when it starts to go a bit more rocky. Bigger chords come in and I'm not sure that's necessary. I think we're seeing the dichotomy of, "Right, we've got two guitar players here and we don't really need them in this song. Okay, let's just have a big riff party halfway through." It doesn't need that. I think that early part works, where they're just coming in for licks, fills, stabs. They're much more effective as texture rather than the big wall of sound itself.

In Phil's lyrics though, we meet characters like Miss Lucy and Johnny Cool. These sorts of people would be avatars of Phil's that he would use in songs over and over again. Johnny is going to become a Phil Lynott icon, standing in for Phil sometimes, being an allegory sometimes or being a wish fulfilment sometimes. So, Johnny makes his debut here. He's probably the most underrated member of Thin Lizzy, Johnny himself. The chorus is very simple, but the song shows a lot of taste. And that's probably demonstrated best in the first part of the song. It's full of groove and vibe and funk, again, especially in the opening part.

Peter: "Showdown" sounds like a film soundtrack—*Shaft* comes to mind, the blacksploitation films. And with the female backing on it, that vibe is even more reinforced. But then all of a sudden, this heavy riff comes out of nowhere and then kind of disappears again. The backing tracks definitely sound a bit dated on this one. It's got strong bass playing on it though, and then there's a nice double-time section that takes the song to completion as well as a great outro solo. And the guitar tone on that section is really glorious to me—that's a sound I could listen to a lot. I think they nailed it right there. Too bad it's on its way out.

Martin: How do you tell Scott and Brian apart?

Peter: Brian is a fierier player, if that makes sense. It's hard to describe. It's like the differences between K.K. and Glenn from Judas Priest. Glenn has his fiery moments, but Glenn will be more of a legato-phrased kind of player. Scott is that way, while Brian is a little more riffy and aggressive, although he's very melodic. And they always have a bit of difference in tonality. Of course, the panning helps you lock into which one is which. A good stereo mix will help you go, "Okay, that's Scott over there; that's Brian over there." Brian's always a little more distorted than Scott is, as well.

Martin: Next is the band's only instrumental, "Banshee," which I always compared with ZZ Top's "Asleep in the Desert."

Rich: Yeah, definitely; I can see that. There's a version of this with a lyric on the *Rock Legends* box set, which is great. It's about four minutes long. I asked Brian Downey about this when I interviewed him about the box set and I commented that it might have been a stronger album with the vocal version, and he somewhat agreed. He said that Phil wasn't happy with his lyric for the vocal version. But

Brian said he didn't see anything wrong with it. But yeah, it's great. It's a shame that the full version wasn't put on because the 1:27 we get here is really enticing and it's a great little track for what it is. I don't know why they didn't develop it more fully, but at least that demo version has come to light all these years later.

David: With "Banshee" it's funny, because even on an album where they're going to overtly American places stylistically, here we have an instrumental where they didn't need to call it something so overtly Irish, but they did. It's the wail of the banshee from Irish folklore. One important thing about it, it's got probably the first really overt twin guitar parts that we can hear that aren't overdubbed. We've heard a little bit of twin guitar earlier on the record, but this is the first time we fully get that Thin Lizzy sound. You just hear that and go, "That's Thin Lizzy." Identifiable as hell. It's intricate, it's pretty, its dainty, it's even Celtic. And I kind of want it to be a full song because I think there's enough here to sustain a lyric. It annoys me that it was chopped down into an interlude, if you will. Although maybe part of the appeal is in that, in the idea of "should have, could have."

Martin: And that title is much more violent and dark than the music itself, right?

David: Yes. I don't even know how popular the term is, but I think people generally know what the wail of the banshee is. In Irish folklore, when someone's dying, the banshee will appear as a kind of harbinger of death. When you see the banshee, someone's going to die, basically. So, it gives you that overt atmosphere of, when you hear the wail of the banshee, deaths on the moors. So, it's old-school storytelling. They've called it that, but you're right—I don't particularly hear in the music at all. Yeah, I would never have guessed this would be called "Banshee." But hey, it's just a little, "Call it something Irish." I kind of like that. Call it something that reminds people of Ireland.

Peter: It's almost Spanish acoustic guitar music with dual leads over the top—very nice. And then this more country kind of style emerges. There's Hammond B3 under there, which is a nice touch. It's not really anything fancy. The drums are very straightforward. And at 1:27, I would just have to ask the question, what were you trying to prove? What were you trying to accomplish?

Martin: Well, "Philomena" is a bit Celtic, so let's just frame "Banshee" as an intro (laughs).

Peter: Sure, and indeed this is very Irish-sounding, and written for Phil's mother. I like that Phil's bass kind of takes the main role in this one. If you performed a song with just a bass player and a singer, this is what it would sound like. But it opens with a dual guitar part, tripled by Phil on bass. It's a very melodic but straightforward kind of song, one of the stronger tracks. There are double-tracked vocals as well, which would be an element that they would use later on. It's interesting that they chose to fade this one out in the mix, because they were plainly starting to retard and slow down to come up with a proper ending. But they faded out the ending (laugh), which seems kind of odd compositionally, almost like a misstep.

Rich: I love this track. We get that Celtic feel that was quite prevalent on *Vagabonds*' title track, and it comes up again later on in "Emerald" and tracks like that. Phil is singing about his mom here. It opens with the twin guitar harmonies; very Celtic feel to those as well. It's quite sturdy and rousing, and that kind of thing will be there on the next album, with "Wild One." It's almost folk rock, the way it's done here, but there's quite a loose and blustery feel in the rhythm. With a bit more punch, this could have been more of a rock track. But I love it as it is, to be honest. Great drumming from Brian and some very skillful bass playing from Phil. The record's funk feel creeps in with the clean guitar chords, and it sounds like there's sort of wah-wah or phaser effect on the guitar.

    I actually played this song going back about 18 years, when I played some Phil Lynott tribute events. I was asked to sort of open the show with a friend of mine, just do acoustic versions of tracks like this and some of Phil's solo songs. And Phil's mum was there, so that was quite terrifying. Thankfully she liked us, and she invited us to Dublin to do a show the year after they put the statue up. They don't do it anymore, but they had a statue memorial gig. So again, that was quite nerve-racking in front of Phil's family (laughs). And I just remember saying, "This is for our guest of honour" and she just sort of saluted from the side of the stage. Yeah, so having worked this song out to play it, there's some great chord changes in it, and again it shows Phil's skills as a songwriter.

David: I like the movement from "Banshee" into "Philomena." The guitars seep in. Recall that on the first record he's talking about his mother's hotel and he's not being too overt about his love for his mother. But here he's doing a song named for her. But even then, he's not being ridiculously overt. It never comes across as cloying or, "Okay, we get it, you're a mammy's boy." No, it's more about what Philomena gave to him and his lineage musically, and so he sings in a much more pronounced Irish accent than he ever would after this. It's almost a pastiche of an Irish accent. He's almost saying, "I'm gonna sing this like I'm in The Dubliners or the Clancy Brothers. I'm gonna be really Irish here." Because Philomena is obviously very Irish.

And we do get the lyric, "If you see my mother, please give her all my love/For she has a heart of gold as good as God above." So, he does throw in some slushiness. But the song itself never crosses that boundary, as I think he would later on when he starts singing about Sarah and things. I think that did cross over a bit into the "Okay, we get it, you love your kid." No, this is brilliant stuff, paying tribute to old folk songs as well. So it's not just paying tribute to Philomena herself, but he's paying tribute to the music that she gave him. It literally starts with him singing, "I've been a wild rover." You don't get much more Irish than, "I've been a wild rover for many's a' year." He's literally putting in little references and making up verses comparable to old folk songs that he had learned from Philomena.

And you get some brilliant Robbo and Scott interplay as well, plus some lovely and yet frenetic drumming from Brian. Sometimes even on the quiet tracks, Brian Downey's drumming can be ridiculously heavy, if you isolate it and just listen for that intently. But it works because that's part of Irish culture too, where they have the Irish drum, the bodhrán, which is sort of played continuously or constant. He's not playing this with brushes or being laid-back. It's very rhythmic and pounding. That informed Brian Downey's drumming throughout the Thin Lizzy catalogue and I love it to bits. Some people think that's a bit problematic in places, where he's playing heavier than the track demands. I think it's just Ireland seeping into the music.

Martin: Nice; I like that. Next is "Sha La La," which is definitely not a heavy metal title for a heavy metal song. In fact, that's something quite amusing across sort of the first half-dozen heavy rockers from the band. It's actually the opposite of what we just talked about with "Banshee."

Rich: Come to think of it, that's true, isn't it? Great track again. This is a really good showcase for Brian Downey—just phenomenal drumming on this. Again, like "It's Only Money," this is more what we associate with classic Lizzy as they became for what they call the Magic Circle lineup of the two Brians, Phil and Scott. Great guitar solo. It's on the live album too, which kind of shows the strength of it. Only "Sha La La" and "Still in Love with You" from this album are on it. Although now we have the box set, and we know they did play "It's Only Money." But I think that shows what this track is made of, that it's included on *Live and Dangerous*. Again, this one supports what you were saying about this whole progressive influence on the riffing and the arrangements. And then there's a key change at the end, with sort of ascending twin leads and Phil's bass goes up to match. So yes, very accomplished musically. I think this would have been a better closer for the album than "Dear Heart."

David: I mentioned earlier, on "It's Only Money," that there are two tracks the non-*Nightlife* fans will glorify and say, "Well, it's got those two." The other one is "Sha La La." I've got a problem with "Sha La La," and it's not a problem with the song itself, which is solid. But someone pointed out to me that the opening for it is the exact riff of "Crazy Horses" by The Osmonds. And once heard, that cannot be unheard. Donny bloody Osmond is not something you want to be thinking of when you're listening to Thin Lizzy. No thank you. But it's a sign of things to come in general. The twin guitars are perfectly in sync. Brian is just frantic on the drums. There must have been gigs where he came off and he needed to put his hands in buckets of ice to deal with the blisters on his fingers, to quote Ringo Starr. Yes, the rocker indeed. So again, one for the non-*Nightlife* fans. At least they could have had a double A-side single made for them, if nothing else.

Peter: Now we're in the wheelhouse. As a drummer myself, I think this is one of the most important tracks. It has all the Thin Lizzy trademarks in it. It's driving and propulsive and Phil's bass playing is on full display. Great riff, love the dual lines and the moving parts from Robertson and Gorham. But to me, it's all about Brian Downey and double bass work and the beautiful, syncopated ride pattern that he's doing. One of the things he does on this track is that there are so many upbeats where he does crashes on the off-beats—and that really pushes and propels the track. I suppose there's not a lot of real melody. It's more of a vehicle, I guess, for Downey, and that's okay.

Martin: We conclude with "Dear Heart," a real closing time kinda song, if you ask me.

Peter: Yeah, it's a very typical, early '70s pop track. The use of the Fender Rhodes is instantly recognizable, where you think Bob Mayo from Peter Frampton. It's a subdued vocal from Phil. In fact, it's kind of buried in the mix. We get extensive orchestration again. The backing musicians are strong, but the song doesn't really go anywhere. I don't think it's a strong closer. They've reused some of the same chord progressions that they've used on earlier tracks. "Sha La La" would have been a great album closer. "Dear Heart" seems like an afterthought.

Rich: Yeah, very laid-back, with the strings. There's something in the lyric there about a "man with the golden arm" who's "taken too much junk." I don't want to read too much into that, but obviously Phil would talk about that more blatantly on songs like "Got to Give It Up." You've got this darker lyric on quite a sweet-sounding track; quite the contrast. This reminds me of a song from that era called "Sad Sweet Dreamer" by Philly Soul Corporation. Not a huge fan of this track, but it works well for what it is.

There was actually a song left off the album called "Rock 'n' Roll with You," which was played live around that time as well. It's very much a stage number like "Me and the Boys" or "Baby Drives Me Crazy." But it's a more substantial, better-written song than those. Those two latter tracks are on *Live and Dangerous*, and I tend to skip over them. They're very good for the atmosphere and I'm sure if you were there in the crowd, it was great. But "Rock 'n' Roll with You," which was left off, this was one of the tracks that when I talked to Brian Downey, he agreed it might have been a good idea to stick on *Nightlife*, maybe even in place of "Dear Heart." It's kind of a lost gem from that era.

David: "Dear Heart," the title itself, is gushy and treacly and very Phil. Like most Irishmen and most Celts, he's not afraid to put his emotions on the line and then sing about fighting and drinking two seconds later. So, a song called "Dear Heart"—perfect. But it goes in straight away to Phil soul mould, not quite Philly soul mould, but Phil soul mould. It could be Gamble and Huff from this kind of period. Spinners, Harold Melvin. But it's an example, again, of Phil being hopelessly romantic, while at the same time writing about something quite bleak—we've got heroin addiction and overdoses. Which, again, take the lyrics away and they're singing in double Dutch. You would never expect this kind of bleak and dark lyricism presented on top of a gorgeously arranged soul ballad. Bruce Springsteen was doing similar things on the second album, *The Wild, the Innocent & the E Street Shuffle*. Van Morrison's doing similar things, although he was a bit more esoteric in terms of lyricism and wasn't singing this kind of street poetry that Bruce was and Phil was. Phil is certainly evoking that kind of dichotomy of just because we're singing about really dark subject matter, it doesn't mean we can't sing about it beautifully.

I think it's a lovely way to round off the record. It sounds like a mission statement: "Okay, this was our soul record, folks. Is this what you wanted? Is this the one that's going to break us?" No. But it does very much feel like, "Okay, have they passed the audition this time?" And ultimately that's a no as well. For the public. The only way we can measure it is, did this break them? No, it didn't. But it didn't destroy them either. It gave them the chance to become. We're still very much proto-Thin Lizzy but in a different way. We have the folk, we have the overt romanticism even in the face of bleakness, we have the twin guitars being added. We have Gary Moore coming in for a cup of coffee every so often. We've got all the elements that become the Thin Lizzy ethos.

Also, they're singing about Philomena every so often and hearing Irishness and presenting Irishness in a period where, as I mentioned earlier, concerning Irishness, they broke the boundaries in terms of Catholic/Protestant, north/south. This was also a period where being Irish was very difficult for people in the UK, where Lizzy were obviously trying to break, because this was the height of the IRA bombings and tensions and the troubles. So, every record company would have been daft to not at least suggest, maybe tone down the Irishness a little bit. And there's this constant defiance of nope, we're going to make it authentically. We're going to push it even more or we're not going to make it at all.

There's never a sellout moment. They could easily have just ditched the Irishness after albums one, two, three and four and they never did and never would, which is fascinating, I think, in the face of potentially career-ending stuff where being Irish would have been the equivalent of, I don't know, a Muslim ban post-September 11th, or somebody trying to try to stay true to their Muslim roots. It's quite difficult to see how they pushed through that and always stayed that way, even when, as I said, their real power would come from the twin leads of a Scot and an American. But they retained their Irish roots—that never goes away. And I think that's testament to Phil's leadership. As we know, he had his problems, but he would always retain that, even when he was struggling. The Irish identity informed everything about Phil and about the music itself.

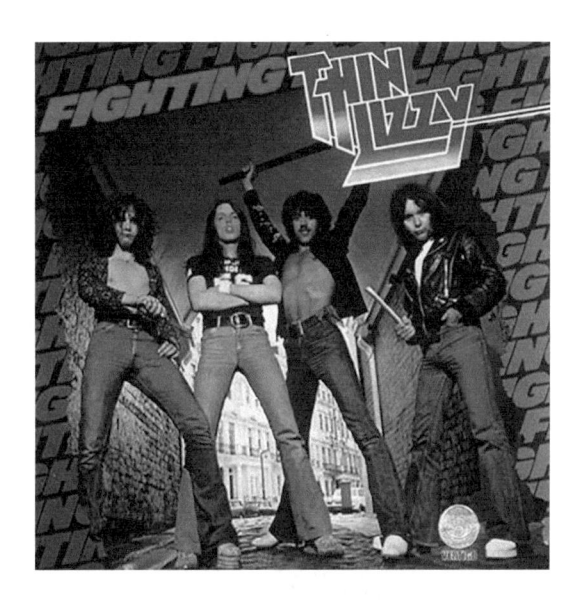

FIGHTING

September 12, 1975
Produced by Phil Lynott
Engineered by Keith Harwood
Recorded at Olympic Studios, London, UK
Personnel: Philip Lynott – lead vocal, bass guitar, acoustic guitar, Scott Gorham – lead guitar, guitars, Brian Robertson – lead guitar, guitars, vocals, Brian Downey – drums, percussion

Side 1
1. "Rosalie" (Bob Seger) 2:56
2. "For Those Who Love to Live" (Downey, Lynott) 3:08
3. "Suicide" (Lynott) 5:12
4. "Wild One" (Lynott) 4:18
5. "Fighting My Way Back" (Lynott) 3:12

Side 2
1. "King's Vengeance" (Gorham, Lynott) 4:09
2. "Spirit Slips Away" (Lynott) 4:41
3. "Silver Dollar" (Robertson) 3:26
4. "Freedom Song" (Gorham, Lynott) 3:30
5. "Ballad of a Hard Man" (Gorham) 3:16

Honesty Is No Excuse: Thin Lizzy on Record

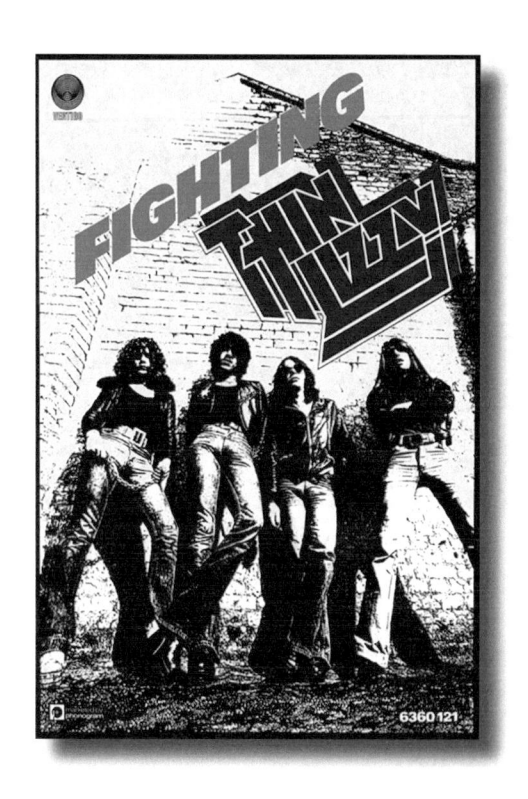

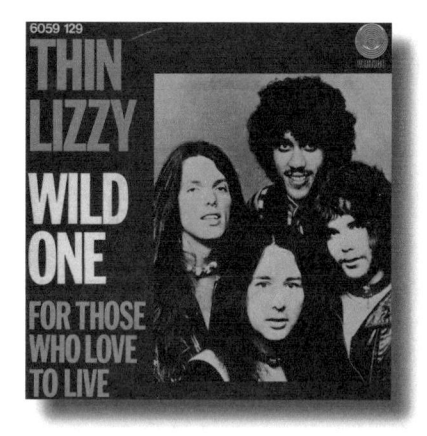

Martin talks to Andee Blacksugar, Tim Durling and Steven Reid about *Fighting*.

Martin Popoff: So, what do you think? Is this Thin Lizzy's first album?

Andee Blacksugar: Essentially, sure; I'll go with that (laughs). *Nightlife* is the first time they have those two guitar players in the band, but it's also a relatively restrained, kind of soulful, mellower album. And this, for 1975, is a pretty muscular, hard rock production. I don't think Judas Priest records sounded this heavy in 1974 and 1976, with *Rocka Rolla* and *Sad Wings of Destiny*, in terms of just the recording and the distortion on the guitars, although I'd say both are more in a heavy metal space than *Fighting* is. But yes, strictly production-wise, I wouldn't blame the production for anything on this album. There's some productions that they have going forward that have distracting elements, but this one sounds like the band playing, so it works for me.

Tim Durling: An additional impression with this album, I can hear the influence of it on other bands, either near contemporaneous ones or certainly bands from the New Wave of British Heavy Metal. There's an admiration for Thin Lizzy that starts with this album. I think it's a decent-sounding album, and the credit goes to Phil, because he's credited as the sole producer.

Steven Reid: The general conception about Lizzy is that they never captured their hard-rocking best on a studio album. For '70s Thin Lizzy, *Fighting* is as near as we get, I think. The production is credited to Phil, although Rob's suggested many years down the line that it was as much Keith Harwood as it was anybody else that produced the album. Sure, you could beef up the guitars, you could make a lot of these solos a bit gnarlier, a bit more aggressive and in-your-face, but I'm really delighted they didn't, because it would lose an awful lot of atmosphere.

It's funny because when we spoke for your *Dominance and Submission* Blue Öyster Cult book, I told you that I'm a sucker for a band where in your head you think, "Oh man, heavy stuff." There's so much aggressive about them that you should be frightened and scared. And then you listen to them and go, "Oh, they're really subtle; they're really clever." It's as much in the perception that you take away from these albums than it is in the actual execution. Don't get me wrong, there are heavy moments, there are some great riffs and some biting solos. But most of that perception of heaviness I think is something you create yourself as you listen to these albums.

But I mean that as a positive and as a compliment rather than a negative. Now it's used to justify, ah that's why they never went mega, because other than the live album, which captured that heft and that real aggression, they never captured that. The point is, I don't know if they ever really tried to, even though members of the band, certainly the guitarists along the line, would have liked a bit more of that push and urgency about it. I'm really happy with where it was, to be honest for you. But again, at least on the heaviest songs on this album, they never sounded thicker and as aggressive, save for *Thunder and Lightning*, which is a different story altogether.

Martin: There are two different album covers, sending essentially the same message: pick a fight with one of us and you'll be dealing with all of us.

Tim: Yeah, there's the UK cover where they're all brandishing some sort of weapon, actually except for Scott. It reminds me of Twisted Sister's *Under the Blade*, where they re-shot the cover and it wasn't much different. But here's the thing: for 1975, no matter which cover you get, it looks like a hard rock album. Whereas *Shades of a Blue Orphanage* looks like I don't know what, a children's book.

Steven: The US cover wasn't any better than the UK one. It's kind of the same thing, just more brown than blue. Maybe the US picture is marginally better. Ours over here was just bad. It's badly intentioned. Never mind just badly executed, the whole idea is poor. I know that Phil's trying to look really mean. Don't get me wrong. I wouldn't mess with him, especially not with a baseball bat or a big stick, whatever he's holding. I ain't getting involved in that, Phil.

But he's got a smile, like he's going, "I'll pose, but… really?!" (laughs). On the US one Scott Gorham looks like a hairdresser that got lost on a building site. So, the US one is hilarious and the UK one is hilariously bad. The notable thing though is, am I right in saying this is the only official Thin Lizzy album released until *Life/Live* that's got this classic Thin Lizzy logo on it?

Martin: Well, Steven, the funny thing is—and Jim Fitzpatrick explained this to me for my book—that logo first appeared on the back of *Nightlife*. But you're right, for a front cover on a proper studio or live album, we don't see it until the end.

Steven: Yeah, there you go. It's such a great logo and so under-used. But the cover is rubbish. I have to say there's nothing about it that is good, other than the fact that my UK version has got the Vertigo swirl on the front (laughs).

Martin: All right, into the album and Thin Lizzy sequencing strikes again—it's a song they didn't write.

Andee: Yes, *Fighting* has kind of a false start with "Rosalie" because it's not their song. They do a good job with it, but it doesn't exactly play to their unique strengths as a band; it's a serviceable cover at best.

Tim: "Rosalie" has a cool Canadian connection, Rosalie Trombley, Canadian CKLW DJ and mother of Tim Trombley, who went on to become an engineer. It's written by Bob Seger, and I think it's important to remember that at this time, Bob Seger wasn't exactly well known. He was an artist that took about eight years to really break, and this was about a year away from him breaking through to the masses with the *Night Moves* album. So, at this point, I think a lot of people were just going back and covering his songs because they thought it was good music. Most people are more familiar with the song because it's on *Live and Dangerous* and it got some airplay in 1978. But we're opening with a cover, which is an interesting decision.

Martin: I just never thought it sounded very much like a Thin Lizzy song.

Tim: No, it's not like it's got some amazing riff. You wonder, did they do it to get a boost in airplay from Rosalie Trombley and decided, well, why would we write another tribute when there's already one waiting for us? I don't know. I don't know what led them to do it and what led them to open their album with it. They still hadn't broken through. In that light, it seems like a sensible move to try something new.

Steven: Well, over at this end, I think "Rosalie" is a bonafide Thin Lizzy classic. I would guess most people don't even know it's a cover. It's got that jangly, ringing riff and that kind of straight-ahead rumble from Brian Downey. I like *Nightlife*, but they've moved up a step here. And when it hits the chorus you go, okay, hold on, something's happening now; this is different. It would be maybe more memorable in the live arena because they're such a great live band. But this is fantastic.

Interestingly, they don't really unleash that twin guitar sound in the first song on the album though. The guitar solo isn't one of those. But memory is a strange thing. You just presume that that's inherent in every Lizzy song and it's not. The solo is well-reasoned and overall, they keep the song to under three minutes. There are hooks all over the place. This should have been absolutely ginormous. Maybe it's better that it wasn't. It's a classic rock piece of gold now, as opposed to the kind of over-heard "The Boys Are Back in Town." I prefer this because it still has that kind of life about it.

And I like Bob Seger's original too. It's close between the two of them. The original has a real kind of Creedence Clearwater Revival feel about it. It's an interesting lyric because it's very of its time, for the radio. They had a real say about what bands you were going to hear. Who's going to make it? Who is going to be ignored because they don't get the airtime? It's about Rosalie Tromblay and what a big player she was at that point. She's mentioned overtly and covertly in quite a lot of different ways in songs and books and various things; she really was a player. And I suppose for Bob Seger and for Thin Lizzy, if you don't get radio play back then, you don't get very much, do you? There's no outlet for a video. So yeah, it's not a song about a girl in the usual way. It's actually a song about, let's make it—can we make it? Yeah, we've got the songs. You've got the power.

Martin: Next we have a tight and profession shuffle, along the lines of "Dancing in the Moonlight."

Andee: Absolutely, and "For Those Who Love to Live" is the first time we get that majestic guitar harmony signature from Thin Lizzy on this record. It has a lot of light and shade and dynamics in the verses and there's some complicated and intriguing playing in the end jam, which really rises to quite a busy and loud crescendo. But yeah, even though it's not a particularly hard-rocking song, it's still the classic sound.

Tim: Pretty funny, but go listen to "The Time Is Right for Love" from three years later, on Whitesnake's *Trouble*, and it really sounds like someone was listening to "For Those Who Love to Live" (laughs). This is a co-write between Phil and Brian Downey, and Brian's only credit on the album. It sounds like he had a lot to do with the arranging of the tune—it's a shuffle. It's an interesting song to have as the second track, but again, it's still early days of what would be known as hard rock. So, I don't think there was any thought of, well, yeah, we gotta keep the momentum up. You could go into a mellower song with track two. It's almost like they just put them in a bingo ball and whatever, spit it out—okay, here's the track listing.

Steven: And there it is—there's the twin guitars. They're careening into view. That set-up they do introduces the future of the band. It's such a statement. It amazes me that it's not the first song on the album. It's probably right not to be, but you do think if you'd been in that studio, you'd go, "Do we not want to let everybody know right from the off that this is what we're about now?" You hear "Rosalie" and then you go to this song and it's almost like the album has started again.

There are these little flurries from Brian Downey where it's like he's piling that song onward; he's so busy but economical at the same time. His style is quite clipped. There's no looseness; it's really very tight. What a great player, because it's like a steam engine running through the song. But he's very, very on it—he's absolutely on it. And we're beginning to hear some really versatile bass now. Phil's locked in and there's a lot of work that is happening now. To me, this is a song where it feels like everybody has the freedom to do what they want. Brian Downey's playing lots of rolls and flicks. If the bass wasn't there, he couldn't do that.

The guitars, they give you that feel of, "Do you know what? We're two guitarists, we're both brilliant, we're doing something different." They can do whatever they want here, but then again, they can't. Phil's knocking them about and keeping them in place all the time. That bass line is just saying, "There's the boundaries; there's the limits." But it's not in a way that makes you think, well, everyone's really constrained, and they know their job. It feels natural. It's really, really good. And when they do kind of dart in and out of each other, during the solo, you can feel magic happening. It's just coming alive. This is it. We found it.

Lyrically, I know that Phil dedicated this song to George Best when he would talk about it. Best was a really famous—maybe an infamous—Northern Irish footballer, who won the European Cup with Manchester United. I'm too young to have watched him in the flesh, but I've seen clips of him; the guy was a genius. But he certainly wasn't understood, and he wasn't appreciated because he was very much a kind of flawed genius. He had those character flaws where he loved the highlife and couldn't rein it in, didn't want to rein it in. And the more he tried to rein it in, the more rebellious he became.

And him and Phil knew each other, because George acquainted the Clifton Grange, which was obviously run by Phil's mum. So, they knew each other and they were kindred spirits, in the same but different worlds, where it's all about talent, it's all about flash, it's all about show. It's all about capturing the audience's attention, that somebody somewhere wants you to play the game. You 've still got to score the goal, you've still got to have the hit. You've still got to do these things but look spontaneous and sound spontaneous and be dangerous and be wild and stand out and entertain. But you have to do it by this time or by that time, and make sure that you do make it happen. You can clock off, but we need you here first thing tomorrow morning.

Martin: Sweet. Next, we have another shuffle, but now we're in a heavy ZZ Top zone with it.

Andee: Yes, "Suicide" has got like a standard kind of shuffle, a one-four-five blues skeleton to it. But it's got these killer guitar lines that sound almost like Iron Maiden too. So yeah, you get this really cool thing building up, where they're really starting to have fun with the guitars, the harmony parts. I gravitate to the guitars because I'm a guitar player, so I'm going to focus on that stuff a lot. But yes, Brian and Scott are really locked in here, and as a bonus, we get a modulation in key.

Tim: This one is as heavy as the production allows—it's a heavy song, probably the heaviest thing on the album. And I like how it stops and starts. It's a pretty gutsy song for 1975 and I like Phil's delivery on it, very actorly.

Steven: I really like the way that these songs work into each other, "For Those Who Love to Live" into "Suicide." I think it's one of the best one-two pairings in the Thin Lizzy catalogue. There's that opening guitar growl; we are aggressive here. And those drum rolls are threatening, quite stark. It's been quite refined up 'til this point in the album, and if any track illustrates the tightness of this band, it's "Suicide." That groove is just so locked in place, it drags you along with it—you've no choice.

And Phil has found a bark that matches his bite. This is not someone who is trying to sound aggressive—he's just aggressive now. There's a real edge to this; you're either on board or you're not. And I'm on board. And those little twin guitar runs that fill the instrumental section kind of replace the first guitar solo, although we get one later. That is a really good example of how to add drama and anticipation into a song. It's just enough for me to say, "Wow, what was that?!" And then it's gone.

But Brian Robertson is on fire here. I often feel that he's kind of left in the shadows. But he's such a powerful force on this. I do think at this stage, that he was the more aggressive of the two. Scott was more about refinement and carrying the melody into what's happening, ride it, get back into the song, bring it together. And it really works. Having that balance and having two guitarists that are competing but that want the same result is really special. You never felt like it was all about, "I'm better than you." It was very much about, "We're better than everybody else." And that's a really good thing.

Lyrically it's hard-hitting. It's about a shoddy police investigation, I suppose. Peter Brent, who appears to have committed a murder, called the police, who didn't want to investigate. So, he's got away with it. Then you've got the line, "The autopsy proved that Peter lied/But they never could find the gun." It feels really on-the-nose. But there's a darker theme here. It's very much about society. It's about inequality. It's very much about who fits in and who doesn't fit in, who is worthy of justice and who isn't. And I do think that Phil is always looking at society with a wider scope but honing it down into something that's more easily digestible. But these are ideas that people, certainly when this was released, didn't necessarily want to acknowledge. So rather than shove it down your throat, you put it in a way that people go, "Yeah, I know what that is." But then lyrically and musically, it's a marriage made in Heaven. It's just such a clever connection between aggressive lyrics and music—really good.

Martin: Nice. And it's a song they'd had around for a while.

Steven: Yeah, with different lineups and under different titles as well, I think. Yet it doesn't sound like it comes from the olden days, does it? There's nothing in it that nods to those old albums. It's been somewhat reworked. The ethos is very different between *Fighting* and everything that's come before. Although there are traces of it earlier, this is the album where Phil seemed to take on board that maybe he needed to create a character for himself if he wanted to get himself noticed as a frontman, and so he heightens just the whole mythology around the band as much as anything else. Maybe too much so, in many ways.

Martin: Andee, as a guitarist yourself, how about a look-in at these two guys as players?

Andee: Absolutely. I actually wanted to say that to me, Scott Gorham is the Thin Lizzy guitar player, and nobody really talks about him as much as they talk about the guys that occupied that rotating spot. People talk about Brian Robertson, they talk about what Gary Moore did when he was in the band, they talk about John Sykes. And granted there's a novelty factor in those guitar players and some of them are kind of stars in their own right. Some of them are volatile characters. So that's fun to talk about.

But meanwhile, you have this really calm, steady guy who is there throughout the whole thing, who to me is the consistent glue in the band. The difference between him and Brian Robertson, I think, is that Robbo sounds more kind of wild and violent, almost. He's a really bluesy guitar player but he has a lot of fury in him. And Scott is just in the pocket, a really disciplined kind of player, but he's still got this amazing sense of melody and phrasing and playfulness. He's kind of like the Adrian Smith to Dave Murray in Iron Maiden, where it's just really controlled and with beautiful phrasing and really nice tone.

So yeah, he's the first-chair guitarist but he never gets talked about like he's first-chair. It's like a secondary thing after you talk about the drama of Brian Robertson breaking his hand and whatever. Or Gary Moore coming in and chewing up the scenery with these wild virtuosic solos. Gary has kind of sucked up a lot of oxygen. Same thing with John Sykes. Anyway, on *Fighting*, it sounds to me like those two guys really are having a lot of fun with this interplay that they've discovered, playing whole solos in harmony together but also having the push and pull of their individual styles.

Martin: And I suppose on twin leads, it's a through-line from The Allman Brothers, Wishbone Ash, Thin Lizzy and then Iron Maiden, right?

Steven: Yeah, but Lizzy are just the best at it. And to be fair to other configurations of the band going forward, they manage to capture that even with different lineups. I think Gary Moore's probably the best of the foils that come to the band. Once we move down the line, that changes a little bit, and we shall see that the dynamic definitely changes at the end. But yes, I think the magic comes from that lack of competition. I'm not saying that all the other bands have guitarists that didn't want to work with each other—I don't mean it like that—but I do think there's often a feel of, "If you can play that, I can play this." Whereas Thin Lizzy seemed to be able to get their shit together in a way that they decided *they* would play this. *We're* going to play this. These are *our* songs. And if we do *this*, we make them better. By being natural. It doesn't sound created or contrived.

Martin: Next is "Wild One," my favourite kind of Thin Lizzy ballad.

Andee: Yes, and arguably one of the first quintessential classic Thin Lizzy tunes. Because it has that soaring quality with the guitar theme. It's got this ache to it because you get the sense that it's from a mother's point of view, and it's easy to imagine it as Phil's own mother. It's got that kind of dichotomy that makes Thin Lizzy so powerful. It's really strong. It's got a certain heft to it that's satisfying to headbangers, but then there's this vulnerability and honesty in the lyrics and in Phil's delivery. "Wild One" really captures that perfectly. And they do the fully harmonised guitar solo where the whole thing is like both guys playing in harmony, which is really cool.

Tim: Here's another song that was obviously influential. The first time I heard this song was from John Norum, the Europe guitarist; he covered it on his first solo album, *Total Control*, in 1987. It's very melancholy, especially the Lizzy version. It's sounds like it was written as a traditional lament. It almost harkens back to earlier Thin Lizzy. It's an early-days song people know, because there have been other covers as well. Plus, there's a high-profile compilation called *Wild One*, even though this song isn't on it. Plus, it's a term—one of many—that has come to refer to Phil himself.

Martin: So, the myth-making continues.

Steven: Yeah, absolutely. And again, it's quite a measured song to have such an intense lyric. But that twin solo that kind of introduces everything, that's a stop and stand still moment the first time you hear it. There are lots of twin guitar bands, and there have been twin guitar bands prior to this, but this is a moment where you go, wow, this is something different to what you're going to hear basically anywhere else. "Wild One" is an excellent example of that. And Phil's bass work is really pushing, again on such a gentle rocker. And I talked about juxtaposition before—there's lots of that here. Because you expect this to be really ramshackle and raucous. It's much more subtle than that. There's an awful lot more going on.

Lyrically you can see this as a love kind of gone astray but longed for. Is it more to do with family? Probably a mother trying to steer her son right, with danger lurking around every corner. Somebody's trying to bring you back from a world that there's no way back from, I suppose. And already we're beginning to maybe follow Phil's own journey. Are we looking at the troubles of his homeland? Do you have to leave to give yourself an opportunity? Can I stay in a situation that's wrong, whether that be a home or family or with a partner? Or just the location that you happen to find yourself in? Because that's where you live and that's where you were born, to then go and flourish and be what you can be. It's a really open-ended lyrics in that sense, because you can easily read all of those things into it. And you're never quite given the solution. You have to work it out for yourself. And that makes it, I think, more powerful, because you can touch more people. As a listener, you draw for yourself different lessons based on what you put into it.

Martin: Side one closes with a quirky one, a sort of sing-song thing, and I guess it's also a third "approximate title track" in a row.

Andee: Yeah, "Fighting My Way Back" is an interesting one, because when you pair it with the cover of the album, it seems like a macho swagger thing, but the song is actually talking about just trying to survive and pulling yourself up from the depths. And you're right; melodically it's very odd.

Tim: Like you say, you could call this the one the quasi-title track. Phil was such a unique vocalist and interpreter. He actually manages to make a hook out of just going "Fighting!" and then the band emphasises it with this rapid-fire rhythm. And that melody, to me those are Who chords, like "Baba O'Reilly." It's got that sort of cadence to it. Yeah, I really liked this one. It's hooky and it's heavy and yet it's melodic. You begin to see why they had so many songs that people latched onto, especially in the UK, and why they were such a great live band and why people really wanted to hear these songs. Yeah, this is a really successful endeavour as far as writing a good hard rock song goes.

Steven: Again, "Fighting My Way Back" feels like a response to the song that's just come before. Because this is now, "It doesn't matter what you throw at me; I can overcome that." Maybe you have to do difficult things in your life to get to where you want to go. But now it's, "It doesn't matter what shit you've thrown at me. I'm still going to be able to be who I want to be and do it the way I want to do it."

But there's also a theory that says, "We're not one-hit wonders; it isn't all about 'Whiskey in the Jar.' Actually, we're going to fight back from being pigeonholed as that sound. That was then and it definitely isn't now." Not sure I buy that, but it's an interesting idea. It's a track that I suppose gives the album its name. not overtly, which I quite like as well. But yeah, the vocals here are uncompromising. It reminds me of the album cover in certain ways. The song works better than the album cover. But it's trying to convey a threat without really being all that threatening. Does that make sense? It's maybe not the way I want to word it. It's angry and it's in-your-face, but it's refined; it's nuanced.

Martin: That bouncy castle melody always bothered me, ever since I was twelve actually, and had this album as a new release. Even then it sounded like children's music.

Steven: I'd be a little kinder than that (laughs). I think it's maybe a little too straight and narrow. And it's not really a straight and narrow album. There's still a good groove there. But yeah, I can take on board that it's a bit twee. No, that's going too far. But it does kind of stick out here as one that doesn't fit melodically. I can see that.

Martin: I guess if we were to go back to the album cover, this one lines up more with Phil's slightly incredulous smile there, while the other guys are all about actual fighting, right? The song's not really about fighting at all. So those guys are acting out the album title and Phil's acting out the lyric to "Fighting My Way Back." All right, enough of that. Over to side two, we've got "King's Vengeance," which, to these ears, sounds like a more Lizzy-like upgrade of "She Knows."

Andee: Nice (laughs). Yeah, "The King will have his vengeance." It also reminds me of some of the things they did on *Jailbreak*. It's got that gallop vibe, not a typical heavy metal gallop, but more like "Angel from the Coast." This sounds like a dry run for that song. There's acoustic mixed with electric. It's got this really crystalline, clean guitar in the verse and then they bring in the power chords. It's got the Van Morrison thing and the harmonies. It's just a broadly appealing kind of song, and obviously not very heavy metal.

Tim: Although it approaches that in the chorus, with those big hanging chords. It's a co-write with Scott Gorham and this was Scott's second album, but it sounds like something Phil would have written on his own. The lyrics are almost in the tradition of Robert Plant in Led Zeppelin where they're timeless or at least historical, with Phil writing sort of about medieval times, except, curiously, in the first verse and then never again (laughs). It sounds like it's about the Crusades times or just a combination of things—myth, legend, history. In the end, it's a good example of that sort of writing style where he's keeping it vague or universal.

Steven: There's a country vibe running through this one, mixed with Celtic and even heavier riffs. There's a nod to Queen in there, in the structure and a bit in the sound. It's one of these songs where there's lighter moments that make the heavier moments heavier. And the heavier moments make the lighter moments more melancholy, more worth listening to. It's about the balance, crunch and nuance. And melody lines are always kind of running through everything. You really want to get involved with the melodies on these songs.

I absolutely love that, "Oh my God; oh my God!" that he hollers just before we tumble into the guitar solo. You would hope that that was just off-the-cuff, throw it in, because it's just so good. It's one of those moments you listen out for. It doesn't matter, you hear that, and you've got to join in (laugh). He's keeping things simple lyrically. We're railing against the state. It's wanting retribution against deeds that are done. But again, we're talking about inequality, I think. We're talking about, should we be sticking up for those that can't fend for themselves? And really, we're talking about the perils of modern society, where you don't really give a shit about the average man on the street unless he's got something to give back. But it's done in a very poetic way; he doesn't bludgeon you with the point.

It's interesting that Scott Gorham co-wrote this. He gives it another go with 21 Guns a long, long way down the line, on their third album, *Nothing's Real*, 1997. It's a dangerous thing to do. It's always dangerous to reach back and rework something like this. To take your next band and look back on what is a reasonably iconic song—that's dangerous. They do okay with it, but they were never going to improve upon it, especially with the kind of sound 21 Guns went for in that era. It's an odd move.

Martin: There really is a fair bit of the *Nightlife* sound that's carried over to this album.

Steven: I think that remained for quite some time, really. It might be there in traces all the way through 'til near the end. I don't want to get ahead of myself and talk about *Thunder and Lightning*, but that to me is the only album where you get none of that. We're doing something different. But sure, there's a thread from *Nightlife* right the way through, where it's, "This is Lizzy; this is what we do—we are about the melody line. And we don't mind taking the foot off the gas, because you'll remember us as a heavy, heavy band anyway. Because we have biting guitar solos and a really intense drummer. We've got a great singer that can add that little bit of grit and gravel and danger." You know, all those pieces are going to be there throughout.

Martin: And here comes another one that could have sat cozy on *Nightlife*.

Andee: Yeah, "Spirit Slips Away" is definitely a dark and moody and mellow one, right? It's got the timpani drums in the beginning, that really kind of thunderous, rolling percussion. Yeah, this is a cool song. It has this dramatic intro but then turns to this reflective, contemplative kind of vibe, really spacious, and again, just really nice, clean, crystalline tones on the guitar. There's a guitar solo where the sustaining guitar notes in the background, that droning, might be an EBow. EBows were pretty new at that point in time. But yeah, listen for those sustained guitar notes happening in the background—that's possibly an EBow.

Tim: Here's another example of me being younger, going back and listening to a band that influence bands that I was into. As soon as this starts, I'm reminded of the instrumental "Switch 625" from Def Leppard's *High 'n' Dry* album. It's not exactly the same resolving note, but there's no way that's coincidence. Def Leppard have always claimed Thin Lizzy as an influence; that's one thing that all five of them, or whoever was in the band, had in common. And they've covered Thin Lizzy. So, to me, that's like a slowed-down version of the beginning of "Switch 625." As far as the rest of the song goes, it's not a heavy song; it provides a respite. And that's when you realise that, really, with the exception of "Wild One," this has been a pretty slamming album for 1975. It's not all heavy rock, but the energy level hasn't really let up until now.

Steven: I agree. This is one that doesn't play to type. It's menacing, but there's also a spacey kind of movie soundtrack feel, with grandiose guitars at the opening and that kind of blowing wind. That's atmosphere that really draws you in, and it's a great dynamic on an album that offers you an awful lot of different things to hold onto. It's one of the lesser celebrated tracks, but I really like it. It's clever because it contributes to the album's light and shade. And it's so natural, unforced. The guitars are easy but they're never listless. The bass kind of meanders, but it delivers; there's purpose there.

And same again, the drums are maybe not as versatile, maybe not as dexterous as you're going to find elsewhere on the album, but Brian Downey is just playing for the song. He's doing exactly what needs to be done. People focus on Phil's aggression and his snarling bite, but when he's in a reflective mood, what he's saying is maybe even more memorable. And he's singing a song here where you might think hindsight is a wonderful thing. But it's eerily kind of prophetic. He's singing about darkness falling, angels rejoicing, spirit slipping away. To me, all these years down the line, it adds a poignancy to what really is a set of beautiful lyrics. In retrospect, I see it as one of the cornerstones of this album. There's an atmosphere and a gentle confidence about it.

But yeah, to me, he's beginning to reveal, with decades' worth of hindsight, maybe too much of himself—already. We're quite early on in the career here and he is putting his heart on the line, whether that's about politics or something on a grander scale. But yeah, with a song like this, you tend to think it's about him and that he is actually letting you in. He's not just using imagery to suggest something where you then go back and think, hmm, that was maybe about him. He sings it like he's singing a song about himself. It's dangerously open, I would suggest.

Martin: Next is "Silver Dollar"—I can picture this on *Nightlife* as well.

Andee: Yeah, there's a standard boogie woogie feel here. When that song starts up, I instantly don't like it, and that feeling stays until the chorus, where there are these yearning chords. I don't know how to describe this, but it's like the rest of the song sounds like any band, and it doesn't really sound like Thin Lizzy to me until you get to those hits, those strokes in the chorus, where he's kind of belting those aching notes. But overall, "Silver Dollar" sounds like any number of bands from the '70s just doing this boogie woogie-lite thing. It's not a favourite.

Tim: I hear an influence on April Wine here, specifically the song "Ladies Man" from *Harder... Faster*, with those "hits," as Andee calls them, and also "Roller," which comes from an album, *First Glance*, that also has a song called "Silver Dollar." But that just makes me think bands were listening to Thin Lizzy and taking notes. Plus, I think, incrementally, Thin Lizzy did a bit better in Canada than they did in the US. I know that *Live and Dangerous* was at least partly recorded at Seneca College in Toronto. So, it would make sense that a Canadian band would be onto them. This is the only one written by Brian Robertson, which kind of goes against what we hear of his personality and reputation.

Steven: As Tim says, this is one of these odd ones where Phil did not get involved. There are not many in the catalogue. There's two on this album. Are there only three in the whole catalogue? I think Eric Bell's got a sole credit on the debut and I don't think there's anything else. So yes, Brian Robertson wrote "Silver Dollar." It's maybe the least memorable song on show. It feels perfunctory and a little simple, certainly by this album's standards. I do like the sort of liquid guitar tones in it. The guitars are really fluid; they are doing something different from what it's surrounded by.

Lyrically it's the man wronged by his woman and busting in to sort things out. There's not really much subtext here. It has an ad-lib with the shout of, "All I got left is my old guitar," which doesn't really feel like it fits with the rest of the lyrics. And that sentence, like the "Oh my God; oh my God," it's just before the solo kicks in. You kind of think that it was just thrown in to give it some measure of mystique. There's not much mystique about this song. It's possibly the only thing on the whole album I could live without.

Martin: And everything we typecast about who we think Brian Robertson is versus Scott Gorham, this does not sound like a song Brian would write. You'd think it's a song Scott brought from California or something, right?

Steven: Yeah, absolutely. That's a really good way of putting it. It's a strange little track. It's okay, but this is a better album than just okay. You're cheering for them. You want these songs to shine once they take them on the road. You want them to win, don't you? But this one isn't going to do that for them.

Martin: All right, now we're back in business. "Freedom Song" isn't heavy, but it's still inherent and intrinsic Thin Lizzy to the core. It feels like a languid amble en route to "The Boys Are Back in Town."

Andee: Sure, yeah, and when the double guitar harmony part comes in, it's almost like that part is functioning like the chorus. It's an instrumental section but it feels like that's where a chorus would be. Yeah, you're right. It's got a similar quality to "The Boys are Back in Town" although not quite as sophisticated. Still, they've got multiple sections where they're playing with this harmony guitar idea with these rising trills going up the neck. Another thing about Thin Lizzy is that they always tuned down a half-step. So, their sound is a little deeper and heavier just by virtue of that. It's sort of where Van Halen would be tuning their guitar. You also hear it in Dio-era Black Sabbath. A lot of bands eventually did that. But I don't think a lot of bands were doing that in the '70s. But Thin Lizzy always did it as far as I remember. That's their standard tuning. So, when they play what looks like an E chord, it's comes out as an E flat.

Tim: I would say that to the average listener hearing *Fighting*, this is the song that would be the most Thin Lizzy-sounding. They'd hear the similarity to "The Boys Are Back in Town." It's a shuffle with twin leads, although it's more casual, I guess. It's written by Scott and Phil. I like that Phil actually says "Freedom song" in the lyrics. Although Phil's song precedes it, I've always associated this song with Bob Marley's "Redemption Song."

Steven: The key treat here are those twin guitars, which make their mark all over the place on this song. It's an interesting balance: hard rockin', trademark Thin Lizzy but at the same time, they're sort of carefree about it. It's got that ability to caress you, and then it kind of knocks you sideways. And that, to me, sums up Thin Lizzy in many ways.

But yeah, it's a freedom song, a liberty song. It's about standing up for what you believe. The consequences may be dire, is what you get from the lyrics. It's brave words, but Phil was brave. Life doesn't always work out, though—I get that impression about it. But yeah, it's an interesting song because it's got so much from before, plus the signpost of what comes after. I don't necessarily know if it ticks all the boxes and yet it still works.

Martin: All right, we close with a heavy metal rocker, and yet again, one that is kind of fussy and note-dense, even framed upon an odd time signature.

Andee: Yeah, "Ballad of a Hard Man" is maybe the heaviest song they had recorded up 'til that time. That sounds to me as heavy as Judas Priest circa 1976 or so. The heaviness definitely gets ratcheted up as we exit this album.

Tim: And Brian Downey definitely keeps things interesting with the big drum pattern. I like this one a lot. Now, what I find most interesting about this song is that it's very Phil-sounding, even though it's solely written by Scott Gorham. And I wonder if Scott wrote it about Phil because Phil lived hard. I like to imagine Scott writing this in response to the family back home in the States going, "Well, what's been going on, Scott? Tell us about it; tell us about Phil Lynott." And he writes a song (laughs).

Steven: As Tim says, this is another one without Phil involved in the writing. You do wonder if they were kind of giving Scott a shot, so he turns in a kind of harder, tougher track. It's a guitar-based song that lives up to the hard man intentions. It growls and it howls and the drums and bass are sounding simpler here than they are on most of the rest of the album, although they have to deal with that time signature.

The lyric is lean and mean: don't mess with me. There's also a suggestion of sort of scrapping in the back alleys and the pubs. We've got lines like, "Well, they got a scheme to sell you kids/The silver screens and glossy magazines." It's a different fight being played out here, isn't it? It's not just about fists, it's definitely about trying to get voices heard, rather than being duped into the easy path, a trivial life, being placated by the masses. I think it's more relevant now than maybe it was even then, in that sense.

But the song isn't depressing in any way. It's absolutely bulging at the sides with a real kind of mean intent. There's a willingness to take a real swipe at you. If you dare to walk in the song's path, it will knock you out of the way. It's straight to the point and it knows what it's all about. It's fitting that *Fighting* closes on a song that is this strong in its attitude about where this band is going to go. I guess it's back to the front cover. We're here for the fight. We're tough, we're rough, we're ready and we're going to win. And this song closes the album exactly on that note. The whole album doesn't need to do that to you, but they do indeed close on that note.

Martin: It's funny, because, again, "Silver Dollar" sounds like a Scott song and "Ballad of a Hard Man" sounds like a Brian song.

Steven: It's also funny because Brian's song is called "Silver Dollar." That's not a Scottish term in any shape or form; it's American—like Scott. A hard man is very much a Scottish term. There's a kind of funny crossover there between the two. I see the phrase "hard man," and as a Scotsman I'm left with no doubt about what I'm coming up against here. This is not so much about a hard time; this is about someone that's going to knock you in the face. And that's what this song does. It just clobbers you in the face and it's not gonna apologise for it.

Martin: But like you say, the rest of the album doesn't have to do that, and it certainly does not.

Steven: No. Although *Fighting* is aggressive in places, it's hard rock. There's maybe one toe into the world of heavy metal. And even still, it's '70s heavy metal, because the term back then was barely formulated, and it covered a wide gamut of song styles. Sure, Lizzy were probably viewed as heavy metal back then, but it's not really, is it? They never gallop. They never kind of fall back on those tropes. There's never that machine gun riff. There's suggestion and perhaps parts of songs, but they never fall into all of those kinds of tropes that the '70s threw at us. And I love them all—don't get me wrong (laughs). I'm on board with all of those. But I'm really delighted that Lizzy resisted it. Because it really would have changed them drastically. They're not a heavy metal band; they're a heavy rock band. This is a band that rocks. It's about groove, it's about melancholy, and even when they're heavy, they're subtle. Those guitars are often suggested as much as they are insistent. It was never an out-and-out charge or racing across the battlefield. It was rough and tough inside the pub.

So yeah, I think *Fighting* is a fully realised album and a really successful album, one of the strongest albums in the catalogue. And maybe that's partly because the guys are still searching a little bit. But that doesn't invalidate it. The goal is in the hunting as much as it is in the finding. They don't quite get to their identifiable sound, but they still have a sound nobody else was doing. There are other twin guitar bands around. You're not going to confuse them with Lizzy.

Honesty Is No Excuse: Thin Lizzy on Record

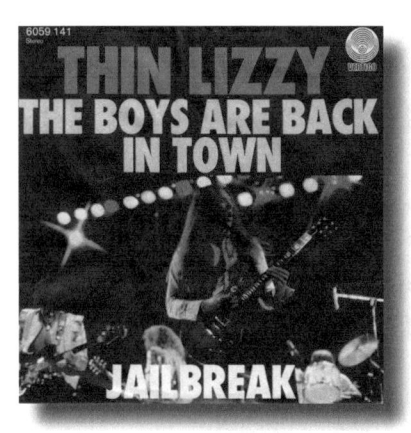

JAILBREAK

March 26, 1976
Vertigo 9102 008
Produced by John Alcock
Engineered by Will Reid Dick
Recorded at Ramport Studios, London, UK
Personnel: Phil Lynott – bass guitar, acoustic guitar, vocals, Scott Gorham – lead guitar, guitars, Brian Robertson – lead guitar, guitars, Brian Downey – drums, percussion
Key additional personnel: Tim Hinkley – keyboards on "Running Back"

Side 1
1. "Jailbreak" (Lynott) 4:05
2. "Angel from the Coast" (Lynott, Robertson) 3:40
3. "Running Back" (Lynott) 3:25
4. "Romeo and the Lonely Girl" (Lynott) 4:20
5. "Warriors" (Lynott, Gorham) 4:05

Side 2
1. "The Boys Are Back in Town" (Lynott) 5:00
2. "Fight or Fall" (Lynott) 4:45
3. "Cowboy Song" (Lynott) 5:15
4. "Emerald" (Gorham, Robertson, Downey, Lynott) 4:00

Honesty Is No Excuse: Thin Lizzy on Record

Martin talks to John Alapick, Tim Durling and Sean Kelly about *Jailbreak*.

Martin Popoff: All right, so what is the significance of *Jailbreak* in the Thin Lizzy catalogue?

John Alapick: I like to call *Jailbreak* a universal album, because this is the first album you should listen to if you are asking to be introduced to Thin Lizzy. It's their *Moving Pictures* or their *Back in Black*. It's their Boston self-titled debut. This is where you start. Something that's been popping in my head today, this actually went gold in the States which is actually a shame, because what really killed the momentum was the fact that Phil had hepatitis and they had to cut the tour short. If they'd been able to keep going and if he was able to stay healthy and they were able to put more singles out and do a lot more dates, *Jailbreak* would have gone platinum in the first year that it came out, in my humble opinion.

Think about how big a hit "The Boys Are Back in Town" was and yet this was only a gold album. Because this album had legs. There are other songs Mercury could have pushed at radio. Sure, there's nothing as catchy and as memorable as "The Boys Are Back in Town" and "Cowboy Song," which was a No.77 song here in the States, but "Running Back" is there. That was originally considered as a single. That could have got some airplay on the R&B stations even. They could have reached a different audience there. And then a song like "Romeo and the Lonely Girl" is pretty catchy. That could have got some airplay as well. Of course the title track is fantastic, and we still hear that today.

But it's really a shame that that killed their momentum cold, because after that they made all these great albums, and yet they never came close to the sales of *Jailbreak* ever again. They never really got to that point where they played the big arenas. If you're gonna play a big arena, you're special guests to Queen. You're probably playing 2000-seaters to maybe 5000-seaters back then. You had a lot more mid-sized arenas. You don't have those much in the States anymore. But yeah, it's really a shame that happened. We did get another great album in 1976, *Johnny the Fox*, which was released really quick. That's a fantastic album as well, but I think they could have gotten more mileage out of *Jailbreak*.

Martin: And the other thing about this record is that it's recorded for radio in the sense that it's very toppy and bright and it doesn't have a lot of bass. When you hear an album like that, the producer's defence is always, "We mixed it for radio play."

John: Exactly, so it sounds great on radio, right? And *Jailbreak* does. Yeah, I agree. I think they made albums that were recorded better, but none better in terms of hearing it over the radio. This was John Alcock producing for them. He produced this and he produced *Johnny the Fox*. He did some John Entwistle albums there in the '70s—not his best albums—and he did some work with Earl Slick as well. A bit of a resume but this was definitely his biggest success, with these two albums.

Martin: And Tim, how have Thin Lizzy changed or improved since *Fighting*?

Tim Durling: I'd say the songwriting has solidified. And that goes back to that wonderful fact that record labels back then allowed bands not just one or two albums but multiple albums to develop and get better and hone their craft, playing the long game, saying, if we stick with these guys, they might make us some money. And that's just such a different world than it is now. And it's different than it would become in the '80s. Because in the '80s, you always heard that if you haven't made it by your third album, you're going to be dropped. So here they are on their sixth album, and it turns out it's their breakthrough.

Martin: What do you think of the production? It's pretty bright and trebly, isn't it?

Tim: It is. I thought *Fighting* sounded like a decent enough production for 1975. It's not going to make you forget Roy Thomas Baker or Jack Douglas, which brings to mind, what would these guys have sounded like if they'd had those guys or Ted Templeman, someone like that working with them? But it's decent enough. It's a friendly enough production, so that when you'd hear "The Boys Are Back in Town" on AM radio, it wasn't overly threatening. But yeah, it's not offensive to the ears, certainly. It's a very polite production and it kind of contains everything, save for enough bottom end, I suppose.

Martin: Sean, how about a few introductory words before we look at the tracks?

Sean Kelly: Okay, well, I'd say that with *Jailbreak*, you're finally starting to see some crystallization of what they're all about and what their commercial aspirations are. Because when I went through and listened to this record again analytically, I started to hear all the things they were taking from their touring experiences, plus the bands they'd seen and what was happening on FM radio in the States. Like, I hear The Doobie Brothers and BTO and Edgar Winter. But I also hear, finally, the classic Thin Lizzy guitar sound captured. This is actually when the tones started to get as tough as the band could be live.

Because previously, the tone was more of an early '70s thing. They were trying to capture the ferocity of loud tube amps from the live setting in recording studios, but that was going against what engineers had learned to do. They didn't want to distort things; they wanted clarity. And so you ended up getting that first Kiss record, these kind of wimpier versions of what the band was actually trying to put across. And on this record, I felt that the producer, John Alcock, who'd worked with The Who, he kind of got it. So, you're hearing the Marshall amps and the Les Pauls captured. It's tough, but it still has a lot of that great clarity that came from '60s and '70s recording. So, you get all the nice, intricate chord voicings ringing out, but the guitars are tougher, and I think that that's really key.

Martin: Okay, and as a strummer yourself, what's your general sense of the personalities of the band's two guitarists, Scott Gorham and Brian Robertson?

Sean: Well, I'll start with Robbo, because he's the dominant figure here. He's the aggressive one and by all accounts, the more schooled guitarist. But I can't say enough about Gorham and his role as the glue in Thin Lizzy. He's highly adaptable. He has no ego, so he didn't ever seem concerned with having to assert himself. But he's also got an incredible melodic sensibility and this laid-back Californian thing in his playing that keeps it all reined in. And if you actually listen to him and his various guitar partners, he adapts and kind of rises to whatever technical challenges are thrown out, while holding it all together. But yeah, Robbo is definitely the fireworks here. And Gorham is the rhythmically and melodically laid-back sensibility that makes the romance in Phil's lyrics work.

Martin: What do you think of the album cover? On some that window on the front is die-cut, but on cheaper editions, it's just a plain old album cover.

Tim: Yes (laughs) and some versions have three guys, and some have all four of them, running out of that television in the middle. Mine's a '96 remaster, and it's just got three of them.

Martin: Yeah, it looks like it's Scott that gets cropped out when only three make the shot. It's closer up and the runner to the right gets edged out.

Tim: The cover reminds me of *Destroyer*, and it's the same year. Even though it's by Jim Fitzpatrick, it looks like one of the Marvel Kiss comics. It certainly stood out. Plus, it looks like a heavy rock album.

Sean: It's interesting; I always thought the album cover was kind of weird, and I couldn't really get what was happening. It's a sci-fi thing, and at one point it was actually going to be a rock opera. So "Jailbreak" was kind of the title track of this rock opera that Phil had in his mind. From what I understand, Phil in a nutshell was going, "I've got this great idea guys. We're gonna do a rock opera." And then you forget about it halfway through and then you just kind of make it all work anyway because you've got to get the record done.

Martin: And the title track of this lost rock opera opens the album.

Tim: Yes, it does, and "Jailbreak" is one of their signature songs, arguably the second best or biggest Thin Lizzy song. It's pretty hard to go wrong with an F sharp riff. And that's what this is—it's a simple but effective riff. I like the little cadence at the beginning, just the one note and the cymbal crash and then they're off to the races. It's very much in the spirit of Phil telling tales. This could be a Western or a mob movie or a film noire from the '40s, like a Jimmy Cagney movie or something like that with a bank robbery and they're trying to get away. It's evocative. It puts you there; it puts you in that little TV screen in your head. Musically, it's simple but it's heavy. I think it's a great way to open this album, not just as a title song, but as a statement of purpose. It's like, well, we kind of mean it this time. We want that hard rock audience. And here we go. This is what we've got.

Martin: It's kind of their "Smoke on the Water" because it's got that riff. "The Boys Are Back in Town" isn't so much about riff than it is chords.

Tim: Yeah, "The Boys Are Back in Town" really doesn't have much of a riff. It's got a hooky twin guitar lead that serves as a riff, I suppose. As for "Jailbreak," I'm sure that in 1976 tons of prospective young guitar players were wanting to learn it as maybe the first song they ever learned—that wouldn't surprise me at all. And there's your link to "Smoke on the Water." It's also interesting that it's called "Jailbreak" where of course AC/DC has a song called "Jailbreak" from the very same year. But that didn't become widely known in North America until the EP came out in 1984. There isn't really a solo in the song. It goes through the different modulations and that's enough of a break from the singing. I guess you could call the twin lead a solo, but it's not your typical solo. It's more of an ensemble piece.

John: Agreed, and overall, with "Jailbreak," you hear the Brian Robertson/Scott Gorham twin guitars in full flight. Phil sounds so confident on the vocals. He's throwing in ad-libs. The song makes you feel like you're in a jailbreak, the way he writes it, the way they're playing, the way he's singing. It's just a menacing song and it's stood the test of time. Like Tim says, it's the second most famous song by them next to "The Boys Are Back in Town." They're the only two songs I ever hear on AOR radio here in the States anymore.

Martin: Which is kind of surprising, because it's one of their most heavy metal songs.

John: Yeah, and people who are not really into hard rock or metal, the people in my life that I've run across over the years, they all like "Jailbreak." I've never met anyone who said that they didn't like "Jailbreak." You might hear somebody say, "I'm sick of that 'Boys Are Back in Town' song." But I've never heard anyone say anything bad about "Jailbreak." What a fantastic track. And what a show-stopping opener it was on *Live and Dangerous* as well.

Sean: I'll tell ya, every guitar player goes to a soundcheck and says, "What should we jam? Why don't we play 'Jailbreak?'" That's like every band I've been in. Coney Hatch, actually, we always end up playing that riff at soundcheck because it's so perfectly suited to the power chord. It's like, that riff was made for a power chord. And once again, they're finally able to capture the power of the guitar tones, coming up with riffs like that. And also a big part of that song is the wah-wah pedal. Brian Robertson has his Coloursound wah-wah pedal, and those perfectly interspersed little bursts of melodicism that he brings are perfect energisers. So, this is Thin Lizzy finally asserting themselves as the stadium rockers they aspired to be.

The song totally works lyrically. Thin Lizzy, the bad boys, are gonna break out and "Listen to me," the women better be waiting. It's a great bad boy rock anthem but classed-up with romanticism. Classic Lizzy riff, great breakdown, powerful and like everything on this record, it's all being underpinned by Brian Downey, who is the most dynamic of rock 'n' roll drummers in my book. There's his ability to play fills and then you can actually hear it crescendo, right? It's unparalleled. I don't know, the whole thing swings and grooves and rocks at the same time.

Martin: I didn't get your comments on the production. Do you find it toppy?

Sean: Yeah, absolutely. It's glassy. They were using Les Paul Deluxes. And they had the mini-humbuckers, which add a lot of clarity, a little punch here, like a Strat or something. It wasn't the big, thick, beefy, full-on Les Paul tones that you'd hear later on with *Black Rose* when Gary Moore joined the band. So yes, it's toppy and it's bright.

Martin: Next is the enigmatic "Angel from the Coast." Is it about a hit man? Maybe it's a hit lady or possibly a more paranormal angel of death.

John: Yes, it's written so skilfully that it's hard to tell. At the music end, it's got a little Springsteen in it, meaning those guitar chords. I like that after they go through the second verse, they play those three chords, but they really stretch them out; that's a different thing. They were adding these little things by this point to their songs, these little hooks that would make them distinct from other songs that were on the radio. It wasn't just verse, chorus, verse, and the occasional bridge.

Martin: And they're also showing a tendency to mix it up with guitar tones, right? You get very clean mixed with distortion pedal here.

There's almost an implied acoustic, and often overt acoustic in this catalogue. Rush and Kiss did that too.

John: Yes, they do, which goes all the way back to the first album. They did a little bit on *Bad Reputation* as well. But yeah, that's another nice thing about them. You usually hear a sort of single-minded structure: this is an electric song; this is a folky acoustic song or a ballad. They present that added sense of texture.

Sean: This is one where I hear BTO and Edgar Winter, the jangling 16th note strumming guitars. But it also alludes to what we hear later on in Iron Maiden with these almost Gothic harmonies. The harmony break is quite unusual. So you're hearing, I think, the crystallization of the twin guitar approach here, but also the attempt to get on American radio with the very funky strumming thing that's happening. It's a nice mix of jangle and heavy riff. There's actually some elements of like *Houses of the Holy* in there. I hear Zeppelin, especially in that brief solo at like 1:56, which is very Jimmy Page. But yeah, there's this kind of Who-ish power chord thing that emerges after I thought it was already pretty satisfying on the verse, with that funk playing mixed with these fired-off licks. It makes for a nice blend.

Martin: "Running Back" sits in a similar space to the one before it, i.e. very much up-tempo pop, but thoughtful.

Sean: Right, plus Phil is definitely in the whole Bruce Springsteen/Van Morrison camp with this one, especially Van, with those laid-back vocals and the kind of Celtic soul approach. They brought in a session guy to play a little Fender Rhodes part, and Robbo hated it because he initially was the guy playing piano and slide guitar. This was initially a much bluesier kind of tune, but Phil wanted to crack American radio—he was going for it. And that was lined up to be the first single and it sounds like a single to me. It sounds like an attempt at a single. The heaviness was starting to take over, but they were still very much angling to get on commercial rock radio in the US.

John: Totally agree. This sounds like a blatant attempt at radio. Now, when you think about this album, this was album number six and the third album with Vertigo, distributed by Mercury in the US. And Vertigo went to them and said, okay, you guys need a hit right now. You guys got good albums, but they're not selling. You gotta give us a hit. And so, you've got "Running Back" with that overt and simple guitar lick and the horn part. It's very catchy, an easy song to remember. Great vocal from Phil here, and some very nice sort of circular solos here from Brian Robertson as well. As for the Van Morrison, I'm hearing a correlation with like *Astral Weeks* and *Moondance*, as well as *Wavelength*, which is actually later, 1978.

Martin: "Romeo and the Lonely Girl" continues this overt blending of guitar tones, to the point where it's becoming a bit of a trademark.

John: Yes, strong track as well and also effortlessly catchy. "Poor Romeo sitting out on his own-ee-o." It sounds a little silly, but it works. Phil always knew how to write a great story song; his lyrics are really peaking here. He knew when to bring in emotion and he knew when to hold back. He was becoming a star at this point. And you're right, the guitars sound like they are in full bloom, where we get almost like a garden of sounds, a panorama, as we move from track to track. It's a wonderful song.

Tim: "Romeo and the Lonely Girl;" this is Phil creating characters—there's two right there in the title. That's another reason Thin Lizzy had such an influence on bands like Bon Jovi, which in turn was a Springsteen thing, or Southside Johnny. It's the idea of, maybe a person is writing about themselves or their own relationship, but they're using aliases to say, oh no, this is about someone else. This is about something that happened many years ago. You could say "Layla" is a song that's autobiographical but in disguise. That's a classic Phil Lynott device, using aliases almost as metaphors.

Sean: Yeah, I get a Doobie Brothers influence here. But it's very propulsive, because once again, Downey is able to play this busy drum part but keep it dynamic and never overpower. Typical Phil lyric. He feels sorry for himself that he has to go and run around with a bunch of women but, like, why does the woman always leave me? I can't believe it. I can't believe she did that to me. All I did was go and have a million affairs on the road. So, it's got that kind of macho thing. Like, I do believe Phil was a very sensitive guy, but he came up in a certain time and a certain place in this kind of '70s rock 'n' roll environment that informs the lyric. But he's the only guy I know who could get away with saying "own-ee-o." Some of the wordplay, no one should do, but you just accept it from Phil. He really was that guy who could sell you anything.

Martin: It's back to the strafing metal now, with side two-closer "Warriors."

Tim: Absolutely, and I used to think it was just called "Warrior," because the lyric is so singular and clearly enunciated that way. I wanted to reiterate the storyline that goes with this album, that it was briefly considered that they would do a concept album, and so you see the tie-in with the cover art.

Sean: Yeah, and I also read something with Phil where he said words to the effect of, "Oh, what I was trying to write was kind of a tribute to guys like Hendrix and Duane Allman who took lots of drugs in the name of pushing it to the limits." But to me, that sounds like a justification after the fact, because this was a piece for a concept record that was no longer a concept record. But I can see the parallels, drug-users as warriors, rock 'n' roll warriors. Incredible guitar solo here by Robbo. He's just a master of the wah pedal, the way he can sweep through all the frequencies while playing those classic licks. Beautiful.

To me, the song is almost progressive in scope; there's incredible drums happening, new riffs coming in and out. And there's like these big, angelic background vocals. I wonder if there was a Rush influence. Like, if at some point they listened to some Rush and said, hey, let's throw some of that in. It was probably too early for that, although both bands were on Mercury in the States. But it sounds a little progressive. And that's part of the Lizzy thing anyway, musical intricacy.

Martin: And as I've mentioned before, Sean, a surprising number of their early heavy songs are quite note-dense and rhythmically complex.

Sean: I guess when they dive in, they just really put a lot of thought into it and try to excel, basically, right? I guess it was a time when there was still much value placed on musicianship. You still had to cut it live and you had to step above, so you did that. It's so funny. I go back and listen to Kiss and people talk about Kiss being caveman rock. Go back and listen. There's some stuff going on there too.

There's Motown, there's riffs, there's some technically challenging things. But definitely with Lizzy, yeah, you could tell there was a musical element in there, and I suspect a lot of that came from Downey.

John: There's a lot of echo on "Warriors," which as a song is heavy, exhilarating and menacing. But the echo on here, I think they overdo it sometimes. But if you like the heavy Thin Lizzy, this is where you go—"Warriors" is for you. Love the ending. After the solo at the end, the last solo, they go into that different movement which ends the track, and I agree with Sean, that it sounds like a Rush thing. But there's focus, compared to something like *Caress of Steel*, which they might have heard, or their own *Nightlife* album. As much as I love *Nightlife*, there are a few songs that are heavy and the rest of it is very R&B. This is focused. This is a try harder album, as you would say. The record company's coming to them saying, "Okay, there's a lot we like, but you gotta put it all together." This is where they put it all together.

Martin: It's so predictable that it's almost sad, but as angry young metalhead kids, we loved the chorus on "The Boys Are Back in Town" but checked out completely on the verses.

John: Yeah, it's intriguingly kind of half-heavy, isn't it? But it's the universal Thin Lizzy song. It's very easy to see how this became a hit single. It's a Bruce Springsteen lyric and vocal with these Who power chords. But there are these hooks; that "Spread the word around" part isn't something that you would normally hear. And then there's the big wind-up drum fill. And then the fact that he's talking about where they're hanging out, like Friday night down at Dino's. People who are listening to this song, they're relating it to heading out to their favourite bar with their friends. It's a universal experience, something that millions of people can relate to. And all inside of a song that is catchy as sin, a wonderful song.

Martin: Also interesting, John, is that if you could say the song has a riff at all, it's played on the bass.

John: Yeah, that would be it. The key to a great song is the quality and quantity of little hooks like that, plus a memorable chorus and, like I say, a relatable story. Plus, the unison guitar lines are so joyous on here. What a song. I will admit I've heard it too many times. "Jailbreak," I could still listen to on the radio all day, but "The Boys Are Back in Town" I'm a little past it at this point.

Tim: True, we've all heard it too much, but of course it's their signature song. It gave them a career and has kept that name in the public eye. If people know nothing else about Thin Lizzy, they know "The Boys Are Back in Town." There might even be more people that know the song now than they did originally. Still, it was a top 20 single in the US and obviously, a hit single plays a big part in an album's success.

If you look at any lengthy career, it's probably the album that contained the hit single that got more casual people to check the band out. Thin Lizzy never struck me as an impulse buy band. You're either way into them or you don't know anything about them. And so, as someone that goes to a lot to record fairs, if you do see original Thin Lizzy vinyl, it's always at least $40 because people have held onto this stuff. And if they sell it, people will notice it in the bins, and it will be expensive. Lizzy did not sell massive quantities of albums and like I say, the people that bought them, I get the feeling they held onto them and cherished them.

As for the song, I get "Born to Run" vibes, especially the way that Phil crams all of those words into the stanzas or whatever. It's almost like it doesn't matter how awkward it might be on paper, it just rolls off the tongue. It's not surprising the song broke through the way it did. It's surprising to me that they couldn't keep it up. Because it's not like it's all that different than the rest of their catalogue. It's not an outlier in their catalogue. It's an outlier only because it became a hit.

Martin: Yeah, great point. Can you speak a little more to Phil as a vocalist?

Tim: Well, Phil's not a singer's singer, as it were. But as a storyteller and an interpreter, he draws you in. It's like, sit down children, your grandpa is going to tell you a story about how it used to be. And it's, dare I say, friendly. Not friendly in terms of like, it's always good things he's talking about. But it's almost like I'm either going to tell you something fun that happened, or I'm going to issue a cautionary tale. Either way, take notice and pay attention because it's for your own good. That's what makes him a great vocalist. Plus, he doesn't sound like anybody else. Even though he's got influences from all over the place, you never get a sense he's mimicking anybody. You always know when it's him. Which is probably why when Thin Lizzy kind of disbanded and he went on to form Grand Slam, it was never going to sound that different from his old band.

Martin: Sean, thoughts on the big anthem?

Sean: Yeah, lots. It's everything. It's where all the pieces of the puzzle came together, including the harmony guitars, which are more pronounced all of a sudden. It's not just a background harmony guitar part; it's coming to the forefront. They're playing it with real authority. And also, something people talk a lot about with Lizzy are the chord voicings. They're not just playing power chords; they're playing sophisticated chord voicings, like sixths and major sevens and things against driving rock, and that just adds class and sophistication.

And romanticism—this song is all about romanticizing what is essentially a pretty typical male experience, right? Going out and looking for girls. Typical lyrical fodder back then. It's all about the romance and it's Phil at his evocative best. He's creating and colouring these characters that you feel empathy for, even some jerk who's like trying to pick up a girl and being a jerk about it. And you feel bad for the girl, but she gets sick of his shit and slaps him in the face. I mean, how do you do that? Because Phil sells it, right?

So, in "The Boys Are Back in Town," it's driving hard rock and it's the right hooks and a sing-along chorus, things which sometimes evade Lizzy. It's amazing to me that this song was almost like a throwaway that didn't make it. I think they called it "GI Joe is Back" or something. But yeah, it captures Lizzy at their lyrically and instrumentally most defined. And I bet there was an "Aha!" moment when they finally saw this song starting to take off. Because moving forward, this is one of their templates.

Martin: It's also a good example of Phil's challenging sense of vocal phrasing.

Sean: Unbelievable. I've tried to cover Thin Lizzy songs and if you ever try to play it and sing it, he's singing so far back on the beat while playing on top, it's quite something. It's a real acrobatic feat, really. And he would constantly reinvent that live. If you listen to the live versions, they're all different. And that, to me, is a master vocal interpreter and something we don't really hear him heralded as. But yes, he's conversational. He doesn't care what's going on with the music. He'll let his lines go right over the top of the end of the verse or the chorus or whatever and keep babbling away. He chases the concept. That concept's probably been conceived on the spot, but he'll chase it to the end.

Martin: Next is "Fight or Fall," the most forgotten song from the album, I figure.

Sean: Yeah, it's kinda '70s soft rock. Lyrically though—and maybe underscored by the R&B vibe—I wonder if given Phil's black heritage, this is a song he's singing to other black men to stand up against oppression. Or was it something different, as part of the shelved concept album? I don't know. But I do like when Lizzy blends acoustic textures with the electric side. That adds a level of class that you don't see in other hard rock bands. Nice production elements too; there's some panned vocal things that go back and forth. When Phil was in the studio, I feel that a lot of this kind of thing came from him and not the producer.

John: Phil shines on these slow songs, the ballads. What a soulful singer. I love this track and his delivery on it. The guitars are really sparse, but what they play is perfect for the track. They're not overplaying; it's all just for the song here. I love the solo. I love Phil's lyric on here—"After all this time"... it's just awesome. You talk about albums that have great first halves, but on *Jailbreak*, what a second half. These are all well-developed songs full of hooks. Now, I'm an allmusic.com junkie. I've been reading it almost every day for 20 years or more. And when I was younger, I would get frustrated when these hard rock albums I love so much always got four or four-and-a-half stars. But no, *Jailbreak* is a five in my opinion and they gave it a five.

Martin: Next is arguably the band's second biggest song, depending on where you rank the title track. Although if you look at the stats, on Spotify, "The Boys Are Back in Town" has been streamed about six times as much as "Jailbreak," and then "Cowboy Song" is next, at about a third of "Jailbreak."

John: Interesting. Yeah, when you go to "Cowboy Song," holy smokes. Maybe if they'd cut it down a little bit, it would have been a bigger hit for them, because who can deny that chorus? I love the intro, which is performed like a country western song, with coyote calls and howling winds and lonesome trails—love it. And then it goes into that memorable guitar line and Phil's vocal, which he sings with such emotion and expression. The first solo is excellent, and then they bring back the twin lead they had in the beginning. We get the breakdown, where things get quiet and Phil sings, "It's okay, amigo/ Just let me go" and then it gets loud, and it gets soft again. Next, we get that wonderful second solo, more chorus and then "The cowboy's life is the life for me," last chord—scene (laughs). There's nothing else left to say.

Tim: Yeah, a classic, a popular song, and a bit like "Wild One" for me, sort of a lament. And the whole idea of "Cowboy Song," I know you hate Bon Jovi, but this song is a precursor to "Wanted Dead or Alive," with the idea of the touring musician being like a cowboy, roaming the trails out on tour and being away from home. That's the vibe I get here. And as much as there's the traditional Irish stuff in Phil's lyrics, there's an awful lot of Wild West imagery too.

Sean: For sure, Phil loved his American cowboy stuff, right? This is my absolute favourite Thin Lizzy song, more so for the *Live and Dangerous* version. Because it's a pure romance. And I could see where being in Ireland watching these cowboy movies and everything, it must have felt incredibly romantic to think of America, the new frontier. And I love it; it's so naïve. "I was took in Texas"— great line.

And from the music end, what's interesting is that Phil would change the bass line underneath these pretty standard rock progressions and create sophisticated harmonies that were more suited to the romantic things he was singing about. Just by changing one note on the bass, underneath the guitars—a very Beatle-esque type of thing—you can create a richer harmony in the guitar parts. And that happens here. This is Phil at his most human, you know what I mean? It's kinda like, well, I'm this type of guy. I run around and I make my mistakes. But it's all in the pursuit of this kind of naïve freedom. He's looking for that freedom that I think a lot of people look to America for. And to me, this is his tribute to America as much as anything else.

Jailbreak

Martin: Side two wraps up with "Emerald," covered by many metal bands, Celtic, blustery, classic, and in three/four time.

John: Yeah, if you're a metal guy, you love "Emerald" because "Emerald" has that fantastic riff. We're going back to Ireland again, the trials and tribulations, the fighting in Ireland—great lyric. And then it's got this triumphant sort of march beats in the verses that takes you in. They have this free concert on YouTube that they did in Australia, and there were like 30,000 people there and they're all just clapping with that beat. They're taken right in, and the guys know it—they've got the crowd right there.

Tim: I'd say this one's heavier than "Jailbreak" because it's got that military feel to it, not just in the lyrics about the Emerald Isle, Ireland, but in the delivery. It's got some great lead guitar work and really speedy drumming, specifically on the high-hat, the ride and with some of the snare fills. Love the twin lead guitar at the end of it. Yeah, this is a song I can imagine people in '76 being very excited about when they got to the end of this album, thinking wow, this is heavy. Years later, Ace Frehley did a really good version of it on his covers album *Origins Vol. 1*, where he actually trades licks at the end with Slash. It's a pretty faithful rendition.

And Brian Downey, man, he's arrived. Maybe not to the maximum of his abilities, but at least most of the way there. It's like he said, "I'm just going to set the pace. Everybody can catch up." It's a shame he rarely gets mentioned in the pantheon of great rock drummers. But man, the stuff he would do on the high-hat and the really quick turnarounds on this album, everything he plays just suits the material. He doesn't overplay and he doesn't underplay. Striking that balance is tough to do as a drummer.

Sean: Yeah, man, "Emerald" is definitive Thin Lizzy Celtic rock. It's when the Celtic rock thing and Phil's love of legend and Irish folklore come together, and you can tell this means something to him. It's something innate in the Irishman, this feeling of, hey, man, we've been we've been oppressed and we're gonna rise up and fight against the oppression, right? Heaviest track on the album. The guitar interplay, that duelling solo, is so beautifully done. And it's funny, because you've got Robbo, clearly the Young Turk, bringing the fire, but Gorham pushes back against Robbo's more fiery approach. But eventually Robbo takes over the whole solo and runs rampant all over it.

Martin: Nice. So, to close, I'm wondering, where would *Jailbreak* rank in the canon for you?

Tim: Well, it would have to be in the top five for me, just because I think sometimes there's a reason for a record's mass appeal. *Moving Pictures* is my favourite Rush album, and I know it's the one that the masses appreciate too, with five million sold in the States. *Jailbreak* is Thin Lizzy's only gold album. It's a good place to start and it's a good place to keep going from chronologically if you want to keep going. It's just a good rock album and I'm glad that it continues to be made available. I wish people would dig deeper with this band. This is not an album that you listen to and then you hear another Thin Lizzy album and think it sounds like a completely different band. No, this is the purest distillation of what makes Thin Lizzy tick as a band. It's sensible to think that if you like this, you'd likely be on board with anything from *Fighting* through to *Renegade*, certainly.

Martin: That's true, yeah. It's absolutely representative, right? It basically covers all the bases. Which makes it more irritating that there aren't another couple of golds in the collection. Out of interest, what would be your others in the top five?

Tim: I would put *Fighting* there because this is a logical step up from that one. I know it's a bit of an outlier, but I really like *Thunder and Lightning*. And for the other two, I'd go with *Johnny the Fox* and *Bad Reputation*. Those are continuing the good work of *Jailbreak*. It's like, hey, it worked. Let's not repeat it, but let's refine what we just did and keep going. It just amazes me when I think of Aerosmith, at least today, when it takes forever to get a new album out of them. The fact that Thin Lizzy put out three classic albums in two years just boggles the mind.

Martin: The *Jailbreak* tour is where Phil contracts hepatitis and they have to come home.

Tim: They were so plagued with bad luck, to the point where they became almost a cult band. But there are things that happen in artists' careers where the stars just don't align for them. And Thin Lizzy never recover from it. Even someone as well-known as Alice Cooper represents a similar example. Alice took sick and there was no tour for the *Goes to Hell* album, which up until that point, pretty much everything he had done had gone platinum. And he didn't have another certifying album in the States until *Trash* in '89. He never quite recovered from that. And with Thin Lizzy, especially being behind the eight ball coming from Ireland, they were finally starting to break and I think that they could have. They just didn't get on that same level. If they'd had two more albums that did as well as *Jailbreak*, they may have had a longer run. You never know.

Sean: *Jailbreak* sounds like a band who's still very much on the same side and working towards a common goal. And then usually after a big, successful album, you go out and send the numbers even higher. But this is the tour that got shut down and that was a big blow. Because these guys would have gone and conquered; there's no doubt about it. So this one gets hampered from hepatitis and next he's sitting in the hospital writing *Johnny the Fox*. And then for that album, Robbo cuts up his hand in a bar fight. Hard luck stories, right? All feeding into the pressure to crack America. Remember, America is always the goal here, with Phil, I think. *Johnny the Fox* is a great record too, but *Jailbreak* is extra special because it's the exciting discovery of a sound and everybody's hopped up and enthusiastic about it. The tour lurches to a stop and like Tim says, they never really recover.

Honesty Is No Excuse: Thin Lizzy on Record

JOHNNY THE FOX

October 16, 1976
Vertigo 9102 012
Produced by John Alcock
Engineered by Will Reid Dick; assistant engineer – Neil Hornby
Recorded at Ramport Studios, London, UK
Personnel: Phil Lynott – bass guitar, acoustic guitars, lead and backing vocals, Scott Gorham – lead guitars, guitars, Brian Robertson – lead guitar, guitars, Brian Downey – drums, percussion
Key additional personnel: Fiachra Trench – brass and string arrangements, Phil Collins – percussion, Kim Beacon – backing vocals.

Side 1
1. "Johnny" (Lynott) 4:25
2. "Rocky" (Lynott, Gorham, Downey) 3:42
3. "Borderline" (Lynott, Robertson) 4:34
4. "Don't Believe a Word" (Lynott) 2:16
5. "Fools Gold" (Lynott) 3:51

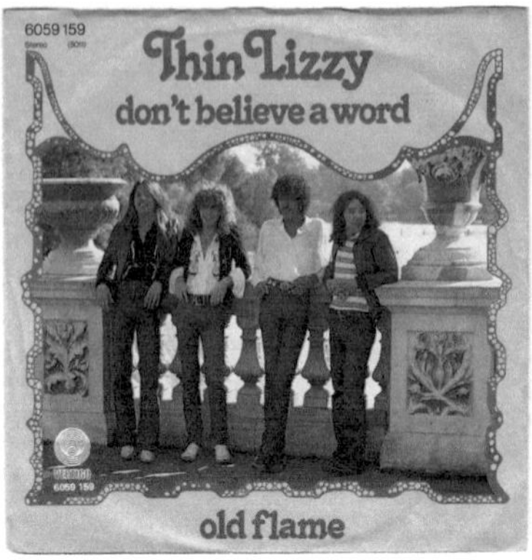
6059 159
Thin Lizzy
don't believe a word
old flame

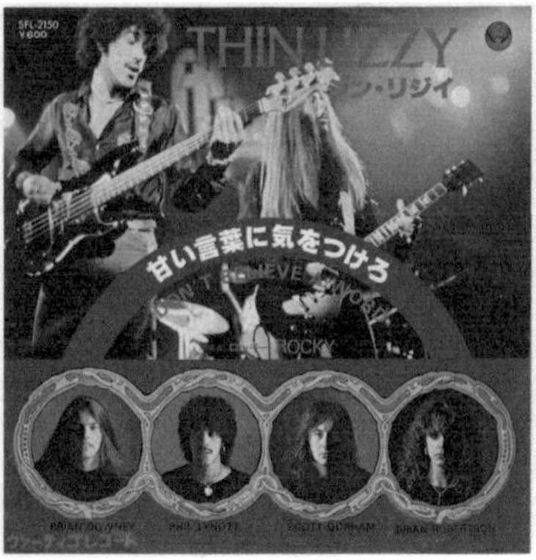
SFL-2150
¥600
甘い言葉に気をつけろ
ROCKY
PHIL LYNOTT
SCOTT GORHAM

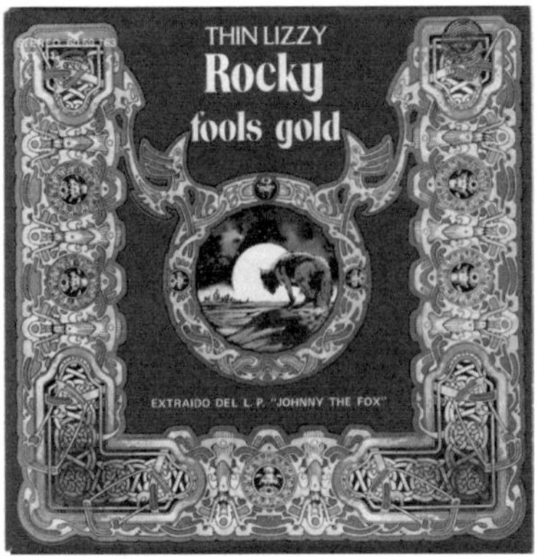
THIN LIZZY
Rocky
fools gold
EXTRAIDO DEL L. P. "JOHNNY THE FOX"

WORDS
(BARRY CLARKE & NIGEL BUTLER)
QUEENSWAY CIVIC HALL
DUNSTABLE
THIN LIZZY
Sunday, October 24th
at 7.15
+ From U.S.A.
CLOVER
Tickets £1.50 from Pavilion Box Office. Tel. Hemel Hempstead 64451 or £1.75 on door
BAR-FOOD

Side 2
1. "Johnny the Fox Meets Jimmy the Weed" (Lynott, Gorham, Downey) 3:42
2. "Old Flame" (Lynott) 3:08
3. "Massacre" (Lynott, Gorham, Downey) 2:59
4. "Sweet Marie" (Lynott, Gorham) 3:55
5. "Boogie Woogie Dance" (Lynott) 3:08

Honesty Is No Excuse: Thin Lizzy on Record

A couple of record company promo shots. Both, left to right, Eric Bell, Phil Lynott and Brian Downey.

Phil and Eric going to work, October 8, 1972, at the Jahrhunderthalle, Frankfurt, Germany. © *Klaus Hiltcher*

Phil and Gary, March 8, 1974 at the Leicester Polytechnic. © *Prakash*

A promo shot featuring Phil, Brian, Gary and a "little darling" to promote "Little Darling."

Phil and Brian, Reading Festival, August 24, 1974. © *Vin Miles*

Phil and Brian, hometown gig, May 17, 1975. © *Kelvin Fagan*

Promo shot, left to right, Scott Gorham, Brian Robertson, Phil Lynott, Brian Downey.

November 17, 1977 at the Liverpool Empire promoting *Bad Reputation*.
© Alan Perry Concert Photography

The twin guitar attack, June 22, 1978 at Wembley, UK. © Alan Perry Concert Photography

The improvised twin guitar attack, September 3, 1978 at the Cape Cod Coliseum, South Yarmouth, MA, US. © Rudy Childs

Snowy and Scott, April 22, 1980. © Helge

Phil looking metal, December 9, 1980, on the *Chinatown* campaign. © Albert Kreis

Another shot from the December 9, 1980 show at the Ontario Theatre, Washington, DC, US.
© Albert Kreis

Two shots from February 6, 1981, at the Scandinavium in Gothenburg, Sweden. © *Mats Odman*

The following night, at the Johanneshov Isstadion, Stockholm, Sweden. © *Mat Odman*

This is the end. March 29, 1983 at the Manchester Apollo, Manchester UK. © *Harry Potts*

Martin talks to Brian Balich, Andee Blacksugar, Peter Jones and Reed Little about *Johnny the Fox*.

Martin Popoff: All right, so the band manage a second album in 1976. What's the story with *Johnny the Fox*?

Brian Balich: Phil had a lot of time while he was recuperating from his hepatitis to work on the record, although interestingly, I guess they said that even with that, he was still pulling songs together and finishing them at the last minute. This is a more confident band, I think, coming off what I'd argue is their best record. But for me, *Fighting* through *Black Rose* are all 10s. But *Johnny the Fox* picks up where *Jailbreak* left off. By this point they knew what their identity would be, and they knew how to get the mix. But it's still a diverse record. On *Jailbreak* you had "Emerald" set against "Running Back." Here you've got "Johnny" and "Rocky" set against "Old Flame" and "Sweet Marie." So, it's a band that's still diverse, but they're leaning more towards the hard rock stuff, and they are working well together and are tight. The musicianship is top-notch across the board. There's a swagger to this stuff. Phil is telling stories in "Johnny" and "Johnny the Fox Meets Jimmy the Weed," in a bunch of them, really.

Andee Blacksugar: Yeah, it's an interesting follow-up. I think *Johnny the Fox* stands in the shadow of *Jailbreak* because I think *Jailbreak*, although it's got sort of an even balance of their heavier and lighter approaches, every song just has this undeniable, anthemic quality to it. All the melodies are really top-notch. We get to *Johnny the Fox* and I would say there's some songs on there that maybe don't sound as fully realised. But on balance, it's a harder, leaner and maybe more muscular and tight album because it's on the heavier side, maybe not quite as eclectic.

Peter Jones: *Johnny the Fox* arrives only seven months after *Jailbreak* is out. And I'll just say flat-out, this is by far my favourite Thin Lizzy record. It's produced by John Alcock, who also did *Jailbreak*, and Jim Fitzpatrick supplies the cover art again. It's the studio record that to me defines the band operating at their best, although overall, if I had to keep just one Thin Lizzy album, it would be *Live and Dangerous*. I just think top to bottom, it's more consistent that *Jailbreak*. It's the work of a band that is on solid footing, at least from the public point of view.

Because as we know now, there was just a whole lot of crap going on in the background that we knew nothing about at the time, most notably all of the snake-bitten bad luck, the tours that get cancelled, the illnesses and bar fights and all kinds of crap that keep this band from taking their rightful place as one of the higher echelon bands of the '70s. They should have been way bigger. They had all the elements, including a charismatic frontman, a great look and they were visually really exciting live. But man, it just didn't happen. Life got in the way.

Reed Little: Yeah, they were in such a strange place. I always tend to say that *Johnny the Fox* is my favourite Thin Lizzy album, but it's a strange one. I think it's the most American-sounding album that Thin Lizzy ever did. I'm not in Phil Lynott's head, but I have to guess that's because he was set to tour the US. He's on this big package tour with Rainbow. They've got an album that's doing well, and this is going to be their big break. And then one of those infamous Thin Lizzy self-inflicted wounds happens. He comes down with hepatitis, the tour is derailed, he goes back, he's in the hospital writing songs. And for some reason lyrics about American things are what comes out of him for this album.

Martin: How about a couple adjectives to describe the production versus *Jailbreak*?

Brian: That's a good question. I think it sounds strong. I feel like *Jailbreak* is maybe a little clearer, a little more powerful-sounding. This one's a bit claustrophobic, if that's the right word. It's more pulled-in and not quite as clear as *Jailbreak*, although they're pretty close. These two plus *Bad Reputation* have a similar vibe.

Martin: I feel like *Jailbreak* has better high end and this one has better low end.

Brian: Yeah, that's a good point. And maybe that's what I mean by clarity. The highs definitely stand out more on *Jailbreak*. On *Johnny the Fox*, you definitely hear the lows, especially on "Boogie Woogie Dance." But sure, it's missing some upper end, although it's still a fine-sounding record.

Andee: This does have a really nice production, as good as any of their '70s productions. I think it's even up there with the Visconti productions in terms of just being hi-fi, although it's nothing fancy. Just a good capturing of the band. There's a little bit of window-dressing, like in "Massacre." There's some spacey kind of delay throws on the vocals and stuff.

Peter: They're both similar. John Alcock's production is consistent between the two. Brian's drums were never really that big. The toms, especially, always had a slightly, dry deadness to them. On *Black Rose* they have a little more ambience that's created artificially, in post-production, but they've always been kind of dry. But to me the guitars are the stars of *Johnny the Fox*. They sound great and are just a notch back from what you would expect live just because of the sheer volume. I agree with you that there's a good amount of low end on this. Right off the opening riff on "Johnny," it sounds more supported underneath. It's hard to think of *Jailbreak* as a transition album, but it kind of is, in terms of having some elements from the past. But "The Boys Are Back in Town" clearly sounds fully formed. But you're right, it doesn't have a lot of bottom end. I certainly noticed right away on "Johnny," that it's got a fuller kind of tonality to it.

Martin: Come to think of it, *Jailbreak* and *Nightlife* are similar in terms of being bright, and you can add *Bad Reputation* in there too, while *Johnny the Fox* is fatter, like *Fighting*.

Peter: I could see why you would make that argument. I haven't compared them in that sense. I was comparing them more chronologically. But that does make sense. You think of something like "She Knows," and it's very toppy and open.

Reed: I think *Johnny the Fox* sounds fantastic. Thin Lizzy generally sounded pretty good, with great separation on the instruments. To me, this album is Brian Downey's shining achievement with the band. He never gets more space to stand out. He never gets a better drum sound. He's so far forward in the mix. You hear every little click as he's riding the cymbals. He gets so many drum breaks. This is really Brian Downey's album in a way that the others are not. And for that you need a fantastic drum sound, right? Or it's just going to ruin everything. Yeah, luckily they get a fantastic drum sound. So, sonically, I think it's wonderful.

Martin: What are your thoughts on the album cover?

Reed: Oh, I love it, although it's a little busy. But that's a pretty weak criticism. There's so much going on in the margins, which is very strange. I would think that you would want your eyes to be drawn to the centre image, and my eyes are always drawn to what's going on around the edges. And that's a little strange if there's not something more specifically meaningful to what's going on in the margins.

Martin: It's funny, I always thought in the lower corners there, on each side, those things looked like hacksaws!

Reed: Oh, yeah, I can see that (laughs). But I guess this is classic Celtic knotwork. I'd say this and *Chinatown* are their best covers. They're just so colourful and eye-catching. It's definitely an attention-getter, and yes, in the middle, you get this fox to think about—is it Johnny the Fox or the fox in "Fools Gold?"

Martin: Okay, once past the wrapper, what do we get with the first track?

Brian: "Johnny" is the tale of this troubled guy. I'm supposed to be a singer and know all the lyrics because we actually covered this song, but they are failing me right now (laughs). It's about a guy who gets in trouble with the law. It's up-tempo, it's heavy and I love the melody to it, plus the way Phil turns a phrase, like near the end where he gives the odds of him surviving the shootout with the cops. I just like the way that Phil phrases those things. It's a good opener, strong, upbeat.

Instead of singing straight-up about rock 'n' roll or sex or other typical tropes, he gives us this story. It's the kind of character you'd see in a road movie and Phil just dialled up these lyrics for him. It's cinematic. It plays out in your mind like you're watching this. You can picture James Dean or Marlon Brando hunkered down somewhere on the waterfront amongst a bunch of crates, having a cop shoot at him. Phil's so good at visualizing these things in his lyrics. He sets up the scene in the first verse and then you get all you need to know with respect to his backstory, delivered in just a few lines, like his sister being a nun, who stands in stark contrast to Johnny.
She's on the quote unquote "good" side of things and he's the bad seed, although he's a sympathetic character at the same time, an

unfortunate case who doesn't do the things he's supposed to do and gets caught in a situation. Whereas other people maybe would get out without trouble, he finds himself in it. Ultimately it's tragic and I love that. It would have made for a good video; that's for sure.

Peter: Great opening track, and one of my favourite riffs they've ever done. And no acoustic guitars anywhere to be found here. Yeah, this is a straight-ahead, aggressive riff. And Brian Downey is just so solid and creates such a great foundation. And now it's this great combination of riff with chords underneath Phil's vocals. It's a vintage Thin Lizzy song to me.

Martin: It's sort of a secret agent riff, like the first track on the last album, and they both start with "J."

Peter: Yeah, you're right. It's a riff that creates motion and it does have that stealth-like secret agent man thing going on (laughs). Great solo section too, where we get another Thin Lizzy staple: wah-wah pedal. Brian Robertson, especially, loves to use that wah-wah, especially live. It's my favourite opener of their catalogue. So yeah, two "J" songs and they're both crime songs too. So much fuss over such a small amount of dope (laughs).

Reed: It's a little strange in that you've got an album titled *Johnny the Fox* and the first song is "Johnny." So, there's a little cognitive dissonance right at the beginning. As a guitar player, I tend to focus on that more, but the guitar lines are pretty simple. It's the drumming that is amazing. Right off the bat, I'm thinking, oh, this is going to be an album of great drumming. Plus, apparently Phil, any time he needed a name with two syllables in it he chose Johnny for whatever reason.

It's a pretty standard Phil lyric about a junkie who kills a guy trying to score by stealing drugs from a drug store. It's not exactly a story, just a slice of life vignette, right? It's got twinned guitars, although to me it just sounds doubled. But they might genuinely be playing twin leads. At a certain point, it's impossible to tell, the way it's produced. But there's definitely a ton of wah-wah pedal on the guitar solos. That's all over this album.

Martin: You're a guitarist, Reed. How would you contrast Scott Gorham and Brian Robertson?

Reed: Brian's a straight-up British blues boom guy, right? He's very much in that Peter Green, Eric Clapton mould—blues blues. Now it's fast blues, its aggressive blues, but it's still blues. And that's what you get from him for his entire career, whether that's Motörhead, Wild Horses or Thin Lizzy. Scott Gorham is, not surprisingly, a much more California-influenced player. There's more melodic lines, he plays less minor pentatonic runs, there's more kind of country-influenced melodic lines. So, he's more of a melody guy and Brian is the aggressive blues guy. Pretty distinct styles between the two of them.

Martin: Next is "Rocky," and we're off to a flying heavy metal start here.

Brian: Yes, "Rocky" is a straight-up rock star kind of song, supposedly written about Brian Robertson; that's what I've heard. "Cocky Rocky, the rock 'n' roll star/He's got the talent to take 'em far." It's a one-two punch at the beginning there. They played the song live for a while but eventually dropped it. Gorham's involved in the writing on this one and Downey too, so it's good to see the credits being spread around. Those guys had to be more involved than the credits would show. Phil obviously should get the lion's share of the credit, but those guys were involved. And Brian Robertson will tell you so too, that they deserved a lot more credit on the songs.

Peter: Driving guitars and another great unison riff. There's a beautiful dual guitar section that explodes in the middle of this, and then more killer individual solo sections with a great supporting riff. What they play underneath, when it's creative like that, it creates this whole new supportive element to it. It's something else to listen to other than just the solo itself. I love the breakdown section, and this is where the twin guitars really shine. Plus, the guitar tone on "Rocky" is big and beautiful. *Johnny the Fox* is what I call a maximum mix record, where it doesn't really have any limits other than your sound system. You give it more juice on a big system and this thing opens up and really gets big. And I think that's the sign of a good overall mix. Some records can't do that. They just start to break up. But this isn't one of those records. This really has some wide range, which also makes it not as easy a listen at low volume. It loses all its energy. Even though the tracks and performances are great, it's got to have a certain amount of volume, or it just doesn't move. But as soon as you hit that spot, it exceeds all expectations.

Reed: Second song, we've got another hard rocker, which is good because I prefer hard-rocking Lizzy to ballad Lizzy. This time we hit one of Phil's other primary characteristics as a songwriter and that is his terrible doggerel poetry. So, Phil goes back and forth between being a legitimately beautiful lyricist and writing what sounds like English as a second language lyrics. There's this couplet that sounds so terrible to me: "Spent his time just looking for kicks/Whipping out them mean and nasty guitar licks/He knows all the tricks to pull the chicks/Just half a chance and away he rips." And notice rips is not even strictly a rhyme; it's what they call a slant rhyme. It has rhyming elements, even though it's not strictly rhyming, and Phil does this a lot in the songs, and sometimes even both during the same song.

Martin: But in his defence, it sounds like a spontaneous rap, like a rap battle kind of idea, where it's more about the rhythm of the words.

Reed: Sure, and there are stories about him standing in the vocal booth making up lyrics as they're doing the songs. So maybe he did that all the time. And if he did, it's pretty cheap, right? Compare that to the way he's telling the story in "Johnny," where it's got an actual structure and a beginning, middle and end. Thematically—and I don't know if he would have appreciated the comparison—he's the Irish Phil Mogg, right? He writes all of these stories about things happening on the street with petty criminals and drug dealers and Phil Mogg's the only other lyricist from that period that is doing that type of material to the extent that Phil Lynott does.

Andee: I don't know, the general consensus is that Phil's a superlative lyricist, a poet. The main thing about him is that he synthesizes these worlds that weren't really synthesized before, where he does have that Van Morrison and Bruce Springsteen, the woes of the everyman kind of thing, combined with this rock star swagger, that more aggressive side. When I first started listening to Thin Lizzy, I found it worldly but there was a warmth to it that I wasn't getting from a lot of metal bands, because the metal bands were singing about things that I couldn't relate to at all and there was never any vulnerability. It was all either fantasy or bragging or talking about conquest. Or partying.

And I always thought that in Phil's lyrics, he regularly exposed his most inner thoughts, to the point where he's literally praying for redemption. You didn't hear that very often in the swaggering hard rock/heavy metal world. There are some turns of phrase that are kind of awkward, including the famous "Tonight there's going to be a jailbreak/Somewhere in this town." Oh, you mean at the prison? There's pretty much only one place that can be. But generally, when I read his lyrics, I see somebody vulnerable and not afraid to expose his demons in the songs.

Martin: And it's surprising how much of it's about getting out of town fast.

Andee: Yeah (laughs), whether he's using a third person kind of character or not, it always seems to be about himself needing to move someplace else. Like he's this perennially wandering spirit and restless type of person. Which you get in Springsteen as well.

Martin: Well, surprise, on the next song, Phil's in some anonymous city, all on his lonesome.

Brian: Yes, but I like "Borderline" as far as a ballad goes. It's got a cowboy on the range kind of thing going on. I can picture him sitting near a barbed wire fence, lighting a campfire, and playing guitar. It's like if Cormac McCarthy needed songs for his border trilogy, Phil could have supplied "Cowboy Song" and "Borderline."

Peter: "Borderline" is quite lavish for a slower ballad. Follow along with me here, but I hear in this song the template for the '80s power ballad, given the textures and the shades of intensity and volume. I could easily hear this format jumped ahead a decade where everyone's doing their power ballads. I think there's a compositional through-line to that.

Martin: It's in three-four time too.

Peter: Yes, or semantically, you'd say it's in six-eight—same thing. The great blues tracks, a lot of Zeppelin ones, have that, like "Dazed and Confused." It's an important element because it has a rolling feel to it, because anything in three, of course, classical music was the genesis of a lot of that. Strauss was the master. Waltzes were in three for a reason. Because they moved and flowed and had swing. And it works for rock as well. Great singing on this, really impressive guitar licks, great solo section and again, that guitar tone I'll never get tired of. Plus, there's a catchy and hooky chorus. It's a nice change of pace from the two heavier opening tracks. I think it's perfectly sequenced right here. You get a couple heavy ones and then you get this nice, kind of solid but refreshing melodic song.

Reed: "Borderline" is the first of the really American songs. To me, this could be an Eagles track. It's very country rock, which is so strange, because it's written by an Irishman and a Scotsman. And certainly, Celtic countries had hundreds of years of history with ballads to draw on, but "Borderline" sounds straight-up California country rock. Thin Lizzy was kind of famous for throwing you curveballs, right? That's one of the things that maybe I think provided interest and yet tanked Thin Lizzy. People don't like variation. They don't want to buy a six-pack of Coke and find a can of Pepsi in it. To some people, it provides interest and to other people, they're like, why is this song in there? And depending on the track, I fall both ways with Thin Lizzy. But this is a good song, although the lyric is pretty standard breakup stuff.

Martin: Next is "Don't Believe a Word," the most popular song from the album by a factor of nine, if Spotify is to be believed.

Brian: I love that song, and at 2:16, there's not an ounce of fat on it. They get right to the point. You get a verse and a chorus and the solo and then you're out again. Great solo from Robertson. Hard to believe it wasn't a hit. Maybe not quite as catchy as "The Boys Are Back in Town" but it's sure close. I think it's one of the best songs they ever wrote, and again, I like the fact that they get in and out of there in 2:16 but it doesn't feel too short. They say everything they need to say in that time and didn't miss anything.

    They argued about this song. I guess when Phil brought it in, it was a bluesy kind of thing. Robertson objected but then switched it up and made the hard-rocking and up-tempo thing we hear on the record. He didn't get credit for it, which I'm sure didn't help in terms of band relations. We've all heard the bluesy version on the Gary Moore record and the way they played it live in later years. Maybe it's because I heard this version first, I'll always come back to this one. I always prefer the straight-up rocker. And I love the lyrics. It's a guy pretty much outing himself, saying to the girl, you can't trust me. How do you know that I'm not singing this to someone else? Maybe I'm fooling you. It's an interesting lyric.

Andee: "Don't Believe a Word" is one of the stronger songs. Like Brian says, they had the slow blues version and they sped it up and it came in at two minutes when they sped it up. It's a good little song, an upbeat shuffle kind of thing with some fiery guitar solos in. Still, for some reason it just kind of floats by me whenever I'm playing this album.

Peter: Yes, it's a trademark shuffle, and if there's one feel Brian Downey is the master of, it's the shuffle. He's so good at it and many bands aren't. And some people like shuffles—depends how they're done—and others not so much. But the shuffle in Lizzy is a key element, like the gallop in Maiden. "The Boys Are Back in Town" is a shuffle as well. Really tight guitar riff, more great soloing. Between *Jailbreak* and this album, not only is Downey's drumming at a different level, but I think the guitar soloing on *Johnny the Fox* is a step up as well.

Martin: There's another similarity with "The Boys Are Back in Town" in that this song is chordal when he's singing, and quite jazzy chordal to boot.

Peter: Yeah, you'd be stunned how many bands play "The Boys Are Back in Town" and get the voicings wrong on those chords—they screw them up. There are two tracks I hear that are always voiced wrong: that song and "Surrender" by Cheap Trick. They're like, "Have I got the root note right?" "No, there's inversions and extensions up on top, and you're not getting it right."

Reed: So yeah, "Don't Believe a Word"—it's fast, it's happy, but it's got what I'm sure is an extremely confessional lyric. "Don't believe me if I tell you/Not a word of this is true" and "There just might be some other silly pretty girl I'm singing to." That's got to be real life stories. Gary Moore put the straight-up, slow, 12-bar blues version of it on his *Back on the Streets* album and it's 3:53 there. And I'm sorry, Gary, it's terrible. And then this version is 2:16. So they lose a minute-and-a-half of music, and it really tightens it up into this fun, punchy little song that I'm not surprised made at least a bit of a stir as a single.

Martin: Side one closes with "Fools Gold," no apostrophe. It's another tall tale—or even fable—from Phil.

Brian: Yes, "Fools Gold," all 3:51, still manages to feel epic, doesn't it? I made a playlist of the heavily Celtic-sounding ones, and this one made the list. It has the Celtic-leaning double guitars at the beginning and the storyline about the Irish potato famine and coming to the United States to try to find a new life. I like that narration, which then gives way to the regular song. I don't know if I'd necessarily call it progressive, but it has that mentality to it. This is a song that grew on me over the years. Whereas, back in the day I was all like, rah, rah, rah, it's got to be heavy. But I appreciate it now, because it has ups and downs and nuance that I didn't appreciate at sixteen.

I love these lines that they printed on the insert, about the vulture sitting on top of the big top circus arena, right? "He's seen this show before/He knows someone's going to fall." Just that whole section and then "In steps the fox to thunderous applause." I know it's not a concept record, but it's just interesting the way that you've got Johnny, you've got Johnny the Fox and Jimmy the Weed and now here's the fox. Is he the hero? I can almost picture a *Three Musketeers*-type fox stepping in with a flourish to save the woman. I remember as a kid appreciating that little snippet of lyric there. Now I see that it pulls it all together. Phil is being the more literary kind of writer. You could populate novels with these characters he's singing about.

Andee: "Fools Gold" is a great song that's got like one of the ultimate Scott Gorham guitar solos in it. It's just kind of playful and effervescent, and really melodic.

Peter: Yes, great solo. This is one of their most overlooked and neglected songs. It's never mentioned on anybody's list of Lizzy favourites. It's straight-forward, super to-the-point, with flowing and super-catchy verses, wonderful dual leads and as Andee says, one of the great solos of the record, both creative and energetic. Here's Phil with his own sense of time, tumbling over the bar line. If there's a Van Morrison influence, it's prominent right here.

Reed: "Fools Gold" opens with this weird, Americana, sort of Native American-inspired music, and Phil doing this monologue about the

Irish diaspora during the famine. And then when we get to the actual lyrics, the music changes utterly; it bears no relationship to that opening. Other than being a song about people looking for a better life, even the lyrics bear no relation to that opening monologue. So, it makes me go why? Why did they include that opening monologue on there? That probably was his own internal inspiration for the concept, but they could have jettisoned that whole part.

The lyric is three vignettes about, well, people looking for fool's gold. One's a literal prospector, whose partner just died. He's trying to hitch a ride on the freeway, and everyone just passes him by. One's about a drunkard pining for simpler days when he was a child. And then you get this completely left-field vignette about a circus act, with this vulture attacking a tightrope ballerina. There's "Oh my God, is there no one who can save her?" and then this great line about, "In steps the fox to thunderous applause."

So, he's not identified as Johnny the Fox; he's just the fox. But notice, he doesn't save the woman, at least in this lyric. He steps in and people are glad to see him and then the song ends. So, we never find out if he saves the woman. And I have no idea what any of that has to do with fool's gold. So, it's like four completely different songs. Pretty weird. And yet it all works. At the end, it resolves to a minor chord. It's a major structure, and yet it resolves to a minor chord. So, it has this sad ending, which leads me to think the ballerina falls to her death. The fox can't do anything about it, or maybe he wasn't planning to anyway. Maybe the fool's gold being chased in this instance is simply the idea of the crowd expecting a hero to save someone from certain disaster.

Martin: Side two begins with a song that us as kids always compared to "Anne Neggen," which is from Budgie's 1976 album that I bought at the same time as *Johnny the Fox*. Same deal: it's got that album's most crushing and heavy metal riff, which similarly gives way to this nutty, chicken-scratch sort of verse. Budgie goes completely weird and this is funk, but it's the same sort of humorous display of light and shade.

Brian: Nice (laughs). Yeah, "Johnny the Fox Meets Jimmy the Weed" is a straight-up, groovin' funk song with a really gritty, heavy '70s street vibe and loud bass. It's heavy without being overly heavy. It's bad-ass, like, freakin' put your leather on and stir some shit up—it's got that vibe to it.

Andee: This might sound left-field, but "Johnny the Fox Meets Jimmy the Weed" reminds me of mid- to late-'70s ZZ Top. I'm amazed at how well Thin Lizzy play this style. It's legitimate funky grooving and guitar playing in that song. That song really jumps out to me as a refreshing outlier in their catalogue. And Brian Downey, man, he strikes me as an incredibly proficient and disciplined drummer. He has the discipline to really lay back and play unfussy grooves, but then he's got all this firepower in his back pocket for when it comes time to really set fire to a song, like "Bad Reputation."

Martin: He's known as a light touch guy, like Ian Paice.

Andee: I suppose so. Ian is similar in the sense that he can be economical, but then he does have chops to burn when he needs to bring them out. And then you have Phil's bass playing, which is the strumming kind, like elbow-based and with a pick. But he's also amazingly disciplined and really tight. I think I told you this, but I did a Thin Lizzy tribute band just for fun with some friends of mine years ago, and it grew out of a Motörhead tribute band that we had been doing. And the bass player/singer, who was doing this great whammy thing with a Rickenbacker and a distortion pedal, creating this wall of sound, when we moved over to the Thin Lizzy stuff, he had a hard time playing those like tight, syncopated, economical, really disciplined grooves and making that sound tight with the drummer. It's not easy.

Peter: Great drum intro on this song. If something can be both straight-ahead rock and funky at the same time, this is it. I love hearing that heavy riff instrumentally without the vocals. It's just one of the coolest riffs. The drums are so tight and punchy. Downey's kick drum is so prominent in the mix. And I don't know if it's an implied raising of the sonics because it's so dead-on rhythmically with what's going on with the band, but it sounds like it's just way up front. And I think that's a credit to his playing. It's just so in sync. All of a sudden everyone is hitting on that beat at the same time and it's aggressively tight.

One of the things that Downey loves to contribute, his tom work is not typical for a lot of quote unquote metal drummers. Not that I view him as a metal drummer. He's a classic hard rock drummer with a strong swing element to him, which those British drummers had, even if Brian is Irish. Most of them have that because they grew up listening to American jazz drummers because we pushed them over there because nobody gave a crap about them over here at the time. Ian Paice and Carl Palmer and all those guys have that swing element in them.

Reed: "Johnny the Fox Meets Jimmy the Weed" is one of my favourite Lizzy songs and there's nothing else in Thin Lizzy's entire catalogue that is remotely like it. It is so far out there in left field. So, we've got "Fools Gold" on one side, very strange, but still with many typical Phil Lynott elements. And then we get to "Johnny the Fox Meets Jimmy the Weed" and it's so American, so Harlem, so New York. It's the sonic equivalent of a blaxploitation movie. I hope you can still use that term. You've got American imagery, right? He talks about Cadillac cars, he talks about low riders, he says they're hanging out at First Street and Main. That's not a UK street description; that's downtown USA.

And then it's the funkiest thing that Thin Lizzy ever did, even more than "Showdown," with Brian Robertson playing funk wah all over it, that "wacka-wacka" sound that had become stereotypical after the soundtrack for *Shaft*. Everybody associated that with that style of drug deal storyline, that type of cinema. Also, right at the end of the song—and he does this a couple of times over the albums—there's a vocal way, way back behind the music that I've turned up and listened to over and over again. I think he's saying, "Is that real cocaine or is that speed?" He definitely says, "Is that real cocaine?" But I can't hear for sure what he says after that. What a fascinating thing to put in the song, because I wonder if it was actually something going on in the studio (laughs).

Martin: Wicked. Now, "Old Flame" is, again, the kind of ballad I like from Thin Lizzy, because I'm definitely not on board with all of them.

Brian: Yeah, there's a sweet melancholy to it. I love the melody line first of all, but I particularly like the twin lead in the chorus. These little things they do in songs add to them. So, the verse itself is fine, but the chorus melody is just so catchy that it pulls me in further. Plus, it wouldn't be Thin Lizzy if they didn't have a song like this, or like "Dear Lord" on *Bad Reputation*, that's set off from the rest. Plus, they are thinking about running order. It's not coincidental that "Old Flame" comes just after "Johnny the Fox Meets Jimmy the Weed" and before "Massacre," which is one of the heaviest songs they ever did. It makes those two songs stand out even more. Plus, I think there's enough in it for a hard rock guy. It's obviously not a hard rock song, but there's enough going on in the song that would keep your attention through to the next one.

Peter: "Old Flame" is a simple but beautiful, light rock track. There's nothing really remarkable about it. It's just one of those things Phil was good at. It's a sentimental song that could just as easily have been acoustic. I agree with Brian both on the sequencing and the melodic beauty of this particular twin lead.

Reed: To me, the music in "Old Flame" matches the intro to "Fools Gold," and it's not quite as Eagles as "Borderline," because there's more energy and activity from the drums and bass. It's more up-tempo. Brian Downey is so good on this track. He absolutely makes the track for me.

Martin: It's back to the metal for the jittery, skittery "Massacre."

Peter: Yeah, of course, big and epic with thundering tom work. It's like some kind of *Braveheart* rally cry, with this intricate and propulsive riff that's sort of focussed on the off-beat. It's Phil's bass that moves the melody along while the riff maintains an even keel and Brian thunders away. Solo section is strong. Phil's vocal delivery is huge, and when they come out of the verse and back to the riff, they are so locked-in.

   I love the lines, "If God is in the Heaven/How could this happen here?/In his name, they use the weapon/For the massacre." There's some weight in that. You can apply that to a whole range of things that have happened in history, that reasoning and justification. We did it for the Lord. Some may suggest that more deaths have occurred over history defending that theory. I don't know if Phil was very religious, but there's the whole Irish Catholic thing. I know more than a few Catholics that believe religion has been used to hammer and suppress people for centuries and I think Phil's making a statement here about that, set to musical accompaniment that's bombastic and almost warlike.

Brian: I love all the good double guitar work on "Massacre." It's got that Native American/Native Canadian vibe going on in that opening riff and then the heavy shuffle thing during the verse. Plus, it's got the religious questioning at the end, which pulls it all together. When I was a kid, I took it as a straight-up battle song, but Phil finds a way to tie that sentiment to a story and give it some deeper meaning.

And it's great live. We played that live a couple times with some friends. We did one of these things where every band picked a band to cover and me and Matt from Penance played with some guys, and we did Thin Lizzy and we played "Massacre" and it was just so much fun doing that song. I love the rhythms in it and the darkness of it and the effects. Plus, Phil's voice is so passionate: "If God is in the Heaven"—just the way that Phil sounds on that. Phil might not have the widest range note-wise, but he was such a passionate, emotional singer that there's no doubting him. You fully believe what he says and you're pretty sure he believes it. He means that shit. That's the phrase I always use: the singer means that shit.

Martin: I never really thought about that. Phil doesn't exactly holler or go high that often. He doesn't push a lot of air.

Brian: No, he's got some power. Instead of going up, he puts a bit more power behind it. But it's what he does with that range that matters. He keeps it interesting, as opposed to some singers who don't have a wide range who are stuck within a certain group of notes. Then there are singers with a ton of range who just recycle vocal lines. I know you're not a huge fan of Blackie Lawless—I am—but he's guilty of rotating his vocal lines. But with Phil, if you picture a range of notes on a piano, he has so much versatility in that spectrum, including just speaking, talking, like the narration in "Fools Gold" or the more emotional, heavier singing in "Massacre." And then he can do a sweet ballad and even a cowboy vibe.

Reed: Speaking of Native Americans, we open up with that very stereotypical, pseudo-Native American melody, right? The Geronimo sound. Now at no time does this lyric ever mention Native Americans or Indians, but it pretty clearly is about that. He talks about Devil's Canyon and makes a comparison to sleeping buffalo. There's the army general waiting for reinforcements from the rear, which is a pretty clear allusion to General Custer's Last Stand at the Battle of Little Bighorn. So, you've got something else American on the album, as well as a theme that plays to Phil's romance with Western narratives.

Andee: They do something really clever in "Massacre." They start with this opening guitar harmony fanfare thing, and then they get into this kind of tricky 16th-note rhythm where they're all playing in unison. And then when the verse starts, one of the guitars keeps playing that ostinato and then the rest of the band is playing a chord progression underneath it. So, every time the chord changes, it changes the context of that riff. So, there's these cool modulations in the second guitar. Plus, the production and mix on this song is good and heavy. It's a really tight and accurate representation of the band. In a nutshell with this album, it doesn't have as many drop-dead anthems as *Jailbreak*, but it's still the band operating at a peak level and being clever about how they use their instrumentation to paint a picture within the arrangements of the songs.

Martin: Next is the kind of ballad I don't like out of Lizzy.

Andee: Sure, well, "Sweet Marie" has a kind of lazy, tranquil vibe to it. But then it kind of widens cinematically when you get the orchestration, Plus there's a sitar in there. It's a beautiful piece of music. Once you get to the end of it, it's sort of lifted the band into this unexpected place. It goes to show how well they are able to acquit themselves for an occasion that calls for this much sensitivity. It's an example of how they could have a light touch and still be really powerful with it. A lot of hard rock bands just wouldn't be able to pull that off.

Brian: It's interesting to me that when they do ballads, it's never straightforward, like a straight-up love song kind of thing. There's always some unique spin on it, for example, the sitar here. But this isn't Phil at his best lyrically. "My sweet Marie/You mean a lot to me." But again, I love every song on this record, and this one's totally grown on me.

Martin: Can you speak a bit to Phil's sophisticated approach to vocal phrasing? You get a bit of that here, with "And what the sea tells/Only seashells are whispering."

Brian: Oh, seriously, yeah, and it stands out actually more on live recordings of the band. Some of that comes from Van Morrison. I don't know that Phil ever sang the same thing twice. I tried covering "It's Only Money" and I could never match what Phil did with his phrasing and his meter, which is unique among singers. So yeah, part of that is the Van influence but part of it is just this confidence and swagger to his voice, and a diversity of skills. Instead of trying to impress with range, he'd do things rhythmically that other people couldn't do, or weren't doing, that kept things interesting. If you can't go up to a high C, try doing something that is different rhythmically, with the lines overlapping and things like that. It's almost a Motown thing. You get guys like Marvin Gaye in the studio that would record multiple vocal lines, but they are all his lines. Marvin's lines would complement each other; he wouldn't just harmonise with them. He would harmonise but have like a counter-melody to the melody, and that's something Phil dipped into, for sure.

Peter: Okay. "Sweet Marie" is gentle but full-sounding, with delicate guitar work and a confident display of dynamics—it ebbs and flows nicely. The guitar accompaniment is a little recessed, but it works perfectly because it's an accompaniment and not a prominent part. The chord sequence reminds me of the intro section to "Ten Years Gone" by Led Zeppelin, not when he kicks in with his phaser and goes to that section, but the opening riff that Robert sings over the top of. It's well-written and one of their stronger of this type of more melodic song. It's not really pop-ish. I don't really see too much of their stuff being overtly pop. Because I don't think being melodic should relegate you to being pop. Melody is melody, and I think this one really shines and shows songwriting maturity.

Reed: "Sweet Marie" is just light FM rock, not even country rock but just a straight-up ballad. I don't think it's one of the better tracks on the album but for this style of music, it's perfectly fine. Back to the American theme, Scott was in on this one lyrically. Perhaps he was homesick for California.

Martin: All right, we close with "Boogie Woogie Dance," which is basically a progressive metal song with a hugely misleading title. As kids, we considered it Thin Lizzy's "Dissident Aggressor," because of the way the drums clump around the riff.

Brian: Nice, I like that. "Boogie Woogie Dance" serves its purpose by ending the album on a heavy note. I don't want to call it a throwaway because I still think *Johnny the Fox* is a 10/10 record. But it's not the

Johnny the Fox

most accomplished lyric that Phil ever wrote. The music is great, with the odd time signatures, but it loses lustre from the lyrics and deadpanned vocal melody. It's another one like "Old Flame," where I've grown to appreciate it over the years. Phil might have made some different choices on it, lyrically. I don't know what kind of time crunch they were in. Bands back in the '70s obviously had less time to get these records done. And he's convalescing from hepatitis while he's writing this record. Honestly, it sounds like, hey, we gotta get this song done, like they are first-pass lyrics. You're not going to open up Phil's poetry book and find this all polished and staring at you (laughs).

Andee: I don't think "Boogie Woogie Dance" is a satisfying song in terms of being heavy. But as an album-closer, I can't help but compare it to "Emerald," which was the album-closer on the previous album, which had such an epic quality to it. "Boogie Woogie Dance" feels a little undercooked. It doesn't feel decisive.

Peter: "Boogie Woogie Dance" is jarring when you first encounter it. It's like, where's the one? Oh, wait a minute; there it is. And then it just settles in and you just enjoy the trip. Downey is just destroying it on drums, killing it. It's so much fun to play, this track especially, but there's so much on this album that I've played a million times. I love the machine gun-like unison section. I wish the song was just a little bit longer. It's a killer track with a monster riff and just an excellent tour de force to close the album. Lyrically there's not a lot to it, but it's just so good that I don't care. And just the riff alone would put it high up my top songs list. Vintage Thin Lizzy, killer closing track, just a great way to end.

Reed: A lot of Thin Lizzy fans don't like this song, which I understand. It's easily the weakest track on the album for me. Now, the drumming is nice, very tribal, although not Native American. You've got psychedelic guitars; I can imagine listening to this with lava lamps in the background. There's this really stupid lyric about the boogie woogie dance. Boogie woogie is a phrase that never went over well with the hard rock crowd because boogie was associated with disco at this point, right? And when you add "woogie" to it, that just makes it kids' music.

Martin: I'm kinda shocked at the low opinion of this one. I know at the time we respected the hell out of it because of how heavy and complicated it was. But yeah, if a song's reputation can be destroyed by its title alone, this is one of those. Okay, any final thoughts on the album as a whole?

Reed: Yeah. I think that the sad reality for Thin Lizzy was that their shot at the big time in America had come and gone with the missing-out on that tour. *Johnny the Fox* did quite well in the UK. And if you look at various musicians, they sing the praises of this album. Def Leppard talks all the time about *Johnny the Fox* and they covered "Don't Believe a Word" on their covers album. Lots of British musicians talk about it being their favourite Thin Lizzy album, whereas American musicians are much more likely to tell you that *Black Rose* is the best one. But *Black Rose* wasn't a big record in the States either.

Peter: I think this is the apex of their career and I don't skip any tracks. I love the pacing. I've already mentioned that Downey's putting on a clinic here. He holds everything together and the guitars are so dialled-in and I just think it's one of those records that's right place/right time. A lot of times, those second albums in a short period of time, sometimes that second one isn't as good because it's rushed.

Here they had the added issue of needing another "The Boys Are Back in Town." Well, there's no single anywhere to be found. And so, from a record company standpoint, I don't think it helped their cause. You can debate *Leftoverture* versus *Point of Know Return* or *Destroyer* versus *Rock and Roll Over*. Some like one over the other and some are completely different production-wise. *Rock and Roll Over* couldn't be more different than *Destroyer*. But in this case, they were barely on the road for the *Jailbreak* tour, certainly not in the US. And of course, they were lined up to get the opening slot on the *Rising* tour when everything went to hell in a handcart. But I don't see a single on here anyway.

Martin: And yet it's like there are five songs that are 75% there.

Peter: Yeah, it's weird (laughs). A case can be made for many of these songs, but the last 25% is missing and it's a different 25% each time, whereas "The Boys Are Back in Town" brings it all together. We can have endless conversations about why "The Boys Are Back in Town" clicked. Why that track? Because there are other songs that they've written that have similar feels and styles. The most casual fan in the world couldn't put three Thin Lizzy songs together for a million bucks, but they all know "The Boys Are Back in Town."

They didn't even write it to become a single. And accidental singles are sometimes the most detrimental to a band. Because the label is like, "Go do it again." And they're like, "Do what?!" And yet that one is squarely right down-the-middle and on-the-nose Thin Lizzy. It's not a "Beth" or "More than Words" situation, and nor is it "Whiskey in the Jar." It's an accidental hit. So, then it was like, "Okay, we want another one. Write another one." Bon Jovi wrote singles, they did it intentionally, that's the way Bon Jovi wrote, they wanted it to get on the air. On Genesis *Genesis*, were "Mama" and "Illegal Alien" and "That's All" written to be singles? Hard to say. But I don't feel like Thin Lizzy ever wrote a song intentionally for it to be a single. And then in the eyes of the casual music-listening public, they become the dreaded one-hit wonder. But better to remembered for one thing eternally than be lost in the ether with nothing at all.

Honesty Is No Excuse: Thin Lizzy on Record

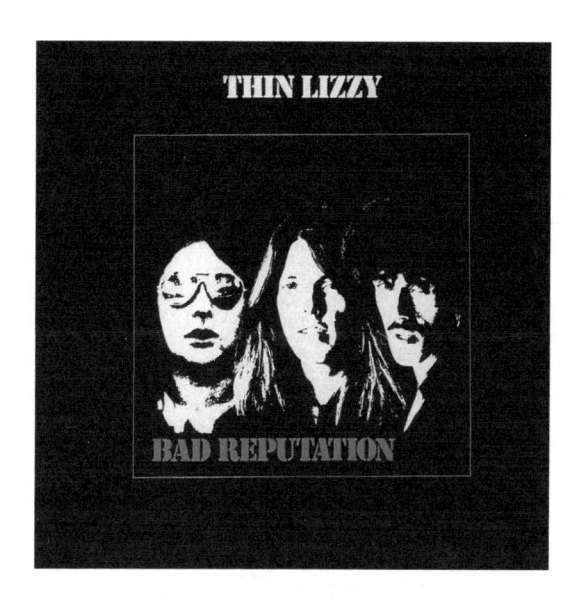

BAD REPUTATION

September 2, 1977
Vertigo 9102 016
Produced by Thin Lizzy and Tony Visconti
Engineered by Tony Visconti; assistant engineers – Jon Bojic, Ken Morris and Ed Stone
Recorded at Toronto Sound Studio, Toronto, Canada and Sounds Interchange, Toronto, Canada
Personnel: Phil Lynott – bass guitar, vocals, string machine, harp, Scott Gorham – lead guitar, guitars, Brian Robertson – lead guitar, voice box, keyboards, Brian Downey – drums, percussion
Key additional personnel: Mary Hopkins-Visconti – backing vocal on "Dear Lord," John Helliwell – sax and clarinet

Side 1:
1. "Soldier of Fortune" (Lynott) 5:16
2. "Bad Reputation" (Lynott, Downey, Gorham) 3:08
3. "Opium Trail" (Gorham, Lynott, Downey) 3:56
4. "Southbound" (Lynott) 4:25

PHIL LYNOTT (Thin Lizzy)

Side 2:
1. "Dancing in the Moonlight (It's Caught Me in Its Spotlight)" (Lynott) 3:26
2. "Killer Without a Cause" (Gorham, Lynott) 3:32
3. "Downtown Sundown" (Lynott) 4:07
4. "That Woman's Gonna Break Your Heart" (Lynott) 3:25
5. "Dear Lord" (Gorham, Lynott) 4:23

Honesty Is No Excuse: Thin Lizzy on Record

Martin talks to Andee Blacksugar, John Gaffney, Peter Kerr and Reed Little about *Bad Reputation*.

Martin Popoff: All right, John, Thin Lizzy's eighth album. Can you set the scene for us? How is the band positioned in 1977?

John Gaffney: Okay, *Bad Reputation*, contrary to the album cover, Thin Lizzy weren't back to being a three-piece. Brian "Robbo" Roberson had fallen out and back into the band, running afoul of Phil after damaging his hand in a drunken bar fight, which forced the cancellation of a second American tour. He is listed as a full-time member on the back, but this would be his last studio album, eventually being replaced by Gary Moore, who subbed for him while he was healing.

The behind-the-scenes drama seems to have little effect on the album though, because they still sound like they're riding on the high on *Jailbreak* and *Johnny the Fox*—lots of energetic rockers, some cool laid-back tunes and one ballad. Everything is clicking here and what helped them sail smoothly into the legendary *Live and Dangerous*, they've got Tony Visconti producing, who delivers on all frequencies and the mix and generally captures the band's energy well. It's slick and sophisticated, distilled, and it packs a nice punch.

Martin: And how would you contrast Visconti's production verse John Alcock's on *Jailbreak* and *Johnny the Fox*?

John: I like the production on this record. I wish the bass guitar was a little louder on *Jailbreak*; the bass gets a little lost there. I do like the production on *Johnny the Fox* but I think this one has a bit of a darkish hue over the production, just enough to make songs like "Soldier of Fortune" and "Opium Trail" sound a little extra heavy. But I've always liked the production on this. It's warm to me, it has a nice low end, and all the instruments are there.

Peter Kerr: I'll disagree somewhat and say that it's not up to standard. If you're gonna call *Black Rose* the benchmark, I don't think it's at that sparkly level. It's a bit midrange for my tastes.

Martin: I'd say it leans more towards the toppiness of *Jailbreak*. So funny, although I think *Black Rose* is better, a word like "sparkly," I'd apply more to *Bad Reputation*. We could do a whole book on trying to describe productions. I wouldn't call *Bad Reputation* warm either—to me, of the three, that goes to *Johnny the Fox*. But really, we're splitting hairs because all three are very good, meaning all it takes is the variety between mediums—LP, CD, radio, Spotify, not to mention pressings—and personal stereo systems to render these comparisons pretty much meaningless.

Peter: Agreed (laughs). Still, that's very much consensus on *Jailbreak*. And that was the sort of sound for AM radio or radio. They deliberately did it that way so it wouldn't be too offensive and would translate for that medium.

Martin: Reed, how about a bit more on the Robbo situation?

Reed Little: Well, as I understand it, Robbo, even when they brought him back on board, he was so uncooperative that he would not allow them to use his image on the front cover. So, I kind of wonder about the vibes that were behind this album. They've gone to Canada to record this, and they've got Tony Visconti producing, which, as a big Bowie fan, I love Tony Visconti. And I am positive that it's him who does a lot of things we'll talk about as we go through the songs. But one thing I don't like is the guitar sound. Tony is not a guitar-oriented producer. Lack of presence may be the correct term. You can still hear the instruments fine, but it's not as sharp and clear.

And speaking of not sharp and clear, other than the fact that you're looking at that cover, and Brian is conspicuous by his absence, you would never get that by listening to this album. But to me, *Bad Reputation* is Scott Gorham's album in the same way that *Johnny the Fox* is Brian Downey's album. There's more Scott on *Bad Reputation* than any other album, to the point where you barely notice Brian isn't there. Because they're doubling the guitar parts, they're adding acoustic guitars and lots and lots of other instrumentation, which again, I put down to Tony Visconti.

Martin: And Scott left some spots for Brian to solo on, correct?

Reed: Yeah, what I read was that Scott did not want to be the only guitarist in this band. They had built their reputation as a twin guitar band, not even a two-guitar band, a twin guitar band. So doing everything himself was obviously not going to work. And I would guess that he didn't want to have to break in a new guitarist. So, he just left some spaces in three songs and told Phil, "We really need to get Brian in," which musically worked out great but probably not in terms of band relations—it literally *didn't* work out. But again, you'd never know that listening to the album. The songs and the performances are fantastic.

Martin: Like you say, the trouble starts at the front cover.

Reed: This is a terrible album cover, particularly after *Johnny the Fox*, which is such a wonderful, eye-catching album cover. Has there ever been a bigger letdown cover? And then it's not even the full band. Well, it was the full band. Rob was no longer a member of the band because he apparently is just a drunken lout. He seems like such a nice guy when he's doing interviews now, but he must have been a total hellion as a young man. Even Adrian Smith from Iron Maiden has a story about talking to him in a bar one time and he thought Robbo was going to clock him because he said something that the man took offense to. So, he apparently had a hair-trigger temper and he drank a lot. He was already fighting with Phil and then he got his hand cut up in a bar fight and he couldn't tour and that's where Gary Moore steps in.

Peter: The album cover, with the grainy silhouettes, didn't do them or the record any favours commercially. This wasn't Jim Fitzpatrick. But it represents the whole Robbo problem, where he's relegated to playing on three tracks.

Martin: Okay, so the album sort of sidles into view with "Soldier of Fortune." It's definitely not a case of smashing down the door.

Andee: No, but on the other hand they are starting the album out sounding ambitious. It has an epic quality to it. It even has this middle section where there's military snare. And the song starts with a gong, which is pretty ballsy. And the first verse is outlined by these synth washes and then the band kicks in and they do the harmony thing. Now it's these big block chords. They're carving out spaces for the vocal to really pop out. The guitar theme that happens at 1:46 is one of their greatest guitar themes; there's a kind of optimism to it.

But yeah, they're really good at knowing when to drop out and play something that's really spare and alternately when to put on the floodlights. There's also a guitar solo section where one guitar player plays a descending line and the other guitar player kind of chases him. So, it's got this round robin effect, where the harmony happens because the second guitarist is starting the same figure a little bit later. It's almost like putting a delay on the guitar.

But Scott is creating this the way Brian May would play a line and these delays would harmonise as he descended. And then, like I say, that military snare gives the song this epic, ambitious quality, and then it ends pretty abruptly and the song starts up again. I find that to be a little bit stitched-together. Like you can kind of hear the seams in that part.

John: Yeah, so "Soldier of Fortune," a massive gong strike leads to Phil reciting some poetry. I guess it's a soldier returning from war who "wondered what he was fighting for." There are a few drum whacks that bring us into some nice Thin Lizzy guitar harmonies, quite upbeat and triumphant-sounding. The verse has some stop/start chords with Phil delivering a passionate vocal. "He will carry on when all hope is gone." I think the mood of the music and vocal melody is letting us know that the soldier here is more of a tragic figure. The chorus is uplifting and catchy and Phil has a cool bass line that moves nicely around the chorus. His playing is often interesting, but it always serves the song; he's underrated in this respect.

Then all this ascending brings a military snare pattern and a really soulful solo, before everything kicks back in, with the harmony guitar theme returning. Man, I always hear highland bagpipes in my head whenever I hear that melody. Love the way Phil sings over the outro chorus. That "I can hear the pipers calling" sends chills up my spine. So yeah, it's a mid-tempo album opener that works when usually they don't.

Martin: Something I've noticed—or maybe Scott explained this to me—but Lizzy are canny enough that when they are doing something simple, like the verses in this song, it's like that's money in the bank to do some more lavish things on other parts of the song. Or like Andee says, it's done to make you focus on a specific part.

John: I always find their chord progressions interesting. They're like you might have heard from The Beatles, or even like something from the Great American Songbook. They're jazz-like at times, but in general avoiding kind of stock blues or heavy-handed simple chord progressions. As for the simplicity issue, here it's done in a way to accent the vocal melody in there as well as the guitar harmonies—that's two very strong and distinct sets of melodies. With Scott and Robbo, you don't get a lot of unnecessary shredding. You just get a lot of melody and tasteful playing, and when Gary Moore is in the band, there's also tasteful blues playing.

Peter: "Soldier of Fortune" has this Gaelic folk melody line and the marching drum interlude and then you've got all this Phil myth-making in the lyrics. It's important to note that Scott is doing all the dual guitars—it's so easy to picture him and Robbo playing away in tandem.

Reed: The first thing that grabs me with "Soldier of Fortune" is the sort of prompt that this is going to turn out to be a stereotypical Thin Lizzy album, even more than *Jailbreak*. And I wonder if *Johnny the Fox* was so far outside and had so many different elements that they needed to construct an album that said, hey, we're still the same band right? "Soldier of Fortune" could not sound more stereotypically Thin Lizzy. You start with a very minor or sparse musical background over which Phil is singing, and then the music kicks in and there are very distinctly two guitars playing in harmony, even though it's actually all just Scott Gorham. Plus, the solo on "Soldier of Fortune" is very typical Scott Gorham, melodic, arguably California-influenced. And when Brian does play, it's just night and day, listening to the two of them.

Martin: Next is the title track, a Thin Lizzy tour de force. When people struggle and arrive at the idea that it's either "Unchained" or "Mean Street" that is their favourite Van Halen song, I think about this being many of my buddies' favourite Thin Lizzy song.

Peter: Yeah, look, this is an album that has two cracker tracks that tower over the whole album. "Bad Reputation" is a great song. It's in the upper pantheon of Thin Lizzy. You listen to it, and you just really want to bang your head. It should have been the opening track. It pushes the boundary of the power trio. It's got that wonderful, syncopated rhythm that kind of harks back to the early Lizzy but sort of upgraded with extra cylinders in the engine. You've got the tasty melodic dual guitar, which was just Gorham double-tracking, plus Lynott's bubbling bass and a heavy groove. It just motors along—top ten Lizzy.

Andee: They had to give Brian Downey the best sonic representation as possible to make that song work and they succeeded. He's got a co-write on it and it's such a feature for him with all those drum fills. Phil is playing muted notes on the bass with a phaser on it, which brings a really cool texture that sounds like a weird percussion instrument or something. But on this album and the one after it, there's a lot of phaser on the bass. That was a really popular thing in the '70s. Everybody was using phasers on guitars and bass and electric pianos and everything. But I think in this particular instance it's a really unique sound that he gets when the guitars drop out in the verses and he's still doing the 16th-note thing with just muted strings on the bass. It adds this percolating texture to the song.

Plus, there's a kind of odd bar duration in the "Turn yourself around" part—such a cool twist. The first time you hear it, it really leaps out; it's very clever. And yet it doesn't sound egg-headed like they're trying to be proggy or something. It still sounds really tough. The guitar harmonies are very anthemic in that song. Like Reed says, this is really Scott's album. He really rises to the occasion, not only with the playing, but also being peacemaker between Phil and Brian. His guitar playing, particularly at the end of the song, the outro, is just is so tight and locked-in and groovy and funky.

Martin: You bring up a good point. When Thin Lizzy does something fancy with time signatures, it's musical. It's never any sort of "prog for prog's sake" thing.

Andee: Right. It doesn't sound self-conscious or "Look how clever we are." It sounded like it was organically happening. I feel like whatever happened within the band, whatever ideas were brought to the table, they went through the Phil Lynott filter. And I know that he was allowing the other guitar players to bring fully-written songs to the table, but up to a point. Then he said, I don't want to do that anymore. If you have an idea, I want to add something to it and then put it through my sensibility and I think the songs improved with that. Plus, his lyrical flair is just a huge part of what makes the band distinctive. I could imagine him not being able to relate to singing someone else's lyrics. So, it's an interesting dynamic. On the other hand, Queen did that all the time. Freddie would sing lyrics that were written by John Deacon or Brian May.

John: "Bad Reputation" hits us right away with a funky 16th note syncopated groove that's, like you say, almost prog-ish, but we know it's not going to get too intellectual on us, right? Because Lizzy is more about a cold Guinness than fancy cocktails. And then the offbeat chord accents in the chorus keep us on edge. I love Phil's almost whispered vocal; it's like two parts menacing, one part cool. But the song is more about Brian Downey, who massages in cymbal crashes between the nooks and crannies of the riffs. His whole kit gets heard and it just sounds wonderfully splashy. This is as close as we get to a showcase for Brian, as I alluded to earlier, maybe his "Moby Dick" or "Toad" or "The Mule," if you will. And yeah, Phil's flanged-out bass is an extra nice touch. But like Andee says, this song proves that you can play with lots of chops and still sound cool and not snobbish while doing it.

Reed: I feel like "Bad Reputation" has got to be about Brian Robertson, right? Is there any other person that Phil could have been thinking about? "You've got a bad reputation" and "You better turn yourself around." But it's a great song and a showcase for Downey who otherwise doesn't get as much space on this album, save for maybe "Opium Trail." I'm putting that down to Visconti, just because in contrast with previous albums, there's so much extra instrumentation on *Bad Reputation*, which leaves less space for each person, except for Gorham who's doing double duty. It's unusual in a Thin Lizzy song to have a guitar solo that goes all the way through the song's fadeout. I imagine that is also a suggestion from Tony. I'm gonna give Tony credit for a lot of stuff on this. I could be wrong, but that sounds to me like a producer's idea. And I suspect it's also the longest solo Scott ever did on a Lizzy track.

Martin: Next is "Opium Trail," another quietly ambitious assembly of parts.

Andee: Definitely. "Opium Trail" has this urgency to it plus a complexity in the riffing. It has this lysergic quality, which is really an interesting trick to pull off, because the song is about opium. So, Phil underscores it with this kind of druggie delivery with long delays on his vocal. It sounds trippy and hallucinogenic. So, it's a smart combination of this tough, urgent, disciplined rhythm happening, and a complex weave of guitars, and then this really spacey, floaty vocal thing on top.

John: First impression is that it's a hard-driving rocker. I love the octave-extending pentatonic runs doubled by guitar and bass in the intro and throughout the song. There's tons of reverb on Phil's vocals, which adds to the element of intrigue and mystery in this one. "The wizard wanders through the world he made from dreams:" Phil takes us on a journey to strange exotic lands, pretty scary, actually. Those long, ascending and descending guitar and bass lines always evoke *2112*-era Rush for me. Scott, Brian Downey and Phil are all involved in the writing on this one and on the title track, while the rest are just Phil and Scott or Phil on his own.

Peter: Yeah, it's a slippery one, because of that serpentine riff. Robbo does all the solos on that one, but I think the rest of the band were well away from the studio. It was very acrimonious.

Reed: Okay, here's a subject on which Phil has a little too much authority, right? And as Peter says, it's Robbo on solos, and it's instantly different. He must have come in at the last minute and just set up how he wanted because his tone is so much sharper, so much more present. And that wah-wah pedal is back, which you don't get with Scott Gorham. And then they play around with the stereo space on this song in a way that's very weird for Thin Lizzy; I don't remember them doing that on any other track. His vocal is on the left and then it's on the right and then it's in the middle. Again, to me, that's a producer trick and I'm going to put that down to Tony Visconti.

Martin: Also, again, that's some sophisticated playing going on at the verses. It's actually hard to pick out what Scott is playing, and I guess Phil takes responsibility for the riff in a sense, or the projecting of the melody.

Reed: Yes. It's funny, because if you read about when Scott Gorham joined the band, he was not considered a particularly skilled guitarist. By the time you get to *Bad Reputation*, he's so good. He has improved so much. And that's why Brian plays so many of the solos on the early albums because he was the accomplished soloist. And also, apparently, the producers didn't like some of Scott's Americanisms, like combining major and minor modes in the same solo. They were like, you can't do that. But that was really common if you listen to things like The Grateful Dead or The Doors. American bands did that, but apparently British bands didn't.

Martin: Side one closes with "Southbound," and although I'm not crazy about the chords on this, the drum sound is just a joy.

Reed: Yeah, mellow track, although not a ballad because you've got this up-tempo rhythm. Pretty average Phil lyric about escaping life's troubles.

Andee: With "Southbound" what drives me nuts is that redundancy in the lyrics, that "I'm going southbound" chorus. If you're southbound you're already going, so you're either going south or you're southbound, not both (laughs). Again, it's got that restlessness lyrical trope, where Phil's on the move; he's gotta get outta town. It's actually kind of simpatico with the *Johnny the Fox* stuff, where you had that gold rush mythology in "Fools Gold" and there's a line alluding to the gold rush in this song, where the town has dried up and it's time to move on. And yeah, it's an example of just how good this band was at playing with a light touch. Brian Downey is really staying out of the way and there's an overall gentleness to the approach. The guitar harmonies sound so hopeful. There's this muscle combined with a little bit of insecurity in Phil playing this character. It's very affecting, and quite rare actually.

Martin: It's a bit like "El Paso" by Marty Robbins, or "Ghost Riders in the Sky."

Andee: Yeah, like an old-school country song, but also rock enough to keep the fans happy.

John: Things definitely mellow out on this one, but we also find ourselves back to more familiar territory of the lonely prairie, "tumbling with the tumbleweed." It's a favourite character in many of Phil's stories, the traveller and vagabond, and here it's actually a lonely cowboy after the gold rush: "The gold rush, it is over/And depression days drawn near." The music and lyrics are chock full of imagery, with nice campfire vocal harmonies in the chorus and even a distant harmonica to emphasise the western feel. "Hey, you're not getting any younger/The Wild West has already been won." This song always felt like "Cowboy Song" part two to me, with our cowboy hero riding off into the sunset as the song fades out.

Martin: Over to side two, we've got "Dancing in the Moonlight (It's Caught Me in Its Spotlight)," which is probably in the top five biggest songs the band ever had.

Andee: Yes, and very nostalgic, very Van Morrison, and nice phaser on the bass in that one. You've got the spotlight on the saxophone. That's a really successful song on this album. Phil's mythologizing his own past, his coming of age. At least that's what it sounds like to me.

John: We've left the prairie for a snappy, sophisticated big city sound. Like Andy says, there's that flange effect on the bass, an effect he uses often, carrying the riff of the song. There are finger-snaps on two and four, which bring that swinging, upscale, Manhattan jazz club vibe. Phil's melody and vocal delivery on this one is one of my favourites. The way he lays back and sings around the beats, it's so melodic and yet natural, like a conversation. Steely Dan and Supertramp come to mind too, with John Helliwell—from Supertramp!—delivering these soulful, rhythm-and-blues sax lines. It's a simple story about a fun night out on the town, but with Phil sort of reminiscing about his youth or young love. That line, "I always get chocolate stains on my pants" is one of my favourites. Not sure any other rock singer could deliver a line like that. How in the world was this not a massive radio hit?

Reed: It's definitely the big curveball on the album, and an example of a hit for a band not sounding much like the band's other material. They're snapping their fingers like the Sharks and the Jets from *West Side Story*. It's got this very Broadway kind of production and swing to it. Strange track. And that chocolate stains line, it's weird, it's oddball. It's also got a big sax solo in it, right? That's a Visconti thing from his years with Bowie. He was a huge believer in saxophone on his albums.

Peter: Whimsical, playful, sassy, sexy—it's Lynott at his most romantic. It's a wonderful track. I'd put that in my top ten. It's one that could have, should have, been a contender to break through in America at AOR and commercial radio. It had all the hallmarks of being a nice pop song and it could have broken through. Wonderful sax line from John Helliwell, beautiful melodic counterpart to Phil's breezy vocals. Teenage romance on the streets of South Dublin. I love it—great.

Martin: Then it's back to the riff rock.

John: Yes, "Killer Without a Cause" starts out dark and menacing on a chugging, New Wave of British Heavy Metal-ish riff. I feel like the sort of held-back tempo is the only thing stopping it from falling squarely into that world, but yeah, here's where Def Leppard got a lot of influence, because this main riff could have fit on *High 'n' Dry*. But then the chorus shifts and modulates to a major key, which feels noticeably uplifting in contrast to the minor key verse and dark lyrics. And what's more surprising is that the riff, so to speak, in the chorus is played on acoustic guitar—pretty weird.

Peter: "Killer Without a Cause:" another street tale. Time to settle scores. It's another potboiler. So that goes into the category of a Phil Lynott story from the streets, this time about a hitman. It's *Pulp Fiction* within three minutes. And that strange chorus gives the listener a bit of a palate-cleanser within the song. It adds a bit of space or airiness, sonically.

Martin: It doesn't make sense emotionally within the song, right? It's like this happy turn inside of this song about a killer.

Peter: Yeah, well, there's a lot of Trojan horse in Phil, where you think it's a happy song, but the lyrics are kind of dark. Or there's some sort of bite or edge, implied or explicit. Or the melodies are in a major key, but the lyrics are definitely in a minor key, a bit sad or mournful. He's unorthodox. He doesn't make the obvious choices and that's why we love him.

Reed: It's a pretty standard track. We're back into hard rock after the rather bizarre digression of "Dancing in the Moonlight." I love the guitar riff on it. Some of the guitar playing is sort of simplified on the album, I feel, but this one goes the other way—it's a great guitar riff. And clearly, it's Brian Robertson playing the solo. As for that acoustic guitar, they're probably just using it to fill out the sound. Even if they didn't miss Robbo sonically because you can just record as many tracks of Scott Gorham playing guitar as you want, they had to psychically feel like there was this missing tooth, right? That they had to fill it up with something, whether it's acoustic guitar or keyboards. The saxophone and harmonica are outliers; they don't count. And I love that "killer without a cause" references *Rebel*

Without a Cause, which was every kind of hard rocker's/punk rocker's favourite '50s movie. And he even says rebel in the lyrics, although he didn't put it in the title. I think he just maybe wanted to differentiate the idea. But killer without a cause doesn't make a lot of sense as a concept.

Martin: Next is a typical up-tempo Thin Lizzy ballad, with a perfectly in-character title.

Andee: Yeah, "Downtown Sundown" is a real kind of "I've hit rock bottom and I'm seeking redemption" kind of song. And that's the kind of song where you really hear Phil's soul laid bare. There's no swaggering there. He just wants help. He's admitting to his wrongdoing and the error of his vanity. It's a pretty vulnerable moment. Also, I want to point out, he's not a showy singer but he's an extremely capable singer. He always had great pitch and his tone is really rich. And unique; he's got a one-of-a-kind timbre in his voice. And he really knows how to communicate, how to telegraph the emotion in his lyrics. He sounds like he's feeling what he's singing.

John: "Downtown Sundown" is the first and only real proper ballad on the album. The background music is light and floating. Phil's lyrics on the power of love are uplifting: "Please believe in love/I believe there is a God above for love/And he is coming." He's almost getting spiritual. A distance clarinet plays, buried far back in the left channel mix; personally, I would have brought it out a bit more. And then sort of melodic guitar harmonies and a tasteful solo help paint the mood of a sundown.

Reed: We're back to soft rock territory, and with, of all things, a clarinet. Excuse me, but saxophone was at least an accepted rock instrument. Clarinet was exclusively orchestra, big band and jazz. So, it's pretty weird to have it appear on a song on a hard rock band's album. And again, I'm throwing that at Tony Visconti's feet, right or wrong. Visconti was such a studio master. And Bowie was so into studio tricks, and he and Visconti would play with reverbs and space, even if it was just one or two notes; it didn't have to be a big thing.

Martin: It's funny, John, you call the last one the only proper ballad on the album, but arguably, there are like five, with "That Woman's Gonna Break Your Heart" being the fourth.

John: Sure, I get your point; it's such a grey scale with all of these. But yeah, we get some big chords and echo-laced toms at the start. So "Downtown Sundown" spoke of the uplifting power of love, but here we are in more familiar rock territory, where women and love lead to disaster and heartache. "That woman will lead to heartbreak/Take the word of one who played and lost in love." The pessimistic lyrics play out in contrast to the Eagles-like major key chord strumming going on beneath, with the chorus going more minor key and the guitars echoing the vocal melody. There's a nice key modulation for the first guitar solo, while the second half of the solo is drenched in some cool guitar effects.

Andee: One of my favourite Thin Lizzy songs ever. It opens up with this harmony fanfare thing and I believe there's timpani drums. And then in the verse, there's just kind of strumming acoustic guitar and the rhythm section is chugging along. But then in the chorus, we're back to that intro music but the electric guitars don't come back! It stays in this kind of airy, acoustic, timpani drum kind of thing. And then the electric guitar doesn't come back until the theme returns. So, what I'm trying to say is that there's a really judicious use of the electric guitar in the song. And yet it's still a powerful song. It's not one of the lighter ones; it's not a mellow song. It's just that the dynamics are really economically executed. So, when the electric guitar comes back in after that chorus for the theme, or the fanfare, it's really powerful because they use the electric guitar so carefully in that song.

For the lyrics, Phil is directly giving advice to someone. But it could be Phil talking about himself. It points out the vulnerability and fear of having one's heart broken. You just get the sense that Phil is somebody that was always ready to jump in with both feet, even if he knew that his heart could and probably would get broken. So yeah, you get this generosity of spirit in the song where he's trying to counsel somebody, but it sounds like he might be trying to counsel himself at the same time.

Martin: And back to the vigorous acoustic strumming, Andee, there's really a country and western vibe weaving its way in and out of this record, isn't there?

Andee: Sure, yeah. I guess there's some overlap between country music and Celtic music. So, I'm sure that there was some kind of appeal there for him. We know he had a romance for American Wild West culture. I'll bet he listened to Hank Williams and Johnny Cash and people like that, storytellers. Yeah, he's a storyteller. And there's an earthy kind of galloping quality to some of these songs that might not technically be country music rhythms and chord progressions, but they do evoke the open plains and the Wild West and seeking out new frontiers.

Reed: Yes, indeed. And in contrast to some of the doggerel in other parts, I think this song has fantastic lyrics. It's very poetic. "It's the wrong card you're using/That deck you're using is stacked against romance." The gambler as lover is an interesting metaphor. Now clearly, it's not the only time Phil would write about gambling; he liked that. I don't know if he was a gambler or not, but he certainly liked that image. And it produces a really nice song. Also, this is the only song where you get a legitimate twin lead between Robbo and Scott Gorham. Last thing, it always struck me as funny that the title of this one sounds like it's going to be a ballad and then it's not. It's a great, energetic song, even if it still has that prominent acoustic guitar.

Peter: Again, it's one of those confessional ones. There are strong guitar harmonies and some heavy bass that emphasises the rhythm. There's a lot of rhythm in this band, which is just not the drums. But it's like the whole bottom end, the syncopated rhythm. The acoustic guitars here are even used for rhythm. He's a wily type of musician, Lynott is, as an arranger. He knows how to get the songs to project. That's the word I'd use: projection. The best songs are the ones that project out of the speakers. Between the eyes, sort of thing.

Martin: We close with our last quasi-ballad, and yet another one with a desperado cowboy vibe to the musical track.

Peter: And yet again, raw and confessional. Somebody once described it as a rock 'n' roll prayer, as a cry out from Phil to a higher power to provide him strength and sanity.

Andee: Yeah, "Dear Lord" is just a flat-out prayer. That's the one where he says, "My vanity is killing me." It's a devastatingly vulnerable moment.

Martin: And when you get to the very end of the song—which is also the end of the album—it sounds like the heavens are opening up.

Andee: Yes, which reminds me that he kind of had other album closers going forward where it sounded like he was ready to just give in, like he was just begging forgiveness and he didn't think he had much time left.

Martin: "It's Getting Dangerous," "Heart Attack."

Andee: And that's really powerful, where he's reaching out to somebody, whether it's like a deity or his own mother. He wants redemption and he's contrite and admitting his folly. He just seems like somebody who was never really at peace with himself.

Martin: But this one, "Dear Lord," really, really sounds like a death scene.

Andee: Yeah, it definitely does. The outro is a really interesting add-on. It doesn't particularly have much to do with the rest of the song. So, it really does bring home this idea of maybe he's preparing himself for the great hereafter. Yeah, it's an epic ending to the album. It's a much more satisfying ending than the way *Johnny the Fox* goes out with "Boogie Woogie Dance."

John: We also get that part at the beginning, but there's also this funky, staccato guitar riff at the very beginning that is then just sort of thrown away. That leads to those long hanging chords with choir-like angel sounds in the background, that part we also get at the outro. The rest of the song fades in and we find Phil being reflective and spiritual. Maybe it's a cry for help, because his drug use was beginning to escalate around this time. "Dear Lord, come gain control/Oh Lord come save my soul." These are poignant lyrics, knowing that Phil's life would soon spiral out of control. The chord sequence is nice and harmonically rewarding. Like I said earlier, Phil's chords always have lots of movement, like something from the Great American Songbook or Gershwin rather than typical blues-based rock. Beautiful guitar solo too. "I'm down deep and need your help/There's no one to turn to and I can't help myself." Those are some poetic, personal and haunting lyrics that end a chapter in Thin Lizzy's history.

Martin: By the way, it closes with Brian bashing the gong, which is how the album started as well.

Reed: Nice, I didn't notice that (laughs). As Andee said, "Dear Lord" is so much stronger of a closing song than "Boogie Woogie Dance." Very confessional lyric and so straightforward. It's so on-the-nose that it's a little uncomfortable, right? Begging God to take him over because he screws up everything if left to his own devices. But then he comes back and says, "If you give your soul to heaven/You won't get it back." Which might mean, I need help, but I'm afraid that if I get help, then I'm going to lose everything. It's an interesting lyric. The music is fine—it matches the vocals. But I think this song is very much about the lyric and about the vocal.

Martin: So how did it all work out of them, this *Bad Reputation* album cycle?

Reed: Well, honestly, with Brian having the problems that he was having, and being kicked out of the band and then brought back to record, and then they did the tour and kicked him out again, they were up against it on this album. *Bad Reputation* was kind of do or die, maybe not commercially, but just in terms of the actual viability of continuing as a band. And ironically it really comes through on the last track, "Dear Lord." I only know that in the US, *Bad Reputation* made no impact whatsoever. I don't remember hearing "Dancing in the Moonlight."

Peter: Look, yeah, two songs for me, "Bad Reputation" and "Dancing in the Moonlight," are gold-plated Thin Lizzy songs and that's probably what this album is sort of remembered for, those tracks. The rest has entered the realm of obscurity unless you're at least a moderate Lizzy fan.

Andee: Still, it's quintessential Thin Lizzy. Phil has a few key lyrical wheelhouses. And fair enough—I've heard this said that any great songwriter is pretty much just rewriting the same song over and over again, with subtle differences. Everyone has their vocabulary. That's what makes somebody interesting as an artist, that out of all the things that are available, if you carve out your own little vocabulary, that's what makes people come to you. They want to hear a point of view, your point of view, and they get that from Phil on this album.

I will add that that's four albums in two years. That's really impressive, right? September '75 for *Fighting*, through to September of '77 for *Bad Reputation*. You think of all the things they went through. He has to write *Johnny the Fox* from his hospital bed because he was told to go home on the *Jailbreak* tour, or he was gonna die. Which is sort of analogous to the Queen *Sheer Heart Attack* situation, where Brian had hepatitis and he was in the hospital when they started making that record. Then Brian wrecks his hand, which is kind of important for playing the guitar. So, it's really impressive, when you think about all the things they went through, and just the level of exhaustion. But I feel like that's the story with a lot of these bands in the '70s that were on that treadmill. It was a thing that they could do up to a point and then they just collapsed.

John: True. They had such huge success with *Jailbreak* and because of that, at least on a small scale, *Bad Reputation* was well received, even though they didn't have any big hit radio hits off of it, at least not here in the US. So, it certainly didn't sell as many pancakes as *Jailbreak*, and for that matter, nor did *Johnny the Fox*.

But I think from a creative standpoint, they're on a roll here. And the drugs, the fatigue and all that stuff hasn't crept in and affected the songwriting. Plus, this album leads really nicely into their big *Live and Dangerous* record. And so, for me, from a studio album perspective, it's the ending of a chapter. Of course, Brian Robertson would leave the band after this, with Gary Moore coming in on *Black Rose*. Brian, I mentioned in the early part that he had damaged his hand in a crazy bar fight. He'd long been a hothead and was rubbing on Phil's nerves and so he was kind of out of the band and back in. So, it's credit to Scott that he took control over *Bad Reputation*. In the end, they turned out a fine record that pretty much every Lizzy fan I know ranks highly.

Honesty Is No Excuse: Thin Lizzy on Record

BLACK ROSE

April 13, 1979
Vertigo 9102 032
Produced by Tony Visconti and Thin Lizzy; "With Love" produced by Tony Visconti and Phil Lynott
Engineered by Kit Woolven
Recorded at Pathe Marconi EMI Studios, Paris, France and Good Earth Studios, Soho, London UK
Personnel: Phil Lynott – vocals, bass guitar, 12-string guitar, Scott Gorham – lead guitar, guitars, backing vocals, Gary Moore – lead guitar, guitars, backing vocals, Brian Downey – drums, percussion
Key additional personnel: Huey Lewis – harmonica on "Sarah" and "With Love" (credited as Bluesy Hughie – harp), Jimmy Bain – bass on "With Love," Mark Nauseef – drums on "Sarah" (credited with "Sarah thanks you anyway")
Note: Extended album title that includes the small-print subtitle: *Black Rose: A Rock Legend* or, as presented in two places on the packaging, *Black Rose/A Rock Legend*. Also, "Sarah" is mis-identified as "My Sarah" on early US pressings.

THIN LIZZY
new single
"do anything you want to"
From the GOLD album "Black Rose" B/W the previously unreleased track, "JUST THE TWO OF US." 50,000 in special colour bag.
Single LIZZY 004
Album 9102 032
Cassette 7231 022

THIN LIZZY
DO ANYTHING YOU WANT TO

Thin Lizzy
DO ANYTHING YOU WANT TO

Side 1:
1. "Do Anything You Want To" (Lynott) 3:50
2. "Toughest Street in Town" (Lynott, Gorham, Moore) 3:58
3. "S & M" (Lynott, Downey) 4:02
4. "Waiting for an Alibi" (Lynott) 3:29
5. "Sarah" (Lynott, Moore) 3:32

Side 2:
1. "Got to Give It Up" (Lynott, Gorham) 4:22
2. "Get Out of Here" (Lynott, Midge Ure) 3:35
3. "With Love" (Lynott) 4:39
4. "Black Rose" (formally known as "Róisín Dubh (Black Rose) A Rock Legend") (Lynott, Moore) 7:03

Honesty Is No Excuse: Thin Lizzy on Record

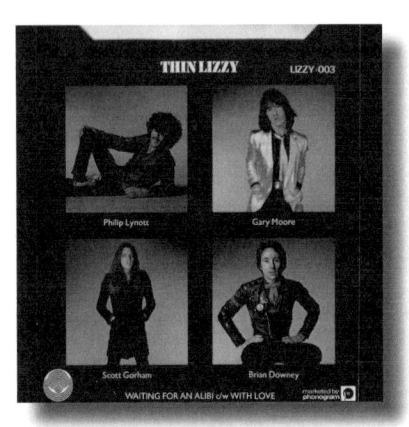

Martin talks to Peter Jones, Sean Kelly and Peter Kerr about *Black Rose*.

Martin Popoff: So big changes are afoot in the Thin Lizzy camp. How do things turn out with their new guitarist on their ninth album, *Black Rose*?

Peter Kerr: Oh, it's my personal favourite. But I'm probably slightly contrarian because everyone I talk to sort of rates it as third or fourth. But I love this album, and simply because we have the wonderful Gary Moore on board. Gary Moore is the enigma in the whole Thin Lizzy story. Is he in; is he out? Is he in; is he out? And they were able to sort of trap him in a studio for a period of time to actually record this. So, I think whatever's on this album is just magic. And he really works well with Scott Gorham. It's absolute bliss hearing them work in synergy on this album. And, you've also got Phil and Brian Downey, and Tony Visconti on as the producer. I think it's a wonderful production—it's sparkling, it's clear, it's a great job.

And yeah, it was the highest charting album in the UK at No.2, but in the US, it only got to No.81. So whatever steam they acquired through *Jailbreak*, which I think hit No.11, had sort of dissipated. Unfortunately, that was kind of a one-hit-wonder album. Here in Australia *Black Rose* got to No.29, but I don't have any sort of personal memories of this. It's just an album that I just got into afterward.

Martin: Gary Moore is kind of a Cozy Powell-type figure, right? He comes to a band with opinions. He's strong-headed and he's going to be right in there helping with the songs.

Peter Kerr: He is, and he's a strong personality. You look at how many people with impressive resumes have played with him. Yes, he has got that Cozy Powell sort of feel. But look, he brings a lot of magic, and there's a lot of magic in his interactions with Scott Gorham.

Peter Jones: I was excited when *Black Rose* came out, because I'd been a huge Lizzy fan since coming on board in real time with *Fighting*, and then directly previous to this, *Live and Dangerous* is one of my all-time favourite albums, and favourite Thin Lizzy album.

Black Rose is clearly an album that presents a different sound, a different direction, a different tonality. Although it's hard to quantify or describe, the addition of Gary Moore makes the songwriting different. But it's vintage Lizzy, and the production is clearly a step up. It's big, lavish guitars, but really clean and powerful. It's funny though, although it was in heavy rotation for me, from what I remember, it wasn't until years later I started hearing anything from this album on the radio, and then of course even then, it was mainly "Waiting for an Alibi."

Sean Kelly: Yes, we've got a significant lineup change. Gary's in for the first time full-throttle, right? And you could call this the steroid-enhanced version of what Lizzy established back on *Jailbreak*. The infusion of Gary brings back excitement, because Gary's just that type of player. You can hear it in the authority of the guitar lines. Like you say, he's another one of those dominant guys. He's going to bring his voice, his presence. Phil and Gary, as they rub together, Phil was clearly the boss, but Gary was going to challenge the throne. And once again, Scott as a guitar player is kind of absorbing all this, sitting back and but also matching his approach to what Gary was bringing to the table. Gary has such an aggressive vibrato and such an aggressive attack; he plays with so much fire and chops. Even when Gary plays the blues, he's not laid-back; he's playing with fire.

Martin: Any thoughts on the album cover?

Peter Kerr: Yes, nice aesthetics. I think the rose really sends a message. And the back of it, where you've got those sort of cartoon caricatures of the band—I just love everything about it.

Martin: All right, with a thrum of drums, we're into the opening track.

Peter Kerr: Yes, and "Do Anything You Want To" was a single off the album, the second one. You've got those wonderful galloping drums—some people describe it as an African-style drumbeat—and that beautiful tone of the twin guitar attack. And you go, "This is Lizzy." This is the Lizzy that everyone knows. It's like putting a comfortable pair of slippers on, on a Sunday morning. This is what we all love about this band. And Lynott is such a wonderful wordsmith, bringing smart wordplay in this song. Add to that the percussive sort of phrasing, and he sings this like he's having a conversation with me.

It's basically about empowerment. And I guess that's another category for Phil—the empowerment song—because a lot of his songs are about personal development and empowerment. You can do what you want to do. You can be who you want to be. You are your own person. It sounds simplistic, but it can be said powerfully in a rock context, especially when you're this good of a communicator.

Martin: It's funny; I can never remember that title perfectly, word for word. And it doesn't help that Eddie and the Hot Rods' biggest song was called "Do Anything You Wanna Do," and we got that one in 1977.

Peter Kerr: Yeah, well, there's a Masters Apprentice album here in Australia called *Do What You Wanna Do*. It's like that, a bit of a tongue-twister, in that vein. Also, I love the fade-out. You turn it up and you can hear Phil saying "Elvis is dead" etc. That's one of his heroes, like Jimi, and he does this little sort of Elvis tribute. Great opening track. The song went to No.14 in the UK and charted for a long time, nine weeks. And if you ask most people their ten favourite Lizzy songs, I'd be gobsmacked if this wasn't in there.

Peter Jones: "Do Anything You Want To" sounds like the work of a band that is more modern, updated, more relevant. Any time an album opens with a great drum beat and Phil thundering away on bass works for me. And right off the bat you've got two killer twin leads, going right into the verse. And again, there's our trademark Thin Lizzy shuffle, which just moves beautifully. Brian is the master of shuffles; he's so great at it.

So overall, the song is familiar, it's comfortable and it's reminiscent of highlights from previous records. Plus, a very catchy chorus—memorable, very sing-along—with these big, slanting chords, like "The Boys Are Back in Town." At the lyric end, Phil is just spouting all this really great prose. And every time he would hit an inflection point with this rapid-fire phrasing he's doing; they'd punch it or punctuate it with this nice syncopation and it flows so nicely. Love the chord change into the bridge. Great dual leads. And then I love the broken-down part with Brian's drums. And then they go into more dual leads. And when they get to the part "Just like I do," that's just really cool. I think it's a wicked song. And as Peter mentioned, before you get to the very, very end, it's "Elvis is dead. I said, one for the money." I gotta keep turning it up because I want to hear some more.

Sean: The opening track is definitive Thin Lizzy. The main riff is represented by a kind of soaring, harmonised guitar line. Like I said, Gary brings out a more aggressive, saturated sound. That's the thing; I find the production of this album more saturated, meaning that there's more sustain on the guitars. They're not fuzzier, but more robust. And then Gorham adapts to that.

Now, this song is another one of those examples of Phil doing his wordplay thing, when maybe a solid idea isn't necessarily there, but he's got an idea like, stand up for yourself and do what you want to do. But he's such a master of vocabulary, he can make it work almost to the point of being annoying, right? Everything's wrong about the premise, or the premise is flimsy, but he finds the words. He embellishes the idea, and he sees it through. He likes to flex his wordplay muscles. To me, it's like sitting around a pub and just being clever. And he does that in spades. But yeah, I love the big tympani, and then the drums give it that classic shuffle feel. It's like a more muscular version of "The Boys Are Back in Town," but there's a romanticism in the sort of descending and cascading chords and twin leads. Going from a major chord to a minor chord; that's something we associate with romantic thoughts.

Martin: All right, next track and we get more of those tough block—or slanting—chords, although we soon learn that the intro presages the chorus, and that in fact the verse offers more of a riff.

Peter Jones: Yes, and in fact "Toughest Street in Town" is one of the few songs in their catalogue that just opens with big power chords. Then we get a driving up-tempo feel that's more like "The Rocker" and things that they had done earlier on. So, it's very vintage, and another one of their signature feels, this driving eighth note thing. There's some super-tight syncopation which, in an upper tempo song is hard to pull off and remain very tight. They're always throwing something at you to get your attention and make it swing.

I like the chorus again, which is simple, a bit of a call-and-response. They change keys when they go into this great solo section, with Downey adding all these drum fills at the tail end of almost every solo lick or seemingly at the end of every bar. So, he's very busy on a straightforward track, but it works. But in that section, the solo is soaring over top of this, so there's a lot to listen to. You can focus on the solo or what's going on underneath, whether that's Downey or the completely new riff we get just for this part. Then there's so much energy as they barrel into the third verse, with these really strong, urgent vocals from Phil.

Peter Kerr: Agreed, and with "Toughest Street in Town" we're into the social observational lyrics. It describes the squalor and poverty of the mean streets. That's another thing. It seems like one song every album he talks about the mean streets, whether it's Chinatown or the back streets of London. He loves doing these little stories about the petty crooks, the hookers, the drug-pushers. That's just part of his... I won't stay shtick, but it's part of his story. Yeah, it's about the haves and the have-nots, all in three minutes, and even though it's a well-travelled topic, Phil's a notch above what you'd get from the average hard rock band.

Peter Jones: It is. It makes you think. The lyrics are interesting and engaging and they paint a picture.

Sean: Yeah, I love it, man. Another thing that Phil was great at was making hardship sound cool and romantic. I wanted to go there. Why do I want to go to this place? It sounds terrible. But he makes you want to hang out there, right? It sounds authentic when he's singing about that, and it sounds like maybe he knows a little bit more about this stuff than is good for him.

Martin: All right, contentious one, "S & M."

Sean: Yeah, I hate this song. I'm a pretty positive guy about music. I look for the good. I find very little good in this song. I think this is an aberration of funk, rock and everything. I find the lyric terrible too. And that's hard for me to admit because I love Phil. There's also the chorus bass sound—obviously someone gave Phil a chorus pedal. It shows up on "Waiting for an Alibi" too. "S & M" is just one of those I skip. I just can't take it. Especially when they say "Ouch" when the girls get beaten. I just can't take it. Brian Downey gets a credit on it; it's Brian and Phil. Maybe if you took away everything and just left the drum track, I'd like it. Because I'm sure that part of it is very good.

Peter Kerr: Okay, on "S & M" we get a sleazy lyric about a hooker, a pimp and her johns, and it's like a pulp novel. It's like a potboiler. It's observational and clever. It's funky and groovy. The bass and the drums are the heroes of this song. People have sort of questioned the lyrics, but when you look at them, he's not being judgmental. He's saying, "Here are the facts and you be the judge of these characters." And that is the sign of a really outstanding lyric-writer. He puts it to the listener. And another thing about Lynott, he asks a lot of questions. A lot of his lyrics ask a question and then he answers it. So it's like in his head, he's got this conflict (laughs), and he casts it out into a song.

Peter Jones: Interesting track, and probably not one you could get away with today without people raising eyebrows. But like you say, I think he's approaching it more from the standpoint of making a commentary than to be tawdry. He's not doing it to be gratuitous. Later it turns to violence, and he includes the female pushback, right? So, he's not just letting that sit. He's saying that's not good, that's not right, we don't want to be condoning that.

We've got even more toms, more drums, going on here. I also want to mention Hendrix here, because we've got like the "Voodoo Child" wah-wah, pick-scraping stuff, atop a very busy drum and rhythm part. It's Phil just thundering underneath what are just smatterings of guitar parts, nothing big or extended. It's very funky—the feel is so infectious—and I love that there's a slight flange to Phil's bass tone on this. Like I say, edgy, powerful lyrics. The chorus brings back what we hear at the intro, like the last track. I also love that Phil does the octave-walking lines, and with that flange effect, it's just a little something extra. There's a smoking-hot solo section and then a great eight-bar drum break that never loses intensity. Then it's just right back into the last verse, tight, boom, done.

Anyway, certainly didn't sound like the first two songs, but it's got something unique about it, and while the lyrics may give some people pause, you can't deny how infectious the feel is. And by the way, as a drummer, it's one of the band's most fun to play.

Martin: I love "Waiting for an Alibi" to death, but I always found it odd seeing it somewhat buried late on side one.

Sean: Yeah, man, great song—a Thin Lizzy classic. It's funny, I actually covered this song with Crash Kelly when I was in England. I went to the studio and covered it and when you start breaking it down, man, that Gary Moore solo is no joke. It's pretty incredible trying to match the intensity and everything. This is when Phil really is firing on all cylinders when it comes to character description.

He connects personally with the characters. That's when it's most authentic. "Valentino's in a cold sweat/Placed all his money on that last bet." I imagine Phil's been in those situations where it's like, okay, Phil, you're in a bad situation here; you've got to get yourself out. And he somehow manages to get himself out, right? It's absolutely quintessential Lizzy.

Peter Jones: This is a stunning piece of music and belongs on anybody's list of their greatest compositions. I feel like this one follows pretty closely thematically to "The Boys Are Back in Town" in terms of being unbelievably accessible. Great bass and drum intro, and then here comes the memorable dual leads. So simple, not a lot of notes, you let the pitch and the vibrato of the two players do the work. And like the very best Lizzy twin leads, it sounds like one guy playing two parts. They do have their own personalities when it comes to solos and improv, but here there's a singular purpose.

Phil's bass-playing is very melodic and very strong here, giving us a great, sexy groove, helped by a lot of real tasty open and closed high-hat work. The riff, so to speak, is structured more as these punchy chords, with the twin leads serving more of a riff-like purpose. I think this album, more than some of the other ones, uses the twin lead as the main weapon. There are not nearly as many solos here.

As for the vocals, Phil goes into his raps and then there's a call-and-response for the chorus, which is one of the oldest and most traditional musical forms. The chorus is just so strong, and you can envision Phil strumming that bass from the elbow, and with a pick, driving the song as he's singing those words. Later on there's a solo section and that's done over the verse music, and then a later twin lead has these cascading runs that remind you of "Emerald." So many little details. Like on the later chorus bits, they've added little guitar lead tails to them. Then they wrap it up with a great ending, and you're like, wow. Super-enjoyable, no wasted space, nothing you wanted to add; it's just leave it alone—perfect.

Peter Kerr: Nice analysis, yeah. And let's not forget, "Waiting for an Alibi" was the first single off the album and it hit No.9 in the UK, so it was fairly appreciated out there in the public. It starts off with the driving bass, counterpointed by dual guitars. It distils everything that's good about Lizzy. Socially observational lyrics about Valentino and his gambling habit, which is maybe about Phil. He's got that warm, conversational tone. So again, this is like I described earlier, where he doesn't actually sing but it's like he's having a conversation with you, a conversation with the audience.

Martin: Closing the side is "Sarah," or "My Sarah" on my early-days US vinyl copy—this is an album I didn't get domestically in Canada, but on a trip to Spokane, Washington. It's a ballad, and of a type I'm not a fan of. Frankly, I can't stand this melody, these chords.

Peter Jones: Yeah, I can understand that. It's a nice, quiet Caribbean feel. We have Mark Nauseef on drums on this one, not Brian. Mark was around Lizzy a lot. He was actually in Elf for a brief moment, and he did a couple live tours for Lizzy when Brian wasn't able to do it.

It's written about Phil's daughter, Sarah, and it's certainly kind and loving and full of admiration. It's sweet and genuine and comes off very authentic, not cheesy or shmaltzy. I love the harmony parts that come in on the second verse and there's a unique solo section which has got an early Jeff Beck feel to it, tonally and playing-wise and in the phrasing. You've got Scott playing a Les Paul as usual, but I believe Gary was playing a Strat; he certainly was a lot at this time, which would explain the Jeff Beck sound. Which kind of tonality-wise works, because there are a lot of great parts. I love the ending of the song; it's a really good change of pace. Very nice, easy listening, well-constructed and well-played and even, I think, perfectly placed on the record.

Peter Kerr: Oh, I love this song. It's a whimsical ballad that shows the gentle, emotional side of Lynott. I think his ballads got better as he got older and matured. I love the warm tone of his voice. It's about his daughter and it's really endearing. Huey Lewis of Huey Lewis and the News is on the harmonica, playing with the key melody line, and Gary Moore harmonises—he sings on this one, apparently. And he does this wonderful finger-picking; it's sublime. "Sarah" was written as a song for Lynott's solo album, but I'm grateful that it actually made the cut on this album.

Sean: Beautiful song, and once again you see the humanity in Phil. This was a real part of Phil's character, the family man. It seems diametrically opposed to everything else you hear about Phil, but he really valued family. And maybe he had an idealistic view of what family should be even, as it sort of ran contradictory to how he lived his life. Besides the sentiment, there are these sophisticated guitar lines and there's just gorgeous modulation in the solo. I'm not surprised that Gary is in on the writing, because it's practically fusion with some of these changes. But the musicianship never detracts from the simple sing-along melody. This is just sensitive Lizzy done right.

Martin: Side two kicks off with a Lizzy masterpiece, and I gotta say, from the day I heard it, it seemed like the meaner heavy metal version of "Waiting for an Alibi." It's got the same verse structure, with the spaces between these chords that in both cases—but more so here—are hard to make out melody-wise.

Sean: Totally. And to me, the vocal delivery is different. I feel like this is Phil suffering, and I think recognizing a creeping-in drug problem that was now taking a hold on these sessions. This is where the drugs really grabbed hold of the band, making this album in Paris. They're now indulging, and the drugs are taking over. And I think he struggled with himself as a drug user—he just didn't want to see that part of himself. Part of him romanticised it and went for it, but part of him really beat himself up about it. And this is him being confessional. This is some Roman Catholic shit going on here. It's like going to the confessional booth and admitting what you've done and looking for redemption. And I can hear it in the vocal. It's an aggressive but dark vocal.

Martin: Like I say, those chords are so coagulated, so percussive. They're almost tuneless. It's almost post-punk.

Sean: It is. It never resolves in the satisfying way that we're used to in pop. It will resolve to a minor chord when you want it to resolve to a major chord, sometimes. It feels angular. Like, you never can quite get your teeth into it. The production is helping cause that dissonance too. It's a little darker. Yeah, that's a great observation.

Martin: I could see an A&R person listening to this and going, "I can't find the hook. I can't hear what's going on. What's the melody?"

Sean: Yes, that's right. It's definitely obscured and complicated.

Peter Jones: Love this one, of course. It begins with this spacey, dark and moody intro, and then we get this heavy riff with weighty, self-inflicted lyrics from Phil. Like you say, it's a choppy, punchy, percussive riff, not a flowing riff. I feel like that's intentional, to make you feel unsettled. Because the topic is like, "I've been messing with the heavy stuff/For a time I couldn't get enough." He's realizing that, hey, I've got this problem, I am in trouble, this has taken over my life. What do I do? Do I just give up? This is him just flushing feelings out of himself. There are not many words more filled with hopelessness than, "I've got to give it up." Not much grey area there. This is a guy who sees his problems and is acknowledging his problems. But the sad part of it is that he's saying he's helpless to do anything about it. It's too on-point to be this larger statement about what goes on in the music business. It's personal. It's poignant.

So, it's very heavy lyrically and vocally but there's some soaring, almost hopeful lead-playing. And then later the chorus pulls back and it's kind of a "Dancing in the Moonlight" vibe with a cool walking bass line. Then the solos just erupt as we move toward the conclusion.

But I see your point about the chords on the verses, yeah. It's more of a percussive effect than a chordal one. There's a sense of chord structure, but it's not very apparent, and it's certainly not very transparent. I'd say it's more jarring than anything. Plus, it sounds a bit processed. Adding to the starkness, there's space between them, where Downey also holds back and doesn't play busy. It's constructed so that we focus on Phil's vocal, really. But when you get to the chorus, all of a sudden everything smooths out. You'd think it would be the other way around. It makes one think, how open is he to knowing that he needs to stop and maybe can't? It's heavy stuff, especially learning what happened later. It's very self-reflective and it makes for an exceptionally powerful track. And it sticks with you, because like I say, this isn't something arbitrary—it's him.

Peter Kerr: For sure. Autobiographical, a call for help. And there's a lot of testimonial that things were really starting to spiral around 1979. Things were starting to close in. You can go through the lyrics and see the decline and pin it to a lot of things that were happening to Phil in his real life. It's him in conflict. I know what I'm doing is not good for me, and I've got to get some help and I've got to give it up. It's tight and it's compelling, and again, you've got that Phil Lynott conversational delivery. But yeah, he's fighting addiction, and his heart is on his sleeve. It feels like this is the song where the rot starts to set in. With the guitar chords, there's a lot of syncopating and punctuating and that also adds drama. I can hear what you mean about the nastiness of those chords. That's a good word for it: percussive. They sort of slam down or punch away at dramatic points in the lyrics. It adds gravitas to the song.

Martin: And while I'm pairing up songs, me and my buddies always saw the next one, "Get Out of Here," as the bookend to "Toughest Street in Town." They're the two with this sort of punk rock energy.

Peter Jones: Yes, I like that. It's another really up-tempo track. They've got two of them on here and they really didn't have these on *Jailbreak* or *Johnny the Fox*. They've put a nice phase-shifter on this, I love Phil's driving bass, it's very wordy. Goodness don't try and sing this one while you're drumming; it'd be impossible. I've been a singing drummer since high school and Phil is the one artist I can't pull off, let alone a song as complex as this. But the rhythmic pattern is similar to "The Boys Are Back in Town" from that standpoint. Love the modulation as well as the echo added to Phil's voice and those couple of electronic punches on the drums during the chorus. Glad they don't over-do them or include them on too many other songs because that can date not so well. But it's a very satisfying track, it's well-written and I think it fits fine on the record.

Peter Kerr: Midge Ure from Ultravox co-writes on the song. To me it's a pseudo-sequel to "The Boys Are Back in Town" and probably just as anthemic. It's that similar free spirit type of song. He's sort of putting his middle finger up in defiance. It sounds like a person who's in a relationship that's abusive and Phil's saying "Be defiant; here's some strength for you. You've got to just get out of here, get out of the situation." So, it goes into the category of his empowerment songs, which prevail all the way through the catalogue. And it's another wonderful one for phrasing. He's completely unorthodox. I don't think you could teach that in music theory. It's his own style, and it's evolved and just gotten more fanciful over time.

Sean: Absolutely—lots of Phil's wordplay. I could see him in the studio not having the lyrics and going, "Yeah, don't worry, man. Just run tape. I got this." Other than the vocals, this one's not complicated, and it's a rare one where I'm feeling a power pop vibe.

But back to the vocals—and this might be presumptuous of me—but sometimes I wonder if he goes in and he improvises something but then doubles it, just to sort of say, "Yeah, I meant to do that, boys" (laughs). I wouldn't put it past him. The other way of looking at it is that his, whatever, spontaneous rap, turned out to be so good it was worth doubling just on its merit.

Martin: Were we wrong as kids thinking it might actually be some sort of response to or nod to punk?

Sean: No, he definitely had an ear for new music and hung out with those guys and even had that band The Greedies. He's like Billy Gibbons in that way, right? He was always looking to the young guys and certainly wasn't afraid of them. He'd go right down there and hang out and try and figure out what was happening on the street.

Martin: Next we have "With Love." See now, I'm not a stick in the mud about all Thin Lizzy ballads. I can listen to a song like this all day.

Peter Kerr: We're back to sensitive Phil. "She broke my heart and made me sad." It's Phil being exposed, raw and vulnerable and from the heart. He's got to be one of the more sensitive rockers. If you look over his career, you think, what are Lizzy? Are they hard rock? Are they heavy metal? I always actually thought that they were classic rock. I don't think they're hard enough to be heavy metal. But for somebody that's perpetuated as being on the heavy side, he has a lot of sensitive songs. He is one of the more emotive lyricists. But that sound of the twin guitars, that to me is the definition of classic rock. It's just made for radio. No, this is a nice palate-cleanser before the epic finale to the album.

Peter Jones: The late Jimmy Bain plays on this. He and Phil were mates, and Jimmy plays on both of Phil's solo albums as well. We get an easy and relaxed but focused groove with really thick-sounding guitars and good, tasty bass playing from Jimmy, I love the tag licks at the end of each verse. There's more great harmonies and a rich chorus, although I do think the chordal pattern is a bit too similar to "Got to Give It Up." Check it and hum those melodies and you'll see what I mean. There are short leads into the next verse and a sturdy bass line that stands out here. It's a good-feeling track, not too heavy, not too light, a nice sonic change of pace and another track well-positioned in terms of sequencing. It's not a downer where you think you gotta skip it. It's authentic and it's genuine and they do it with conviction and it works.

Sean: Yeah, nice acoustic textures and very romantic. "With Love" might represent the ultimate definition of Phil as a conflicted character. "This Casanova's roving days are over more or less." It's like, I found you, I love you—oh, you're breaking my heart again, just because I broke yours?! Ah, geez. But why did you do this to me? I love you; you see. But the "more or less" qualifier is just so perfect (laughs). So, you've still got the macho guy and the sensitive guy all in the same package. And I see that lyrically, but I also hear it musically.

Martin: All right, the album closes with its leviathan of a title track. Is it their "Stairway to Heaven" or their "Achilles Last Stand?" Maybe it's a bit of both.

Peter Jones: Sure, both of those make sense. I love "Black Rose" for many reasons, but let's start with that powerful riff—holy smokes. And figuring out how to play it is a lot of fun. It's in three/four or in six/eight, however you want to look at it, and even more specifically, it's a six, a three, a six and a six. So, it's got this odd meter feel, because everything's based on three, but it grooves like crazy. So, they carry on with that, but Phil is almost singing in four/four over the top of it until they line up every certain number of eighth notes. And you're like, wow, okay, cool. It's very complicated. This is definitely one of the most difficult songs in their catalogue to play properly. But they are such natural musicians, the riffs just roll along so effortlessly.

And then once you get into the post-chorus, now it goes into a full-fledged Celtic swing thing, closer to straight time, where you raise your stein and all that good stuff, and it just builds and builds. And even though there are some individual solo sections, so much of it is based around the dual playing between the two of them. Gary's such a great player and Scott's so complimentary to anybody he's ever played with. Snowy and him I thought were great. Sykes doesn't play well with others, but that's another story. But Gary and Scott really did lock in here.

Lyrically, it's a history lesson, folk tales and legend and legendary figures, tales of long ago, stories that have been told over the centuries. It's part of their heritage, their lineage, what they grew up with. And in the meantime, it's set to this heavy, thundering riff which fits right in with all of the great Thin Lizzy riffs.

Then they hit the final big breakdown and Phil's going, "Oh, tell me the legends of long ago." He takes his time and it just kinda fades. Then all of a sudden there's this huge drum fill from Downey and we're right back into it and it just crushes from there to the end and just sweeps you away. It's an epic, grandiose track, and you don't use epic too much with Thin Lizzy because most of their songs aren't this elaborate. But this is a crowning achievement and it contributes to a lot of the album's legacy and street credibility. Obviously, "Waiting for an Alibi" is really strong too, but "Black Rose" anchors the album. Because some of the other ones, like "S & M," might not be as accessible to the general public. But there's a lot of fans of other genres that could listen to "Black Rose" and go, yeah, okay, I get that.

Peter Kerr: It's their "Stargazer" and those Zeppelin songs you said, Martin, as well as their "Kashmir." It's a classic, an epic and cinematic finale, seven minutes of majestic rock. It's a patriotic history of Ireland and it's got everything you want. Wonderful vocal delivery, and actually quite haunting in places. I love that echo effect in the vocals where he speaks really close to the microphone. There's a bit of reverb on his voice. I feel like he's really getting into it. He's really behind this material. Poetic lyrics, great songwriting, wonderful array of folk melodies. And there were a lot of '80s metal bands who adopted this idea of doing these folk medleys, Scottish or whatnot, and I think the blueprint for that was right here. It's the pièce de résistance of this album. I haven't come across anyone who doesn't like this song. I think it's wonderful and it comes across as completely sincere.

Martin: It certainly is, but if I was to floor a wee bit of criticism, is it a little over the top? Is it a bit obvious? This is why I brought up "Achilles Last Stand." To me, that was Zeppelin trying too hard to write another mystical song—a smartypants song—because they had an album to get done.

Sean: Well, totally, man. It's on-the-nose, right? "It was a joy that Joyce brought to me." "Brendan, where have you been?" Like, that's really pushing it. But I love the fact that it came from a place of love. I think it came from a place of wanting to honour his homeland. You're basically trying to truncate all of Irish history into seven minutes. And it certainly achieves the goal on an emotional level, musically. I absolutely adore the riff, and like I say, I can hear the love in his voice.

Granted, a lot of people don't like the folk medley. They think it's just too much. And it's funny, the tunes that he chooses, in the folk medley, like, one of them is "Shenandoah" and that's actually written by an American, right? He's an Irishman that has chosen a pastiche version of Irish tunes to put in there to represent core Ireland. But those songs were written out of pure sentimentality, and I think this is a sentimental song. And that last reel Gary Moore does at the end... I can't remember which one it is, but it's an old Irish reel. Wow. It's technically brilliant, and super-exciting. I think it succeeds in knocking down any material criticism. It's like *Citizen Kane*. Is it always great? No, but a pretty great effort, right?

Martin: It's ambitious like Rush. Normally, Phil and Thin Lizzy would be thinking in song-sized bites, almost with an attitude that true prog rock is immature because it's driven by ego. But here they relent. They sort of look around and say, "Why not?"

Sean: Yeah, absolutely. To me, it's almost like that thing where a contractor is working on a bathroom or something and screws something up and has to change where he puts a shelf. Then he finds out he's running out of time and goes, oh crap, I gotta get this job done. It sounds like they might have painted themselves into a few corners on this song and then realised, we gotta put this record out.

Martin: Nice (laughs). Any final thoughts on the record as a whole?

Sean: Well, I'll just say that I think a lot of people consider this the last classic Thin Lizzy album, like true classic. It's the beginning of the darkness, which makes it interesting. But they're still functioning, right? So, it's still a functioning band with an infusion of freshness because of Gary Moore coming in as a full creative collaborator. It still has all the romanticism but with a hint of the darkness that was going to come in and obscure the band.

Martin: Sean, most of the songs on here just seem like fresh, exciting, new ideas. They even find new ways to be heavy, right?

Sean: Yeah, that's a good way to put it. And it's also their transition into a more modern hard rock sound. I also think it's a stepping stone guitar tone-wise for a lot of the hard rock that came after it.

Peter Kerr: This is a great headphones album. Crank it up and don't have your headphones on, but it's a great one for putting the headphones on and closing your eyes, and through Phil's storytelling, you can do these little movies in your head. Especially the last track. You can imagine the rolling hills of Ireland and it's just completely cinematic, widescreen. But yeah, overall, I think it's their best album, a stone-cold masterpiece.

Peter Jones: I'll close with a couple more comments on the arrangements. This album sounds resplendent. Everything on it sounds super-clean. They're exceptionally well-crafted compositions. There's no wasted anything on any of these tracks. Huge focus on melody, and maybe more so than on previous records. And there's not as many solos as you think in comparison to previous records. When you do get them, it makes an impact. But they used them sparingly and focused a lot more on tandem lead playing. Super-tight, solid grooves, Downey is exceptional. I don't think Phil has any better performances vocally or lyrically. They're complex but they're interesting, and like Peter says, they convey his meanings so succinctly because his word use is dead-on.

    The importance of Gary joining can't be over-stated. Gary was the guy. And he was always in the wings. By this point, Gary was just about ready to take off on his own stuff and become the guitar hero that he ultimately became. But all of a sudden Gary's in there and the tracks don't disappoint. *Black Rose* is well-produced, it sounds big, the tracks are strong, there's no filler.

    But it's so short-lived, it's just one and done. And everybody's like, "Oh, *Chinatown* is such a left turn." No, it isn't. *This* was the left turn. *Chinatown* just took over from where *Bad Reputation* left off. If you yanked *Black Rose* out of the mix, it would have just gone right on naturally. This is the one that's different. And because it was different, there was an appreciation and a respect for Gary and rightly so. My gosh, he's one of the great guitarists of all time. But none of it would matter if the songs weren't any good. And the songs are good.

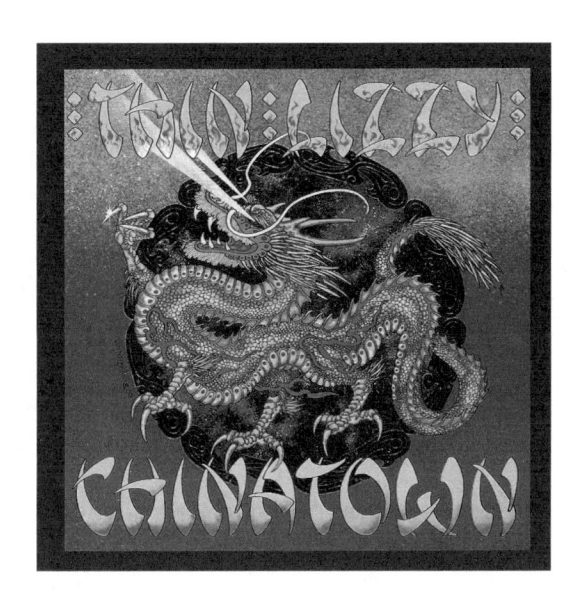

CHINATOWN

October 10, 1980
Vertigo 6359 030
Produced by Thin Lizzy and Kit Woolven
Engineered by Kit Woolven; assistant engineer – Flash Gordon Fordyce
Recorded at Good Earth Studios, Soho, London, UK
Personnel: Phil Lynott – bass guitar, keyboards, vocals, Scott Gorham – lead guitar, guitars, backing vocals, Snowy White – lead guitar, guitars, Brian Downey – drums
Key additional personnel: Darren Wharton – keyboards, backing vocals, Midge Ure – backing vocals on "Chinatown," Fiachra Trench – string arrangement on "Didn't I," Tim Hinckley – electric piano on "Didn't I"

Side 1:
1. "We Will Be Strong" (Lynott) 5:07
2. "Chinatown" (Downey, Gorham, Lynott, White) 4:40
3. "Sweetheart" (Lynott) 3:28
4. "Sugar Blues" (Downey, Gorham, Lynott, White) 4:18
5. "Killer on the Loose" (Lynott) 3:53

Honesty Is No Excuse: Thin Lizzy on Record

210

Side 2:
1. "Having a Good Time" (White, Lynott) 4:35
2. "Genocide" (Lynott) 5:05
3. "Didn't I" (Lynott) 4:25
4. "Hey You" (Downey, Lynott) 5:06

Honesty Is No Excuse: Thin Lizzy on Record

Martin talks to John Alapick, Brian Balich, David Gallagher, Peter Jones and Peter Kerr about *Chinatown*.

Martin Popoff: Now we're up to *Chinatown*, which comes in for a fair amount of criticism. And yet every time I actually play it, I'm hearing so many songs that zoom right up my list of favourites.

David Gallagher: It's a bit of an outlier, as you say, for numerous reasons. But I have never quite understood why it has such a backlash against it, apart from the notion that it's a bit of a retread of what's been done, kind of a safe album for them to make. There's quite a lot of themes and whatnot that have been revisited from previous albums, and there's a lack of ambition in places too. But I think with the lineup changes, with the failure to crack America and, actually, UK sales even declining the last few albums, maybe retracing your steps and seeing if you can recapture the magic of three years earlier is not a bad plan. That amount of time seems like nothing now, but back then for them it must have felt like a lifetime. I don't think there's much of an issue. What we get within the tracks of *Chinatown* is solid to very, very good in places.

John Alapick: I echo a lot of sentiments that I hear from Lizzy fans. There's a very strong first half and the second half is kind of hit and miss as far as Phil's vocals go. Yes, I think he was losing the soul in his voice at this point. He's getting deeper, but his voice wasn't as soulful, and I think that really affected some of the songs here. As far as the production goes, where I find inconsistency is on the drums. Now, this might represent Brian Downey's finest drumming on a Thin Lizzy album. But at times his kit sounds tinny, almost like a drum machine, the way it's recorded. But when he does those great fills, he brings a lot to the songs. But yeah, on a song like "Killer on the Loose," the drums are almost robotic, even though that song is fantastic.

Peter Jones: I look at *Chinatown* maybe a bit differently than some might. A lot of times it's viewed as an outlier. I hear that a lot, but as I alluded to last chapter, I'm going to suggest that it was the album previous, *Black Rose*, that is the outlier. I'm not talking about quality or whether you like it or dislike it. I'm saying that was the bigger left turn from the string of albums that they had been doing since *Fighting*. To me, this album feels more like the follow-up to *Bad Reputation*. Minus a couple of the bigger hits or maybe more classic type of songs, this feels and sounds like it belongs right there. *Black Rose* is the one that takes us in different directions. The addition of Gary Moore, the way it sounded and the way the tunes were written and played prompted a certain expectation that said, oh, Thin Lizzy's changing; they've gone this direction now.

And with *Chinatown*, all of a sudden, whoop, Phil's pulled that carpet out. We're going back over here. Gary's gone and now we don't even have Robertson and we have this new band, and we have a fractured Phil. But to me, these are—and I don't want to use the word disparagingly—these are almost like if they were a bunch of extra session tracks from that era. They have the same feel they have the same agenda, the same modus operandi—it's classic '70s Thin Lizzy.

But it's not going to be a prominent standalone album. I think it suffers from a couple of key things. The departure of Tony Visconti is important. I think the sound on this, while good at times, is highly inconsistent. For example, listen to the guitar tone on "Chinatown"—that's never revisited. That is never used again on any of the other tracks. And so, they utilise various degrees of heaviness, various degrees of distortion. The drums stay pretty consistent. I believe Phil's bass is a little recessed. For my tastes, I don't think there's nearly as much low end or punch in it that there was compared to the previous records, which impacts how these songs are delivered.

Brian Balich: It's hard for me to be objective about Thin Lizzy at this point in my life. They were a band I got into in high school, when I was first getting into hard rock. Like, I loved "The Boys Are Back in Town," but I didn't know much about them until I finally picked up *Jailbreak*. I had bought a *Hit Parader* that had a top 100 heavy metal albums of all-time list in it. I bought the issue because it had Angel in the list, and I had already gotten into those guys. But *Jailbreak* was there, and when I read the paragraph about it, I was intrigued by it. They especially brought up "Emerald," which quickly became a favourite when I got the album.

So then, over the years, it became a matter of grabbing the records here and there. If you'd asked me 30 years ago who my desert island band was, I would have told you right away that it was Kiss and that was it. I couldn't live without those records. But now, that band would be Thin Lizzy. It would destroy me not to have this catalogue. Their music has become that important to me. I listen to it constantly.

So back to *Chinatown*, I love all the records and it's hard for me to give any of them up. I like everything they've done, with the first four records situated down a notch or two. I feel like the stretch from *Fighting* through *Black Rose*, those are all like nine- and ten-star records. *Fighting* is probably a nine for me and the rest are tens up until maybe *Black Rose*, which gets a 9.5 because "S & M" I think is a little bit wonky lyrically. But *Chinatown* is the first time I feel like in that stretch, Thin Lizzy stepped down again. Not far, but if I'm honest, it was a drop from *Black Rose*.

Martin: Anybody have any thoughts on the album cover? Jim Fitzpatrick is back for a second time in a row.

Peter Kerr: It's 1980 and we're right in the thick of the New Wave of British Heavy Metal. And with that lurid album cover, I feel like they're saying, "We're gonna keep up with the kids. We've got to keep up with our competitors." You've got Priest and Maiden and all these young bands and they're all using strong, almost cartoon-y illustrations and they're proud to be heavy metal. So, let's put this bold dragon on the cover and talk directly to the kids. It's sort of like, "Where do we find ourselves? What's the music climate? We've got to assert ourselves." Because the rock geography is changing. So that's why I think, on an aesthetic level, you've got that bright, flashy, and, yes, lurid album cover. And when I say lurid, I mean that as a compliment—I like it. It's one of their better covers. Got ripped off by Mötley Crüe too, for *New Tattoo*. I was looking at that the other day and I thought, oh you fakes—you've done it again!

Martin: All right, so past the candy wrapper, what's the record sound like? I gotta tell you, I'm lovin' the hell out of "We Will Be Strong." It's one of my very favourites in this medium heavy zone they do so well.

Peter Kerr: Absolutely. "We Will Be Strong" is a very convincing empowerment anthem. "I know you've lost, I've won/We will be strong/And getting stronger every day." I think that's Phil ruminating about himself. He's got two personas within his head, one strong, one weak, and he's oscillating between the two in his head. It's really interesting. So it's an empowering statement, but at the same time he's talking about his vulnerabilities, his weaknesses.

It starts off with that familiar twin harmonizing guitars, between Gorham and the new guy, Snowy White, who's a fine guitarist but apparently lacked that X factor on stage. He was just standing there. Beautiful and tough lyrics, but is it the punchy opener that you would put on an album that's got to compete with the new kids on the block driving this New Wave of British Heavy Metal? Probably not. It's a bit notched back. It's got to be out of the blocks like a Deep Purple opening track. I would have swapped it around and put "Chinatown" as the opening track on side one. I don't know what your views are on that, but it feels a bit muted.

Martin: Sure, once you get to the verse, both the music and the vocal are a bit morose. And like you say, that's underscored by the feeling that there's more wishful thinking in what Phil's saying, verses confidence or affirmation. It's more like he's asking for strength than possessing it.

Peter Kerr: That's a good way to put it. Yeah, the sequencing on these Thin Lizzy albums could have been stronger. It's a bit all over the map. "We Will Be Strong" would have been a good number two or three track, in my opinion. "Chinatown" should have been the opening dog out of the gate.

David: Notwithstanding the concerns for Phil's health that you can read into it, "We Will Be Strong" is one of those great kind of party anthems that Thin Lizzy do so well. It's a mission statement kind of track. This is who we are at this time and we're coming out with aplomb. It says the gang is back together, kind of thing, even though, as we know, it's not quite the same gang. And as you say, they're not in the same place mentally or personally either.

John: It's a solid opener but I think if you compare it to some of the other openers that they've had on other albums, like "Jailbreak," like "Johnny," like "Do What You Want To," it doesn't hold up quite as strong.

Martin: Next we get the title track, which is resoundingly heavy and yet operates on a bit of a blues framework, right? It's always reminded me of "Suicide," but it's just so much more action-packed.

David: Absolutely, great rocker. So yeah, we're gonna have a good time here. A friend of mine called Rich, who loves *Chinatown*, the Jack Nicholson movie and also loves Thin Lizzy, he always quotes the last line in that film, "Forget about it, Jake." And then he says "Chiyyy-natown" just like Phil does. But yeah, rousing rocker, and actually somewhat of a classic Thin Lizzy shuffle feel as well.

Peter: "Chinatown" was the advance single, issued like five months before the album, and to my mind, it's a bit of an odd choice. It's the cousin to "Toughest Street in Town," socially observational, a story of the streets. Snowy White's guitar riff is sublime. Beautiful shuffled drumming but like you say, stylised. It feels New Wave of British Heavy Metal but there's also a nod to classic '70s rock, possibly something like Golden Earring's "Radar Love." The production is raw; it's not fussy, not very sparkly. I love the extended solos between White and Gorham. And yeah, again, there's references to what's happening in Phil's world, with China arguably representing heroin. "Living and dying/There is no release" and "Man, you don't stand a chance/If you go down in Chinatown;" it's talking about the mean streets of the city. But like I say, at the same time he may be talking about his social imbibing and his private substance issues. He wasn't shy to put these sorts of topic in his albums.

John: Killer track. This sounds like the more cerebral brother to "Bad Reputation." I love the drumming behind the guitar solos in the outro, especially those triplet fills. It's fantastic. And Phil's lyrics on here, they're clipped and short but menacing. It's a wonderful track, perhaps my favourite on the album.

Martin: An opinion I've had since the beginning is the idea that the next track, "Sweetheart," was almost part of a suite with "We Will Be Strong" and side two's "Having a Good Time." They're almost like amplified, sped-up ballads.

Brian: I see what you mean. I always liked "Sweetheart," although the chorus is a bit substandard; it feels a bit done on the spot and kind of lazy. "We need a chorus here. Let's just repeat this a few times." It's cool, though.

Peter Kerr: I feel like this one is distinguished by very conversational singing, which I've talked about in earlier chapters as a celebrated thing Phil does. Overall, it's a stock-sounding Thin Lizzy song. You've got this ascending melody that holds the song together. It's political observation, which is interesting, with lyrics about leaders and what they stand for and how you have false prophets that provide hope to the people. But it's all just broken dreams. It's dark, cynical, kind of bleak. I like it. This is Phil with his socially conscious hat on, one of these four or five personas that he constantly puts forward.

David: On the first three tracks there's not a footstep wrong. "Sweetheart" is a bit of a rocker but then goes really poppy at the choruses, with really poppy harmonies. I find that preferable to what they've been doing before, which is kind of alternating between really almost sappy stuff like "Sarah" against squarely heavy metal songs. I don't think that's what people wanted from Thin Lizzy. So, to be able to do a song like "Sweetheart" and still make it punchy and rocky and poppy at the same time, I think is really cool.

Martin: Exactly. I guess that's what I was getting at. It evokes both power pop and actually, "The Boys Are Back in Town."

John: Yes it does. Man, those unison guitar lines sound excellent. Snowy White's playing on here is very good, although I don't think he had a distinct sound like Gary Moore or Brian Robertson did.

Martin: Next is "Sugar Blues," a short, sharp rocker I've always paired up with "Leave This Town" from *Renegade*.

John: Nice, yes, I can hear that. Cool, rolling bass line on here, creative lyric, very good track. It's one of those songs that Phil wrote that would turn out to be prophetic. It's in the tradition of the Rolling Stones' "Brown Sugar" and many others.

David: Yes, very much almost confessional, about heroin, with Phil and Scott. But it's a good bluesy track anyway. It's good for what it is and it's not real lyricism, but it's kind of the classic idea of using fruits and foods and whatnot as metaphor for, in some cases sex, but in this case addiction, and specifically heroin.

Peter: "Sugar Blues" is a group composition, kind of a fast ZZ Top-type shuffle. Simple lyrics about drugs and the high life, or arguably the low life. Lynott and Downey, bass and drums, they propel the song along. You've got wonderful, tasty Downey drum fills. "See I'm changing my point of view/Ever since I caught me the sugar blues." And the opening line is "Now I'm not the type to worry, especially if it's concerning my health." Both of those are interesting and they point to conflict, a deeper internal debate between Phil and his conscience, really.

Martin: You'd get these amped-up homages to ZZ Top with the New Wave of British Heavy Metal bands as well.

Peter Kerr: Yes, and I think Phil had his ears tuned to the competition or what was happening in the music scene at any given time. And as you alluded to, *Chinatown* came out pretty much right during the most active period of that movement. They could have been seen as a dinosaur because they started in '69, first album in '71. They'd been around a while, so they had to pull their finger out and do something.

Martin: I gotta say though, Lizzy really are one of the big influences on those NWOBHM bands. The clearest through-line would be from Deep Purple and Judas Priest, but there's a lot of Rush in the regular complexity that you hear, and a ton of twin lead lines, which comes from Lizzy. All right, side one closes with "Killer on the Loose."

John: Yes, this would be their last Top Ten hit in the UK, because at the time this was released, you had the Yorkshire Ripper, Peter Sutcliffe, getting arrested and later being convicted for murdering thirteen people in the UK. He got pulled over for driving with a fake license plate and then later on they convicted him of all these murders, and he wound up going to prison for life. But despite what was going on, it should have been a big hit because it's a very catchy track.

Brian: It's also interesting that that song was somewhat of a hit, because it doesn't have the trademark double lead harmony guitars on it. So, it's an interesting outlier in their catalogue.

Peter Kerr: It's the band's most controversial song. And as John says, the controversy propelled it into the Top Ten, just at No.10. There's nothing like being banned by the BBC. He plays the person of Jack the Ripper around the time of the Yorkshire Ripper. Wow. I don't think you could get away with that these days, my friend. Sonically I like it. There's a lot of urgency in the riff. It could be a soundtrack to a slasher movie. But it's kind of dodgy. The video clip's got all these scantily clad women and he's pointing. In fact, with a lot of these Thin Lizzy video clips, Martin, you could have a drinking game every time he points (laughs). Seems to be a stock Phil Lynott move—he loves pointing. But yeah, I don't know, I think this was just trying to get a bit of buzz. I don't buy that he was trying to stir up the police to do a better job. There are all these different theories of why he put this track out. I don't think there's anything to it other than a little bit of controversy to push up record sales. I'd say it goes into that category.

David: Lyrics aside, "Killer on the Loose" gives us another one of those cool party rockers that Thin Lizzy were really adept at putting out. It's a little more contemporary-sounding. It almost sounds like what Status Quo were up to at this point rather than Thin Lizzy. It leaves out the dual guitar aspect, maybe because Snowy's playing isn't anywhere near as good as what we've seen before when Gary Moore was in the band or obviously when Robbo was in the band in the real classic era. Regardless, we are still getting great guitar playing throughout the album, from Scott and from Snowy. I just think that it shows that Snowy is a more structured session guy rather than someone who's used to playing off of somebody else.

Martin: Side two kicks off with "Having a Good Time." Stylistically or arrangement-wise, it's kinda the same temperature as the opener of side one. Even the lyrics are similar, with Phil putting on a brave face.

John: Sure, except I'm not really buying into the lyrics. From a literary point of view, I think this is the weakest song in the Thin Lizzy catalogue, comparing it to the wonderful and creative lyrics that Phil had written before. I think it's corny and nostalgic and not in a good way. But like you say, there's an air of the prophetic. Maybe he knew that his life wasn't going to be long. But for someone who was 30, 31 years old when he wrote this song, I think it comes off quite lame compared to what he did before. And that even includes the early albums where they were trying to find their sound, because at least those were interesting and really quite endearing and poetry-based. It's very well-played—they're excellent musicians—but I think the song comes up flat.

Brian: Personally, I love "Having a Good Time." I don't know what it is. I love the rhythm of the verses and the way that Phil sets the vocal line in there. The lyrics are what they are. I listen to a lot of bone-headed rock, so the lyrics don't really bother me. Yeah, it's not Phil being a poet and, as has been said a couple of times, when Phil was in the studio, a lot of times he's doing the lyrics on the spot. So it is what it is. I just think the song is fun. It's one of those that has always strangely appealed to me. I feel like I shouldn't like it as much as I do (laughs).

Peter Kerr: I think the title explains well enough the philosophy of the song. It's about comradeship with his buddies, get drunk, tear up the town. He's playing up to Phil, the rascal, the rocker, the rock star stereotype. And I love his humorous ad-libs. There's nothing deep here, but for what it's worth, it's a fun song.

Martin: And there's a bit of a Lizzy trope in here, this mixing in of acoustic with electric that they've done a few times in the past, right?

David: Yes, which tends to put the song in a pop space. Yet another party rocker. It's almost like they're doubling down on what they know they can do well and what sells. The way they all come in and sing the actual line, "Having a good time," I can't get it out of my head that it reminds of Queen singing "Don't wanna stop at all." Surely it must have occurred to them that it sounds very much like that. But hey, Freddie was friends with Phil so maybe it was even a kind of intentional playful homage—who knows? I think it's a really fun track. There's actually quite a lot of fun throughout this record, regardless of the kind of popular opinion that they got a bit dark in their last period.

Martin: Now "Genocide (The Killing of the Buffalo)" is one of those Thin Lizzy songs that you kind of forget about, but then when you experience it, in all its triumphant movements, it's hard to think of a better Thin Lizzy song. It's sort of a microcosm for this record as a whole to me, in that way. Its brilliance is stealth-like.

John: Right, totally agree (laughs). In fact, it's a song I wasn't a big fan of, but revisiting this album I've gained more love for it. I don't think it's as strong as anything on the first half though, but it is menacing.

Brian: It's an "Emerald" or "Massacre" type song, but a step down from that for me, not on the same epic scale. So yeah, it kind of fills an anchoring role similar to the title track on *Black Rose* or "Emerald" on *Jailbreak* or "Massacre" on *Johnny the Fox*, that big historical kind of thing.

Peter Kerr: Well, Phil's talking about the 19th century atrocity of the buffaloes that were killed, and effectively killing the livelihood of the American natives. So, Phil's very socially conscious. He takes on a lot of different issues, whether it's the environment or historical wrongs like the plight of the Native Americans. This falls right into that wheelhouse; he's very much into indigenous rights. So "When they try to tell you knowledge is a dangerous thing;" that really sets the tone for the song. You've got these tribal drums underpinning or kind of driving it along with the twin guitar lines. The lyrics actually highlight the rhythm of the song. He repeats the line, "The killing of the buffalo/The killing of the buffalo." And that's another trait of Phil in his lyric-writing, where he repeats little catchphrases. In some cases, he uses the lyrics as another way of propelling the rhythm. And that's a very rhythmic line. He has these subtle tricks that add to the catchiness of his songs, and that's one of them.

David: The band's friend and cover artist Jim Fitzpatrick helped Phil on these lyrics—and there are a lot of them, wow. Jim, bizarrely, did that iconic Che Guevara poster that every young socialist in the world has on their walls. He apparently kind of told Phil the more historical aspects that he needed to include. But it's a bit on-the-nose trying to write about the Native American plague and whatnot. It just seems a bit outside his wheelhouse. I'm not sure that's where Phil's strengths were. He could write from his perspective, but he's writing for a different continent there. And maybe that was part of the whole, we'll give it one last push to try and conquer America thing. We'll put on a track that reflects an American or an Americana point of view, rather than an "Emerald" or whatnot, which is more homeward bound. So, I don't think "Genocide" works lyrically very well, or musically, for that matter. That's the only one in the album I really don't care for, despite it being perfectly competent. I think there's too much talent involved for it to be incompetent at all.

Martin: Okay, next comes the album's only, lonely, lone ballad, "Didn't I."

John: Phil did the ballads so well, but his voice wasn't as strong at this point. There's also keyboards and strings. I don't think it holds up to past ballads that he did, like "Dear Heart," "Sweet Marie," "Fight or Fall" or "Sarah." I think those songs are tear-jerkers. But this I think comes off a bit shmaltzy. It's good. It's just that they've done better.

Brian: "Didn't I" is okay. I'll take Phil's shmaltzy ballads from the early days any day over this song. But it's fine.

Peter Kerr: It's a return of vulnerable Phil. You've got the Tony Visconti-like strings. It's a ballad. "I didn't think that I would miss you" when you walked out the door—it's confessional. It's the feelings and emotions of a lost love. But he asks questions. This is the typical question-and-answer lyric. Ask the question; then he answers. I didn't think I would miss you. Yes I do. That sort of thing. And it's all contained within a song. It's a clever device he uses quite a lot in his lyric-writing. Fully-fledged, vulnerable Phil.

David: I think "Didn't I" is absolutely gorgeous, and kind of out of place on *Chinatown*, because, like you say, it's the only ballad. There's nothing on here even remotely comparable. And it's rather telling that that was the one track that was considered for Phil's solo record. Because if you take that off, you would have a considerably straight rock album with nothing particularly slow on it at all—it would be bangers from start to finish. But "Didn't I" gives you a good change of pace. Phil sings really heartfelt on it, empathetically, regardless of his voice now being a bit lower than it has been in previous years—he sounds real. I love the pacing of it; it's yearning and it's painful and even when the band comes in, it doesn't feel overblown. It doesn't feel like, okay we've got dual guitars and we've even got keyboard in this lineup. Everybody comes in, but it never goes over the top, and I think we appreciate the restraint shown on it.

Martin: We close with "Hey You," a sort of lunch-bucket, bricks-and-mortar heavy one.

John: Yes. They usually close their albums out really strong and with this one, they don't. It doesn't really leave a strong impression on you.

Martin: It's strange. The first thought I have is that it adds ably to the Thin Lizzy saga, but it's more like supporting evidence of the band's greatness, not at the front edge of the argument.

David: I'll disagree (laughs). "Hey You" is a solid, spectacular closer. It's a good way to go out. That is a track that probably has the most pyrotechnics when it comes to showing off the dexterity of everybody and their granny who is involved in this project.

Peter Kerr: "Hey You" starts off with a bass line that is very similar to "Walking on the Moon" by The Police. So, I looked at the timing, and "Walking on the Moon" did come out earlier. So yeah, this is Phil chucking in a bit of reggae. Persona-wise, this is socially conscious, responsible Phil. He double-tracks his vocals to emphasise the spirit of the song. Now, I got this from an interview he did with NME on July 8th of that year; he said, "Every night I changed the lyrics. Because I haven't got what I'm trying to say. It's about how when you leave your hometown, everybody goes, 'You've got it made, man.' And when you get to London, you haven't. You've just solved one set of problems for another." And he's saying that the kid's saying to him, "I wish I was you. You've done everything." And Phil goes, "If only you knew the problems I have." So that's directly from Phil.

Martin: I really think this song is another one that is a metaphor for the album as a whole. They've managed to make a true, blue Thin Lizzy song—and album—and it's left to us to debate whether that's good enough.

Peter Kerr: Well, sure; was Phil an innovator at that particular time? Was he running with the pack or was he leading the pack? That's the thing. So maybe because the previous albums were so outstanding, so sparkly, so innovative, so almost perfect, that you feel a vague disappointment. Maybe because there are a lot of new kids on the town, he got swamped, and people tended to follow the narrative that Thin Lizzy were old news.

Martin: It might also be because we've heard all these Thin Lizzy tricks before, that this is the first time that it feels a little repetitive, right? Even if they are tricks that they own and they are great tricks.

Peter Kerr: Possibly. He definitely does cover some of the same lyrical themes. He's got the five personas and he's just covering those personas. Maybe people were thinking it was getting a little bit clichéd. Sonically there's a lot to like. Is it as good as the other material? They had a golden run with that mid-'70s to the end of the decade period. The fans might have been comparing it to the golden run and maybe it was somewhat in the shadow.

Martin: What do you think about people not wanting to accept another guitarist change? Maybe they think the wheels are falling off.

Peter Kerr: Well, I don't think anyone sort of writes Snowy into the top echelon of Thin Lizzy guitarists, although he's a fine guitarist. But he was a muso. He played live in Floyd and that's actually where they saw him. I don't think he had that sort of rocker persona that the others had. And he came into a band where people had substance abuse issues, personality issues, and he was this non-heavy metal technician, like a Guy Pratt. He was a support musician that was brought into a four-star, gold-plated rock band. Still, I think people are a bit unfair and they're looking at the rock star aspect of it. He brought a lot of great craft to this album.

Peter Jones: I don't want to be disparaging. The material is okay. There are still good songs. Side one especially, you've got five great tracks in a row that I would have no problem listening to on a regular basis. And a good portion of side two I have no problem with either. It does tend to fall off a bit and get a bit weaker as it finishes out, in my opinion. But it's still a solid album.

And the addition of Snowy White… I never understood the comments that he's the wrong guy or he's didn't fit in or anything. He is a perfect complementary player. To me, it's moving forward with John Sykes that I'd complain about. Sykes doesn't play well with others. He's a solo guy and it's always about him. Snowy fits right where he's supposed to. He plays what he needs to, and the band still sounds tight in the live recordings from this era, of which there's an abundant amount. He sounds great and he sounds solid on the older material too. I never had an issue with him.

Really, if you take a look at these tracks, if any of these were added as an extra track or two across those three records, *Johnny, Jailbreak* or *Bad Reputation*—just take them and split them up and add two to one and three to another one—you'd be okay. They'd fit in all right.

Also, the problem here from a popularity standpoint is that 1980, as we all know, is absolutely loaded with some of the most seminal hard rock albums from other bands. So, it's easy for *Chinatown* to get absolutely buried amongst all of those records that quickly became way more popular and way more talked about. I know this is an unpopular opinion, but I think this band found its legs with the next record—I really enjoy *Renegade*. I think they found their cohesion and what works for that lineup and it's a natural follow-up. And then of course *Thunder and Lightning* is its own thing. So, I don't have an issue with this album. I do like other ones better; I prefer those. But it's a good listen for me and the title track itself is just one of the best tracks they've ever done in my opinion. I like the album and I listen to it often.

David: Unlike previous records, *Chinatown* has got quite a few session players—inside men, friends, cohorts, comrades—joining in on events. The elephant in the room is that Phil not only was in a bad place personally, but professionally he's pulling in two directions because this comes out, what, six months after *Solo in Soho*, the debut solo album from him. So, he's making a Thin Lizzy album that sounds like a Thin Lizzy album intentionally because he's now trying to do different things on the solo side. This lineup also recorded some of the material for that album, for *Solo in Soho*. So, I think *Chinatown* is an attempt to say, "What's the classic Thin Lizzy sound again? Let's just do that."

So, I think that all *Chinatown* can really be accused of is a slight lack of ambition, and maybe being a bit derivative of their own works from earlier and not pushing any significant boundaries. Parts of it do sound very contemporary. I do miss a lot of the guitar interplay, which I just don't think is part of Snowy's skillset.

I like the production on it, although it's quite weird in places. Kit Woolven is credited alongside the band, but apparently all Kit really did was engineer, unlike he had done on previous records. He'd basically tell Phil, "That's the button you press if you want that sound." Phil would give the orders, basically, and Kit Woolven just kind of told him how to do it. So, it wasn't a real production from Woolven.

I know the band were frustrated because Phil was unprepared, and he was coming in and just making up lyrics on the spot in a lot of places. That put him out of sync with the band. I think that shows sometimes. "Killer on the Loose" is probably the best example of actually really just making up what rhymes in his head.

I think the record shows that he's moving aside from the band. I'm not sure what would have happened in the long term, knowing he had a couple more projects on the go after even the solo career. I'm not sure this lineup would have kept going too long with Phil being where he was in his personal life because he's just pulling himself in too many different directions and he's not good mentally or physically enough to do that, to be honest. He's not ready to be in that position.

And as much as "Killer on the Loose" was the biggest hit since "The Boys Are Back in Town," I think that's the track where you can see a bit of the creative well-being dried up. And what's the first line of "Sweetheart?" "If I was to stand in the general election." What?! That's not a Phil Lynott lyric. That is the lyric of somebody just coming up with something off the top of his head because he's cooked up a few things that rhyme with election. So yeah, I think Phil's poetry goes out the window here and we have Phil in "Let's get the job done" mode. We need an album. Let's just make a Thin Lizzy album that sounds exactly like a Thin Lizzy album. He's pragmatic. It's the pragmatist, rather than Phil the poet on this one.

John: First half of the album, I think is very, very good. But it's not one of my favourite albums by them. I think the seven albums they did before it, starting with *Vagabonds of the Western World* right through *Black Rose*, they're very good to fantastic. This one, there are some very good songs, but I think there's an array of Thin Lizzy tropes they've dealt with better in the past.

Brian: I'd agree, and Martin, I like your idea of vague disappointment, like you feel guilty about it (laughs). As much as I like *Chinatown*, if I were putting a Thin Lizzy compilation together and I had 45 minutes to do it or even a full CD, man, I might squeak one or two in from this record only because I feel obligated to have something from *Chinatown*. Again, that doesn't mean I don't like the record; it just means that I like other material so much more than this.

The production sounds a bit like where the '80s was starting to head at the time. I don't know, I'm just the singer (laughs). It's a little bit bright or something. It doesn't have the same vibe as the records before it. Maybe it was because they didn't have Tony Visconti doing the record. By the way, I recently got the Record Store Day edition, which is beautiful, and that includes the non-LP B-side track "Don't Play Around" and a bunch of demos. There's a second record that is all demos. The double CD has this stuff too.

As far as Phil's vocals go, I don't really notice a huge drop-off. But then again, he was in the studio doing two records at one time, *Solo in Soho* and *Chinatown*. Which, as a side note, really irritated Snowy White, because he'd come into the studio to do sessions for *Chinatown* and they'd be working on *Solo in Soho* stuff. But I guess Phil would stay until forever at the mic. He'd just keep going and going until he hit the wall. I was reading some stuff on it, and they'd have to force him to take a break. He's doing two records at one time and pushing himself too much.

Maybe like David has pointed out, that's what this record suffers from: Phil's intentions to get that solo record done. He was funnelling the songs that he felt he couldn't use for Thin Lizzy over to *Solo in Soho*. Which is interesting to me because that never seemed to stop him in the past. *Jailbreak* is full of songs that people who don't know Thin Lizzy would never think were by them. Songs like "Romeo and the Lonely Girl" or "Running Back" or "Fight or Fall" are great Lizzy songs, and yet they're stylistically diverse. There are all kinds of things that make those albums diverse. That was one of the things that appealed to people so much about the band.

So, what ends up happening is he funnels this stuff that is maybe less rock and more soulful or pop over to his solo record, and then ends up with whatever rockers are left and he has to put something out. So, I don't know; maybe *Chinatown* is too homogeneous. I don't think it's ever a good idea to do too much at one time. Maybe he bit off more than he could chew.

That being said, I still think it's a strong record. When I say it's a step down, this is like an eight out of ten for me. I love this record. It's just that I don't love it as much as *Jailbreak* or *Fighting* or all those records that on any given day could swap the number one spot for me. Snowy White is great here and he's also great on *Renegade*. I love *Renegade*. I think that's a step up from this one. Snowy did come into the band telling those guys, I'm not a hard rocker like Gary or Brian. And I think some of that does come across.

But I can't really complain. It's a shame too that they didn't tour the US after *Black Rose*. I can understand why Gary Moore quit. Scott and Phil were out of control with drugs. But they had issues and never toured here again. Who knows what would have happened to the band's success? It's no surprise their profile really started fading in America by this point. Which is a shame, because I think *Chinatown* deserves more recognition than it gets.

RENEGADE

November 20, 1981
Vertigo 6359 083
Produced by Thin Lizzy and Chris Tsangarides
Engineered by Kit Woolven, Chris Tsangarides and Andrew Warwick
Recorded at Odyssey Studio, London UK, Morgan Studio, London, UK, Compass Point Studio, Nassau, Bahamas
Personnel (no performance credits): Phil Lynott, Scott Gorham, Snowy White, Brian Downey
Key additional personnel: Darren Wharton – uncredited, but known to provide keyboards, organ, Minimoog, backing vocals

Side 1:
1. "Angel of Death" (Lynott, Wharton) 6:17
2. "Renegade" (Lynott, White) 6:08
3. "The Pressure Will Blow" (Lynott, Gorham) 3:45
4. "Leave This Town" (Gorham, Lynott) 3:48

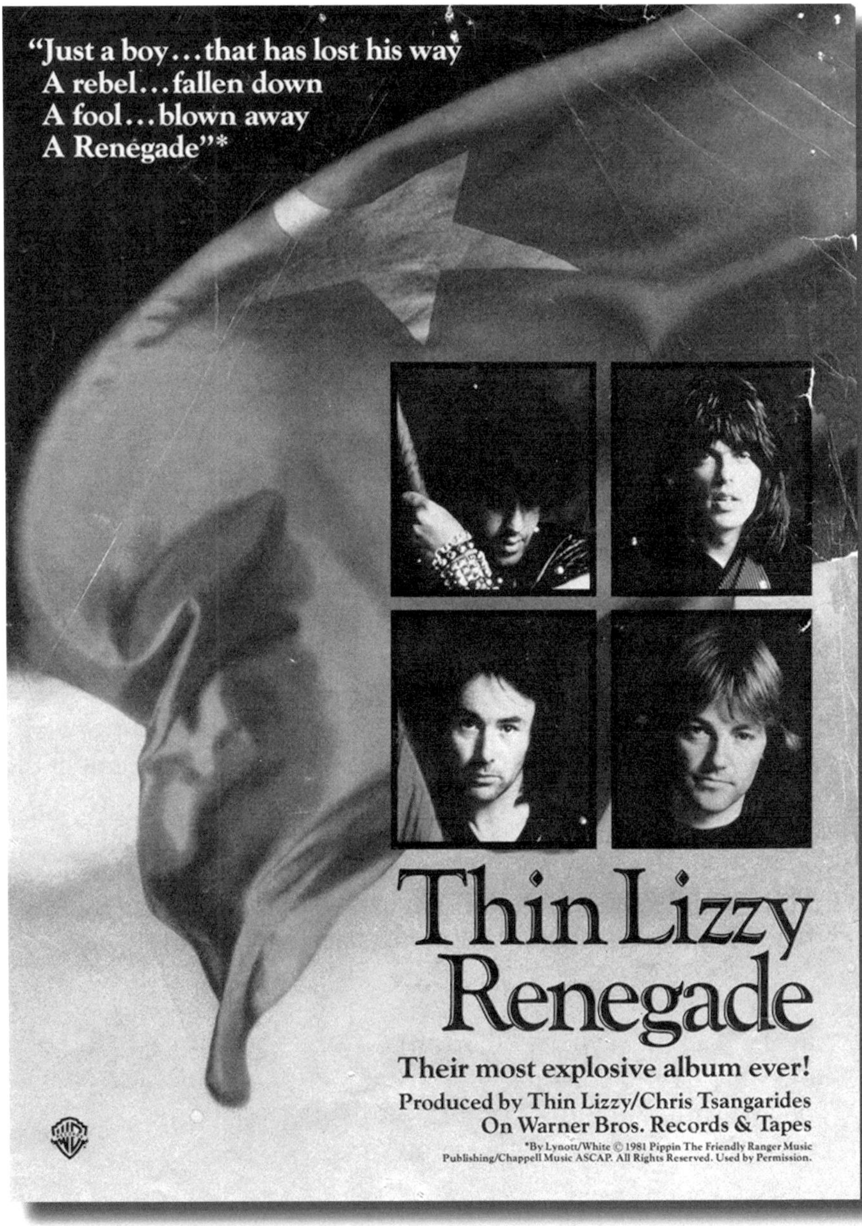
"Just a boy . . . that has lost his way
A rebel . . . fallen down
A fool . . . blown away
A Renegade"*
Thin Lizzy
Renegade
Their most explosive album ever!
Produced by Thin Lizzy/Chris Tsangarides
On Warner Bros. Records & Tapes
*By Lynott/White © 1981 Pippin The Friendly Ranger Music
Publishing/Chappell Music ASCAP. All Rights Reserved. Used by Permission.

Side 2:
1. "Hollywood (Down on Your Luck)" (Gorham, Lynott) 4:10
2. "No One Told Him" (Lynott) 3:36
3. "Fats" (White, Lynott) 4:02
4. "Mexican Blood" (Lynott) 3:40
5. "It's Getting Dangerous" (Lynott) 5:46

Honesty Is No Excuse: Thin Lizzy on Record

Martin talks to John Alapick, Rich Davenport, John Gaffney and Reed Little about *Renegade*.

Martin Popoff: Well, let's stir things up right away and that means going to John. I've been pretty steadfast for years in calling *Renegade* my favourite Thin Lizzy album, but...

John Alapick: Yes, I know you love this album, and I respect your views, but *Renegade* is my least favourite album by Thin Lizzy (laughs). Not to say that there isn't a lot to offer. And I do agree with you on the production—I think it was very well-recorded. The only thing I would say is that I think the drums—just like on *Chinatown*—need a little more beef too them. You can see that Brian's playing up a storm, but I think there should be more bottom end. Now, you can really hear Phil on here, as well as Scott, Snowy and Darren, actually, but I'm missing that gutsy drum sound out of Brian.

Martin: That is so bizarre, because to me, there's ample bottom end. It sounds plush and expensive. Perhaps they are lacking an aggressive heavy metal sound, but I'm still finding the complete sound picture full and regal—like the album cover.

John Alapick: Well, to be more specific, the problem for me might be in the snare sound.

Martin: I can understand that. It's incredibly analogue-sounding. This is a plush, gorgeous production, and maybe that's not what John wants out of a hard rock album.

John Alapick: I just don't think they capture Brian as well as they do on other albums. With the album being called *Renegade*, I see this flag here, I'm thinking, okay, Lizzy's gonna get a little heavier. We're maybe gonna go back to the sound of some of those great rockin' tracks on *Fighting*. In the end, it's lacking.

Martin: Fair enough. Can I get some support from some of you other guys?

Rich Davenport: Well, I love this album. I think it's absolutely fantastic, Lizzy's lost classic, really. I like *Chinatown*. I like both of the albums. I'd say this one's a bit more cohesive and a darker album, which I think reflects the mood of the band. You said in one of your reviews that, not lyrically, but more on an abstract level, it feels like a concept album about the demise of the band. Or it's an allegory for that. Because there's an air of defeat, which starts with *Chinatown*. By this stage, they could sense they weren't going to break through in America.

Martin: I don't recall saying that. Although, sure, I'll buy that. But here's what I feel more strongly about: it reads like a concept album about troubled loners, or even a single troubled loner who goes through all these unfortunate life phases.

Rich: Sure, yeah. And let's not forget, around this time the drug side of things had kicked in pretty heavy. That song title says it all: "It's Getting Dangerous." That aside, something key to this album is the presence of Snowy White. Brian told me that when Snowy joined, Brian was absolutely delighted because he was such a bluesy player. Brian had started out on the blues scene, so he loved that about Snowy. But Brian felt that Snowy was never given a chance. Even before anyone had heard him play a note, some of the British press had the knives out for him because he played with Cliff Richard and Pink Floyd. And people were saying, "This is the wrong guy for Thin Lizzy." He was judged before he even started.

And Scott said a very similar thing, that he wasn't given a chance. Scott also said it had to do with the idea that Gary Moore was running around the stage and Robbo was also a forceful personality, but Snowy wasn't a forceful personality in terms of stage presence. He was such an incredible player, but people maybe judged him on how he looked rather than how he sounded.

So, this album came out in a bit of a depressed period for the band. Also, around this time, Phil's marriage broke down, all while they were working incredibly hard. Also, they used to pay the road crew in between tours, which a lot of bands didn't do. So there was a huge amount of pressure on Phil to keep writing and keep the product coming out, because that was supporting everybody. And Scott was actually quite cutting about the band's management, saying that they kept being told if you come off the road, people will forget you. If you don't make another album, people will forget you.

And Scott said that was purely said on the management's behalf because they wanted the money to keep coming in. He felt that they should have been taken off the road for six months, and told, "You guys need to get well." But unfortunately, they were kept grinding away to keep the money rolling in.

I want to add, I felt Phil was treated appallingly after he died, up until probably ten years ago. He'd been almost overlooked. And when he died, the press in Britain were vile. It was all about how he died. And it's only in more recent years that his and Lizzy's accomplishments as songwriters, and just the quality of the music, has come through. If you look at this particular period, from '79 through to '83, there was *Black Rose*, *Chinatown*, *Renegade*, *Thunder and Lightning*, two Phil solo albums and, in late 1978, Gary Moore's *Back on the Streets*. So irrespective of the drugs, they kept up an incredible work ethic, which often gets overlooked.

John Gaffney: Well, in deference to John, *Renegade* indeed often lands at the bottom of fans' ranking lists, or third to last above the first two albums. The main issue for many is that the songwriting is all over the place, which could be blamed on a few factors, not the least of which is the fact that Phil was also working on material for his second solo album at the same time, thus blurring the lines between solo project and band. These things often get tricky when the primary songwriter of a band leaves to do a solo record.

Declining album sales and escalating drug and alcohol abuse also give the feeling the album was maybe a bit forced. As for Snowy, I don't understand why he gets a bad rap. I find his playing tasteful, bluesy and melodic, maybe slightly lacking on the balls-out rockers. But I prefer his style over the flashy technical stuff from John Sykes, who would follow on the *Thunder and Lightning* album.

Even though he's not pictured on the sleeve, keyboardist Darren Wharton becomes a full-time member, with the keys being another source of tension for some of the fans. I do agree they don't always fit and somewhat date the sound of the album, but at other times they work for me. Chris Tsangarides' production is smooth and slick, maybe a bit too much so, softening up the edges of the guitars. Rather than a full-on jailbreak, we get a polite asking for the door keys, thanks to this production.

Martin: I tend to categorise it as billowy and pillowy, regal. It's heavy but a different kind of heavy. There's ample bottom end, but the edges are rounded.

John Gaffney: Yeah, I like that—regal. But it's maybe a little too slick for Thin Lizzy. It just seems like some of the edge is taken off the guitars and there's a bit too much reverb. And the drums are a bit back in the mix for my tastes. But it's certainly not hard on the ears. It's not fatiguing. I find it a nice correction after *Chinatown*, which to me was very much lacking in bass, both the frequency and the instrument. The guitars on *Chinatown* are way up in the upper-mids, which makes that album a little fatiguing on my ears.

Martin: All right. How about you, Reed? Opening thoughts?

Reed: I agree that *Renegade* represents an upgrade in sound over *Chinatown*, but I suspect that that has more to do with advances in technology and change of studios. I know Chris Tsangarides is producing, but Kit Woolven is still there from the last album. It's just better. It's more high-fidelity. There's more top end, there's more low end and everything sounds great. You've had Gary Moore in and out and you had Midge Ure in and out. Snowy, they had heard as touring guitarist for Pink Floyd. You hear a lot about Snowy not fitting in with Thin Lizzy, but I don't hear that on these albums. I think he fits in great. He's a bit less rock and more blues than Robertson, but that was a style of guitar that Phil was very comfortable with, so it fit the music fine.

Martin: As for the *Renegade* album cover, there's the story in my book about how Phil was inspired by the colours on a Dunhill cigarette pack. Any opinions on the final artwork?

John Gaffney: Yeah, they almost like overcorrect by trying to look as classy as possible. From what I understand about the cover, this wasn't exactly what they were expecting. The red flag forced Phil to have to defend the band, saying that they weren't communists. Maybe there's an element of them looking around at 1981 and the emergence of the NWOBHM and trying to get something that looks a little metal. Then they go a bit over the top when we get to *Thunder and Lightning* with the studded fist popping up through the ground.

Martin: But you could also say that a cover like this makes the statement that the band was above the meat-and-potatoes heavy metal fray.

John Gaffney: Yeah, I can see that too. It could be seen as a flag of solidarity or conversely that we're our own thing; we're planting our own flag, sort of staking our territory—we were here before you guys. Maybe they're saying that they can hang in the '80s as well as anybody else.

Martin: The album begins with "Angel of Death," possibly the heaviest thing Lizzy ever did, *Thunder and Lightning* aside.

Rich: Great track, but I know Scott didn't like it for that very reason. He's commented in various interviews and biographies that he thought it was too metal. But they'd always had that metal element, and given what was going on with the NWOBHM, this is in keeping with that. The lyrics have been called a bit garish or cheesy, but I don't agree. It's still Phil's style and it ties in with his use of religious imagery, although it's more apocalyptic, like "The Holy War." Similarly, it reminds me of "Sympathy for the Devil."

Darren Wharton turns out to be a great fit for the band. The keyboards at the beginning are moody, building atmosphere, and he adds some great effects. He's not obtrusive, and what he puts in really fits. There are some nice cascading effects near the chorus of the song and it's very atmospheric in the middle as well.

Martin: He's not credited too fairly on this album, in terms of the liner notes.

Rich: No, and you wonder, even at this stage some metal bands could be oversensitive about keyboards despite Deep Purple and Uriah Heep and Rainbow. But bands could be so sensitive about actually crediting a keyboard player and making them a permanent member of the band in those more metal-conscious times with the NWOBHM. Yeah, it's unfair, because Darren's contribution to this album was prominent and he plays so tastefully. It's not drenched in horrible, dated, '80s, jarring synths. There's a sound that's all over everything in the '80s called an orchestral stab and it's really jarring and harsh and so artificial. But his keyboard playing on "Angel of Death" reminds me of Tony Carey at the start of "Tarot Woman" by

Rainbow—very appropriate. Nice, rumbling bass line from Phil as well.

As an aside, this album as a whole was a favourite on the tour bus for The Outlaws. Because Freddie Salem, who's a friend of mine, there are a couple of DVDs that have come out of them playing the Rockpalast show in Germany, and Thin Lizzy headlined. The Outlaws were on the bill along with 38 Special. The two bands got on well, and Freddie told me that he and Hughie Thomasson used to listen to this album on the tour bus and that he had fond memories of being in the bus and hearing that intro to "Angel of Death."

John Alapick: I love "Angel of Death"—one of the best songs they ever did, and the best one in terms of featuring Darren. How many songs do you hear that are this heavy, and yet so heavy on the synth? I hear that intro and immediately they have my attention, and then he's throwing in flourishes between Phil's vocal lines during what counts as the chorus.

John Gaffney: I agree with Rich, that when you hear this Moog intro, you think of "Tarot Woman." The fact that both songs open their respective albums makes them feel even more connected. It's Wharton's only writing credit on the album, a co-write with Phil. The galloping Iron Maiden-like rhythm of the verses is maybe Thin Lizzy's most on-the-chin, metal-sounding riff to this point, maybe outside of "Emerald." Heck, even Maiden themselves have covered this song, although it's never been released.

Phil delivers this snarling aggressive vocal. "I hear men, women and children crying out to their God for mercy/But their God didn't listen." Has Phil ever been this apocalyptic? Like a seasoned actor though, he's able to pull it off. Everything breaks down in the middle when we get this Pink Floyd "On the Run" sequencer-sounding 16th note keyboard thing. There are also the steady sixteenth notes on the high-hat. Phil does this spoken word part that's made almost unintelligible by an octave-lowering vocal effect. It sounds a bit cheesy to my ears, and that's a rare thing to say with these guys.

The guitar solos are properly energetic and metallic. It's a really good "come out swinging" album-opener, but I can't help wondering if Phil and the boys were noticing the rising success of NWOBHM bands like Iron Maiden and Def Leppard who eagerly cite Thin Lizzy as a major influence anyway. It's like Lizzy was going a bit too hard on asking for a piece of that pie. The optimistic side of me wants to believe this is Thin Lizzy showing the young kids how it's done. The glass half-empty side thinks it's Lizzy following rather than leading.

Reed: The big change in the band is the addition of Darren Wharton on keyboards, and nowhere do you get that more than on "Angel of Death." They leave him out of the picture. He was a young dude, like 19, when they recorded this album. So, it's a bit like the hiring of Robbo, who was also a teenager.

It's an interesting choice of opening track. You could say that like *Johnny the Fox*, this album is a collection of songs that don't sound anything like each other. I think *Chinatown* was a more cohesive album stylistically. But in this case, it opens up with a keyboard solo immediately bringing to mind Rainbow *Rising*. I also hear Boston and Angel, in terms of the prominence of the keyboards.

But this is a problem too, right? *Rising* came out in 1976. *Boston* came out in 1976 and *Helluva Band* came out in 1976. *Renegade* comes out in 1981. It's arguably out of step with popular music, let alone heavy music. I know *Thunder and Lightning* is the heavy metal album by Thin Lizzy, but this song is really looking in that direction too. So, it's maybe a bit retro for the heavy music of the day and too heavy for the AOR rock music of the early '80s. So it's an outlier, but a fantastic one, and certainly from a 2023 vantage point, it's an amazing song, and of a style I wish they would have continued with.

Martin: And what do you think of the lyric?

Reed: There's a whole verse about his father dying. Which is really weird because his dad was still alive and actually outlived him by 25 years or something. So, you kind of wonder why he put that in there. Other than that, it's quite apocalyptic. Apparently he had been reading Nostradamus. So, it was influenced by his prophecies. I will take this track any day over anything off of Judas Priest's *Nostradamus*. At the start of it, you can hear Phil say, 'Oh my God, there's millions of them!" Fascinating little artifact, and too quiet to be noticed by most people, and yet they left it in the recording.

Martin: Next is the title track, which is also top five Lizzy for me. May as well start with you again, John!

John Alapick: Yes, well, we're really taking it down here. It's a ballad of sorts, but it's got some cool guitar work in it. Not one of my favourites on the album. This started on *Black Rose*, but the hard living was really affecting his voice, making it less soulful. You think about it. He was 32, but then again not as bad as how Jim Morrison sounded at 28. Jim Morrison sounded like he was near death at 28.

Rich: Great track, atmospheric, and having that progressive element we heard on "It's Only Money" and things like things like that. Phil is perhaps singing about himself allegorically. There's a real weariness in the lyric and it's the same sort of tough guy character from "The Boys Are Back in Town" and "Johnny" and "Rocky." The guy's not quite defeated, but he sounds wearier and he's taken some heavy blows, a bit of a battering. So, it's the same sort of character but the character's kind of bloodied but unbowed.

There's a raw emotion in Phil's lyric. There's a bit where he sings, "Oh please, I'm on my bended knee" and it's quite moving, really. We get brilliant rhythm from Brian Downey, with Phil locked in tight. Displaced beats again, so we hear prog chops but they're used sparingly, the way Rush would go in the '80s. There's certainly some very accomplished playing. It's not a typical arrangement but it flows well. There's a really nice twin lead in the middle as well.

Martin: Yeah, well, that's actually my favourite twin lead of theirs ever, on account of the sort of ponderous spareness of it but also the chord sequence that it's played over. Seriously, that bit there, which comes back for the outro, is one of my favourite chunks of music by anybody ever.

Rich: Very cool! Yeah, it's such a shame. There's actually a TV performance of this. There was a TV show on BBC TV called *Three of a Kind* and it was three comedians, one of whom is still really, really popular. One was Tracey Ullman, plus Lenny Henry, who's a black British comedian, who's a real sort of comedy pioneer, and a guy called David Copperfield who hasn't kept up the same profile. But they actually perform the mime to "Renegade" on that. And Phil does a comedy sketch with Lenny Henry. It's actually on YouTube.

From what I remember reading in one of the biographies, when they did, I think, "Trouble Boys" as a single, Phil had some sort of argument with the crew at *Top of the Pops* and that didn't help the album's chances. So, they didn't get a lot of TV coverage on this album. But this is a rare TV appearance, and it comes over very well.

John Gaffney: I consider this song to be a sort of sudden left turn towards pop, but with an influence from The Police, which was happening to a few bands at the time. You hear it in the interplay between the instruments in the opening and first verse. Then the drums sort of pick up in busyness, pushing everything towards more familiar Lizzy turf with those big, hanging power chords. Some nice harmonised melodies lead us to a syncopated riff. The drums hit on the off beats, making it hard to find the downbeat at times. It's almost proggy, but for some reason it still feels smooth enough, given the near pop context. Eventually the Police-like reggae vibe returns, fading in at the end, and actually awkwardly in my opinion. I don't know, too many strange changes in this song; it's like puzzle pieces that don't quite fit. I could never quite get past that intro.

Martin: As teenagers, we always thought it sounded a bit like "Bette Davis Eyes" by Kim Carnes.

John Gaffney: Yeah, right (laughs). To me, it sounds like a song that looked good on paper, but they didn't quite 100% pull it off in the recording. But I do like the verse music and the lyrics. I like Phil's melody and I love that middle section where Brian is playing on the offbeat and the riff is twisting and turning around and you're wondering where the downbeat and everything is. It's just a strange song. I can't unhear the Police influence, or even Dire Straits.

Reed: The tonal shift between "Angel of Death" and "Renegade" is just huge. And that's one of the problems with this album. Every song you listen to, you go, okay, now I know what's coming. And then the next song comes on and you're like, oh, that's not what I was expecting. That can be bad because people don't really like to be shocked that much. It's a good song with a pretty typical Phil, shady side or sad side of the road lyric about an outlaw biker. The music is surprisingly restrained but there are a lot of parts—there are just parts and parts and parts. It's a very different type of composition.

But it's not anywhere close to the heavy metal that "Angel of Death" was. It's a more Thin Lizzy kind of song but a very busy Thin Lizzy song. But this is where Phil starts using a very different vocal style. I don't know if it's age or abuse or just life on the road, but he's rougher. He uses a lot more vocal fry and he's actually less conversational. I don't know if that was intentional or if that's just where his voice was at when they recorded this.

Martin: Next is "The Pressure Will Blow," which is one of those where you hear them turn in a simple verse, but then balance or correct by adding more cerebral parts.

John Alapick: Yes, we're getting back to that glorious double guitar unison guitar sound. This is a very good track with a nice solo in it.

Rich: One of my absolute favourite Lizzy tracks. The twin leads on this are just phenomenal. And again, this is such a sad fact about this album; They're pushing ahead with the twin lead guitar format, using it intelligently, developing it, and it gets so overlooked. Now I actually bought a British budget price compilation called *The Boys Are Back in Town*, and obviously with that title, that track is on it. It was on Pickwick Records, who were a budget label that used to sell albums in Woolworths, but tended to put weird songs on. I had no idea that these weren't the hits because this was my first Lizzy album.

So, the only well-known tracks on it were "The Boys Are Back in Town," the single, plus "Bad Reputation." And then it's got "The Pressure Will Blow" and it's also got from the same sessions, the B-side, "Memory Pain," the Percy Mayfield song, and it's also got a B-side from *Chinatown*, "Don't Play Around." But as it was my first Lizzy album, I just bought a cheap compilation, and I didn't realise that these weren't the best-known songs.

And it just shows the quality of this album that "The Pressure Will Blow" is still one of my favourite Thin Lizzy tracks to this day. I'd take it over a lot of the better-known classics. It's testament to the writing and performance quality that for somebody who had very little clue other than a couple of the singles, this could hold up. I think it's a lost classic, this track.

The solo is great. Snowy and Scott are an underrated team. Scott had really elevated his game as a player. He hadn't been playing very long when he joined Lizzy in the first place, only a couple of years, and then he really came into his own with *Bad Reputation*. I seem to remember reading somewhere that he really practiced a lot when Gary joined the band, and here is, again, such an underrated guitarist. But yeah, great solo, and then it switches to a major key twin lead in the middle. The drumming is great. The whole song is fantastic.

John Gaffney: I love the intro to this, where you get that rockin' start/stop riff and the woofer-activating low keyboard notes dropping in between the opening spots in the riff. Those classic Thin Lizzy guitar harmonies make us feel warm and fuzzy. Scott gets a writing credit along with Phil. I would guess he was instrumental in the nice guitar harmony sections throughout the song. Phil's lyrics get across this pent-up anger ready to overflow, maybe directed at someone that we don't know. "So, I'll keep pushing my position/'Til the pressure builds it well."

Reed: Yes, it's another seedy "slice of life" story, this time about a guy who's mad at his girlfriend. It's a much more straightforward composition than "Renegade." It doesn't have all of those moving parts in it. Now this song to me feels more like 1981; it's even got a galloping guitar part in it. There's one part where I'm pretty sure that the keyboard and the guitar are playing a unison line, which is rare with Lizzy, even after Darren joins the band. Again, Phil's singing with a lot of that vocal fry, rougher and more aggressive.

Martin: Next is "Leave This Town," which, as a teenager, I heard and instantly paired up with "Sugar Blues" from the last album.

John Alapick: Okay, but "Sugar Blues" I like more because it's got the bass in there. Plus lyrically it's graphic and prophetic for Phil's life. He's warning you but he's doing a lot of things he was talking about, like on "Borderline," where he's spending too much time at the bar and on *Black Rose*, "Got to Give It Up." Same thing there. But when I hear "Leave This Town" all I can think of is Molly Hatchet. You listen to this delivery, I'm waiting for Don Pardo—or maybe Pete Pardo—"Ladies and gentlemen, Danny Joe Brown," and Danny Joe Brown comes in and duets with Phil. I'm waiting for him to go, "Whiskey man, don't you play that hand too long." I don't want Molly Hatchet in my Thin Lizzy. I do not care for it.

John Gaffney: I'm hearing more ZZ Top. The main riff is a little too close to "La Grange" for me, but the chorus is energetic and fun. Thankfully, the riff's a bit more ornate or flashy than "La Grange," so it's not a total rip-off. But then again, that low-register spoken bit in there, that's so Billy Gibbons. At this point in their career to be doing something that sounds so much like another band, I don't know, it just doesn't work for me.

Rich: It's another song about the macho guy under siege that needs to get out of town, and if you read between the lines, you can envision Phil and his drug problem, get away from the dealers and hangers-on, try get clean. It plays into the mood of the band at the time. I agree with you about the link to "Sugar Blues." It's hard to do a bluesy riff like that that doesn't sound clichéd and they do it really well. I wonder if that might have been Snowy's influence, with him being a blues guy.

There's a great solo on it, and a brief twin guitar lick, quite a hypnotic-sounding lick. They might be playing in three/four over four/four on the solo. Yeah, I like the track as it is, although I do wonder that if they'd have a little more time, that this could have been even better with a big chorus or if it went somewhere different—it's sort of one mood all the way through, with really propulsive drumming. I wonder if that points to the pressure they were under at the time. Still, they make a blues song sound quite accomplished.

And you really hear the strength of this album's production. Like you say, it's regal, definitely not raw. It's strong, the guitars don't sound blunted, and the riffs hit home. It's a really rich production and the frequencies are full. I think because of the lushness, that's why the keyboards don't smother anything. It's all very well-balanced.

Reed: "Sugar Blues;" that's an English shuffle and this one's a Texas boogie shuffle, very ZZ Top, and I love Thin Lizzy doing this style. I love this song, except for the part where Phil tries to talk Texan. Let's just say he's not totally successful with that. I live in Texas, so I know of what I speak. But I love that "Gotta leave this town" vocal part. Lyrically, again, Phil's on the move. I think that's Phil's entire life. Phil rarely talks about being content. He's always looking somewhere else. It's just that this time he's doing it over an uptown shuffle beat.

Martin: Over to side two, we get "Hollywood (Down on Your Luck)," a title I dislike for a couple reasons: use of the name Hollywood plus the parentheses and even what's in them.

John Alapick: Yeah, but the song kicks ass. This was a single. There's this cool half-time piece of music before they go into the solo, plus a great chorus. One thing I'm not too crazy about—and this is something I find on a few of Phil's songs—he sometimes crams in too many words. In a song like "Fools Gold" from *Johnny the Fox*, it works, but here it's distracting. Plus, it's another one where I hear the degradation in his voice. And I get what you mean about the title; here you've got a guy so associated with Ireland singing about Hollywood. You just don't picture Phil ever setting foot in Hollywood.

Rich: This is the great lost Thin Lizzy single. For me, "Hollywood" keeps up the energy of the punkier tracks on *Black Rose* like "Toughest Street in Town" and "Get Out of Here." Those weren't exactly punk, but they certainly raised the game in terms of upbeat, brash energy. And this has got that same sort of energy, with a killer chorus and a really original sort of staccato riff. I'm totally guessing here, but I wonder if maybe they're using Hollywood as a metaphor or allegory for the music business. The raw emotion in Phil's voice when he sings about being down on your luck in Hollywood… you wonder if he's reflecting about their career being on the decline. I certain do.

Music-wise, there's an intelligent use of the twin guitar format with the rhythm change underneath it, and there's a key change that builds tension in the middle. The keyboards are well-placed. There's a sort of progressive rock advancement but at the same time a continual thread back to the band's heavier tracks. It's such a shame "Hollywood" gets overlooked. And Phil says as much—that "Nobody give a damn" line is just so heartfelt, the way it's delivered.

Martin: Definitely, and along those lines, he goes, "Lady Chance, she won't dance," and then later, in total anguish, "I'm ready for the dance."

John Gaffney: Yes, nice one. The lyrics are comparing and contrasting Hollywood with the two other meccas of rock music at the time, London and New York, the overall sentiment being that it's hard to catch a break, although the lyrics aren't strictly about the music business. In fact, his point seems to be that Hollywood is a cakewalk compared to New York and London. The halftime-feel guitar solo section ends with some beautiful fanfare-like guitar harmonies, which, for me, contrasts the pessimism of the lyrics.

Reed: I've always had a thing for songs that start with naked bass lines, even though it's just eighth notes on the bass. Then the guitar riff kicks in and it's brilliant. So we've got another song from the mean streets. He talks about how people in Hollywood think they've got it rough, saying it's much harder in New York and London. Kind of a strange message. I wonder if that one was aimed at Scott, the Californian. No way to know. Included are some of Phil's sledgehammer rhymes, things that don't quite rhyme.

Martin: Then we get "No One Told Him."

John Alapick: Yes. "Hollywood" is the last song on *Renegade* that I feel is strong. I find "No One Told Him" pretty mediocre. It's like we're singing for 13-year-olds now or something. It's okay musically, but not particularly memorable. It doesn't sound like something that would have made any of the albums up through *Black Rose*, in my opinion. It's like "Having a Good Time," which is also simple and silly.

Rich: I'll disagree and say I love this track, which could have been a single, really. Similar feel and energy to the preceding track. It reminds me a bit of "Dear Miss Lonely Hearts," almost power pop but rock, a power pop crossover vibe. Some nice harmonies from Phil and a kind of stop/start feel to the verses with the guitar punctuations, sort of call-and-response. There's a lot of emotion from Phil, especially his singing on the bridge. He's singing about this guy who hasn't got a friend. Again, it's the sort of down on your luck idea, as explicitly stated in "Hollywood." It's a theme throughout the album, the idea of being a bit beaten down, snowed under.

Martin: It's a little new wave, a little jaunty, like a Cars song.

Rich: Exactly. Phil was renowned for jamming with other bands. He had a lot of friends on the punk scene and apparently used to get up on stage with people like Elvis Costello and Dire Straits as well. He definitely had his finger on the pulse.

John Gaffney: "No One Told Him" is a fun rocker on the surface, but it's actually about a fellow who's lost in heartbreak after losing his girlfriend. Phil takes the interesting perspective of a neutral third person explaining to the woman that, "He's going crazy, he's reckless/ Without you baby, he's helpless." The narrator is also quick to admonish the departing lover that she didn't tell him she didn't want to see him again and that she broke him. He's making the listener sympathise with the guy left out in the cold by his ex-girlfriend. It shows what a creative lyric-writer Phil is for turning a simple breakup song on its head like that.

But his cheerful delivery of that "When I'm upset, my friends they help me to forget" line always puts a smile on my face. You might notice that Phil seems to cheer up when he talks about friends and buddies and hanging out with the boys and everything like that. As much as he sings about sadness, the tone of his voice can be uplifting and hopeful. Like, if you were hanging out with him and you were in a bad mood, Phil would be the guy to put his arm around you and make you feel better.

Reed: Sure, yeah, and words aside, this is an upbeat, happy hard rock song, and quite poppy. It's always reminded me heaviness-wise of "Don't Believe a Word" from *Johnny the Fox*. In fact, when I listen to this song, I think surely, he wrote this to be a single. I read a quote from Chris Tsangarides saying that they couldn't hear a single on the album. And I'm like, what?! What about this song?! And like you say, jaunty is a good word for it. Its biggest problem is that it's not representative of anything else on the album. What if you had bought the album hearing that as a single and then got "Angel of Death" as your first song? You probably wouldn't have been happy. At the lyric end, now that you've pointed it out, I see the troubled loner through-line, but because the music on *Renegade* is all over the map, for me, it masked making those connections. It never really struck me as having a cohesive through-line like that.

Martin: Next is "Fats," which, again, I keep saying this, but even though it's not heavy and actually jazz, I'll take a song like this over "Still in Love with You" or "Sarah" any day.

John Alapick: Yeah, I quite like it too, because it's something different and interesting. And I love jazz too. It sounds like Phil's playing a fretless bass on here. I've heard people say that. It's another song where Darren Wharton is used quite well, on that piano solo on there. And I think Phil's deep, gruff vocal works well here.

Rich: Some people don't like "Fats," but I think it's a nice diversion, It's incongruous, but I think it's a nice break after the more upbeat rock tracks. The chord changes are smart, and actually melancholic, sombre. They've put equally jarring tracks on some of the other albums.

Martin: It's interesting how everybody views *Renegade* as not too heavy an album, and yet "Fats" is the closest thing to a ballad on it.
John Gaffney: True, but also, here's where the lines feel like they're blurring between Thin Lizzy and Phil solo. "Fats" is a swinging jazz number, telling the story of this smooth character. You can picture the zoot suits and watches on a chain. You've got the jazzy acoustic piano solo adding to the '50s-era speakeasy, smoky jazz club vibe.

There are finger snaps on two and four and as John mentioned, fretless bass carries some of the melodic stuff that is laid down over the top of a standard fretted bass part. And it's kind of fun hearing Phil imitate an old jazz singer like Louis Armstrong. Still, it's bit outside the typical rock boundaries of Thin Lizzy for me, very much sounding like something that could have been on *The Philip Lynott Album.*

Reed: For sure, it's a divisive song among Lizzy fans. I happen to love "Fats." And I don't know why anybody who liked "Dancing in the Moonlight" would not like "Fats," because the Jets and Sharks are back snapping their fingers. Admittedly, an ode to Fats Waller is strange subject matter. That's weird subject matter for anybody, let alone an Irish hard rock singer. It includes the word razzmatazz, which is a word that I've always loved and I'm glad to see it appear in lyrics. Darren Wharton does a really believable job with the stride piano part. Again, that's a 19-year-old kid going from Rainbow-styled heavy metal at the beginning and now he's playing stride piano. Such a talented guy at such a young age.

Martin: What do you know about Fats Waller?

Reed: Quite a bit. Weirdly, my wife is a big Fats Waller fan. We've got a box set of Fats Waller's recordings. He was famous for growing up as a pianist in houses of prostitution. His songs are really lewd. He wrote things like "Fat and Greasy" and all of these songs about prostitutes and sex. "Ain't Misbehavin'" was his big hit. Born in 1904, died in 1943, so he's sort of a 1920s guy. And he played piano, stride piano, sort of like ragtime, very up-tempo, kind of New Orleans cathouse jazz. But yeah, Fats Waller was not a well-known musician outside of jazz circles.

Martin: Next is "Mexican Blood," which I love to death. I have no problem with this one, although right after "Fats," I can understand how the stylistic shifts could make the typical fan of Lizzy dizzy.

Rich: This might be testament to Chris Tsangarides and his ability to handle diversity. It's like we're going back to *Vagabonds* compared to the first two, where despite different song styles, it was all distilled into a more unified sound. Because of the arrangement, the players and the production from Chris, it doesn't veer too far toward the point where you think, oh, this is a bit much. "Mexican Blood" is quite skilfully produced, with the sort of flamenco style at the beginning and some of the percussive additions and the deft use of Darren in there. Nothing overwhelms, and despite the Mexican flavour, it still resonates like a Thin Lizzy rock track and fits the album.

Martin: I agree. The production is so rich and consistent of tone across the album—especially the drum sound—that it serves as a significant unifier of these songs into something that makes sense.

John Gaffney: Yes, that's true, although I'm not much of a fan of this song. Spanish-style plucked guitars open this one, and then we get this soft pad sound on the keyboards, I guess imitating or suggesting horns. I find it annoying the way Phil keeps repeating the word Mexican. I don't know; this should have been pushed to Phil's solo album, in my opinion.

Reed: I'd frame "Mexican Blood" as disposable, even though I don't think there are any bad songs on *Renegade*. We're back to Phil's beloved Western motifs, but as a story, it's pretty slight. He tells you right at the start what the ending of it is, and just repeats it over and over again. "His pretty Mexican girl, she died." He sings it in a very conversational tone. It sounds like a neutered version of Marty Robbins' "El Paso." Think about that. Actually, I consider it a missed opportunity. If he had ZZ Topped this song and done it in the same Texas boogie style as "Leave This Town," it might have been a killer track. Good use of Darren again, who is integrated smartly into the mix. I can see why the guy would be unhappy about his crediting because he's all over this album.

John Alapick: The old Phil would have written a much better song about a Mexican girl. This is just undeveloped and even lazy. It's just not good.

Martin: I'm shocked. Not a lot of fans for "Mexican Blood!" Okay, last song.

John Alapick: Now, in my opinion, "It's Getting Dangerous" is a song that could have been saved, specifically by putting the guitars up in the mix instead of just the keyboards playing in the verses and then the guitars coming in for colour. They could have made that song an anthem about the memories you had about being young.

It could have been a more impactful closer, and I would have gone, well, there's a lot of stuff on here I don't like, but at least they ended the album strong. Instead, it ends with a whimper. There are good twin leads in the choruses, but I would have liked to have heard them drive the verses harder and heavier. You're going through a lot of fluff to get to that triumphant chorus.

Martin: I love the song, but I see what you mean; it's a little subdued.

John Alapick: It is. If Phil wants to be a little reflective or pensive, that's cool. But I like when an album ends loud and rockin'. Do Thin Lizzy. Don't go out with a whimper. Okay, you want to end with a great ballad like "Dear Lord," that works because it's grandiose. But if you're going to end it with something that's supposed to rock, it's got to have some meat on the bone. Even those unison guitar lines should have been higher up in the mix. They're so good; they could have carried the whole song. You don't even need Darren on that song. Okay, Darren, you can take a seat for this one. They could have done that.

John Gaffney: I agree. Like other mid-tempo songs on the album, "It's Getting Dangerous" takes a bit too long to get started for me, although it starts to come together with that catchy and melodic chorus. I love Brian's fills on the fade-out. This one feels stuck between a hard rock tune and a pop tune, with the chorus being its saving grace. I can't see this making it onto one of the earlier classic albums. Phil's spoken word section feels a bit uninspired or forced, especially since he's already done the spoken vocal thing a few other times on the album. Brian Downey has some nice drum fills though on the fadeout.

Rich: Another great arrangement plus a dramatic buildup with a quieter vocal from Phil. We're talking about a man being alone for the very first time. He's lonely but he's got to work it out on his own. Again, this idea of being beaten down, "Who in the world would believe/That he's got another trick up his sleeve?" And there's "Which way to the top?" Well, Lizzy had been to the top by this point—at least where I'm from, the UK—and now they're on the ropes. Maybe I'm reading too much into that, but he says that, and I think about the career they've had.

Phil's really putting his heart into the vocal. We tend to forget how relatively young Phil was when he died. He was 36 then, so making this album, he's 31. That's a very world-weary lyric for a relatively young guy. It's nostalgic and wistful. He's talking about when we were young. He's longing for a more innocent time, being retrospective, and it doesn't look like he's putting any of this on for effect. It's quite a lived-in lyric. Which is a sad thing, really, for a bloke as young as he was at that point. To me, the song shows such amazing growth in the band. There's a nice twin guitar harmony, and it sounds like it might have a synth doubled in it. I know Darren used to do some of that, especially live, double some of the riffs. But yeah, it's a very good sort of show-stopper to bring the curtain down on the album—very accomplished.

Reed: Like the two Johns, I don't think "It's Getting Dangerous" starts particularly well, and this is after "Mexican Blood," which is also pretty weak tea to me. So, it starts out lacking promise, but it really picks up, and by the chorus, it's turned into a pretty rockin' song. Now, I find the ratio of keyboard to other instruments on this song really odd. It's very keyboard-heavy. It doesn't have the Rainbow sound of "Angel of Death" but the keyboards are very prominent, more prominent than the guitars. If you just took the guitars out completely, you'd have a synth pop song! I figure Phil must have been listening to the English pop music of the day and maybe experimenting a bit in that direction.

Martin: Funny. Again, as contrarian as it most definitely is, I whack "It's Getting Dangerous" way up my list of favourite Thin Lizzy songs. I agree on the verse—at least when there's no beat—but everything from the pre-chorus, through to the chorus and that sublime twin lead, I'm totally on board. All right, any final thoughts?

Rich: Well, again, in my opinion I just see so much growth and so much progression across the songs on this album. It's in the writing, the playing, the production, the way Darren has been integrated into the band. It's just such a shame *Renegade* didn't get more attention and serious consideration. I think it was purely circumstantial because of where Lizzy were in their career, along with external factors. There was nothing wrong with the album. In fact, "Trouble Boys" may have harmed its chances as this advance single.

Martin: That's pretty much a novelty song.

Rich: Absolutely. It was a retro, rock 'n' roll Rockpile song, and those guys are almost contemporaries of Lizzy. It's like, why are they covering one of their tracks? It's not a bad song, but it's weaker than a lot of Phil's own compositions and it's really nothing special. And I wonder if putting that out first gave people pause. Because obviously in those days, the single was such a big advance postcard for the album. And I wonder if that hurt its chances.

Martin: It caused dissension in the band too. And not only that, it was slated to go on the album and they were even thinking about calling the damn thing *Trouble Boys*. I also wonder if *The Philip Lynott Album* coming out afterward hurt the record's chances? It's a year later, but it's like, oh, I guess Thin Lizzy's broken up. Phil's doing this now, and wow, it sure isn't Thin Lizzy-type music.

Rich: Absolutely. We know about the confusion around *Solo in Soho* and *Chinatown*, so yeah, it's possible that *The Philip Lynott Album* diluted Thin Lizzy's impact in general, whether it's confusion around *Renegade* or *Thunder and Lightning* or even the last live album. In those pre-internet days, people see that solo album and they're maybe surmising that the band's broken up.

It's such a shame because I think *Renegade* is the last great Thin Lizzy album. *Thunder and Lightning* is a fantastic album, but it's very much a different thing. Some Lizzy fans who'd been with the band for a long time didn't like *Thunder and Lightning* as much or didn't like it at all. They felt it was too heavy. Whereas people my age and other northern kids, we thought it was fantastic (laughs). It was a bold move for them, and I think it worked. Whereas *Renegade* is still a progression in spirit and sound from *Jailbreak* or *Johnny the Fox*.

Martin: I don't mean to harp on about this record that only I seem to love this much, but is it possible that it's got the very best collection of Thin Lizzy twin leads?

Rich: Yeah, I would agree. I would agree because, again, Scott's a far more accomplished player by that stage and Snowy is a far better player than people give him credit for. He can get the speed going when he wants to. So, the two of them, it's just the right balance. It's not like a million miles an hour shred stuff, but it's pushing the standard of the guitar playing somewhere new, exploring the musicality and potential of what they can do with the format. And like we were saying, on "Renegade" itself and on "The Pressure Will Blow," they switch from the main twin lead, like the ascending one—that's the main hook of the track—and then there's a major key one in the middle. They're layering leads upon leads upon leads and it's just fantastic. Yeah, I definitely agree. This is the best album for that.

Reed: It's kind of amazing to me that they got another album out after how poorly *Renegade* did commercially, and that they were able to steal John Sykes from Tygers of Pan Tang. I would have thought this would be the last hurrah. Like I said, it's too stylistically diverse by the time hard rock evolves into what it is in the '80s, especially with the NWOBHM. Music had really started to silo and partition into subgenres and Thin Lizzy is trying to keep one toe in like four different silos. That was no longer going to work. They needed to pick a direction, although, interestingly, they then picked a direction on *Thunder and Lightning* and that didn't work out for them either. It's possible that they were simple beyond their shelf life at this point.

John Gaffney: Like you, I appreciate *Renegade* more than most Lizzy fans do. I like it better than *Thunder and Lightning* because I don't care for John Sykes' playing on that record. *Renegade* isn't going to rank higher than any of the classics for me, like *Bad Reputation* or *Johnny the Fox* or *Jailbreak*. I don't even think I'd put it above *Vagabonds*. But yeah, it's grown on me over time. It's a hard one for me to digest because of the production and some of the weird twists and turns. Plus, it runs out of gas for me with the way the last three songs on the album go.

I feel like there are songs that Phil could have used on his solo album, and they just got inserted onto *Renegade* instead. Whenever you have the primary songwriter in a band going off to do a solo album, the lines get blurred even more between solo album and band. It gets hard to differentiate between the two. This is not some case where you have a band member who barely writes anything in the band and then he goes to do a solo album and it seems more surprising. So, in that sense, again, some of the songs that could have been on Phil's records, they still work here because Phil is also the main personality in Thin Lizzy. But he's an adventurous writer, and I'm glad we got those two solo albums before we lost Phil for good.

EMA PROUDLY PRESENTS
THIN LIZZY
THE FAREWELL CONCERTS
NY LP:
THUNDER AND LIGHTNING
JOHANNESHOVS ISSTADION
LÖRDAG 30 APRIL KL 19.30

THUNDER AND LIGHTNING

March 4, 1983
Vertigo VERL 3
Produced by Thin Lizzy and Chris Tsangarides
Engineered by Chris Tsangarides and Andrew Warwick
Recorded at Lombard, Dublin, Ireland and Power Plant, London, UK
Personnel (no performance credits): Phil Lynott, Scott Gorham, John Sykes, Darren Wharton, Brian Downey
Note: original UK issue included a live EP, catalogue # LIZLP3, featuring live renditions of "Emerald," "Killer on the Loose," "The Boys Are Back in Town" and "Hollywood."

Side 1:
1. "Thunder and Lightning" (Downey, Lynott) 4:53
2. "This Is the One" (Wharton, Lynott) 4:01
3. "The Sun Goes Down" (Wharton, Lynott) 6:18
4. "The Holy War" (Lynott) 5:10

IMD 8681
Thin Lizzy
STEREO
also playable mono
thunder and lightning

Thin Lizzy
thunder and lightning
CHROMIUM DIOXIDE 120µS
DOLBY SYSTEM

Side 2:
1. "Cold Sweat" (Syles, Lynott) 3:06
2. "Someday She Is Going to Hit Back" (Downey, Wharton, Lynott) 4:01
3. "Baby Please Don't Go" (Lynott) 5:07
4. "Bad Habits" (Gorham, Lynott) 4:03
5. "Heart Attack" (Wharton, Gorham, Lynott) 3;38

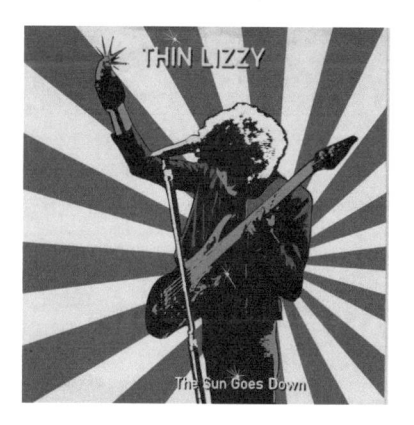

Honesty Is No Excuse: Thin Lizzy on Record

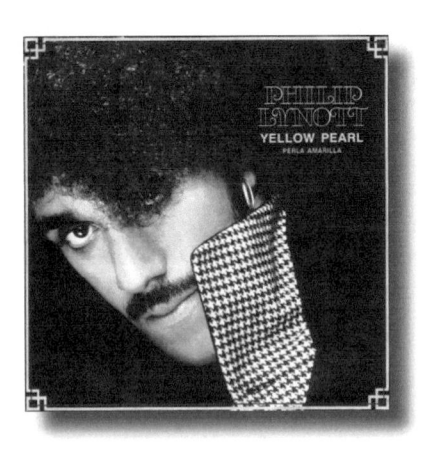

Martin talks to Tim Durling, David Gallagher, Sean Kelly and Steven Reid about *Thunder and Lightning.*

Martin Popoff: We arrive at the end of our journey, and Thin Lizzy throw us the ultimate curve ball, don't they? How do you begin to assess what kind of record *Thunder and Lightning* is?

David Gallagher: Well, it's definitely the outlier in the catalogue, isn't it? It's the heavy metal Thin Lizzy album, really. It's Thin Lizzy attempting to join in on the New Wave of British Heavy Metal, certainly following in that stream or wandering down the same path. And they've got a producer on board, Chris Tsangarides, who is very much part of that. Chris brings from his time with Tygers of Pan Tang, into this venerable band, a guitarist by the name of John Sykes.

Scott Gorham is also contributing, of course, and through Scott, they were always a hard rock band, essentially. But this is where the rock turns into metal. It's the *Slide It In* of their catalogue if you will. Literally we've got a member here that would do the same thing for Whitesnake. So, it's very much the bridge, unfortunately, in this case, to the demise of Thin Lizzy but the rise of Whitesnake. It's the bridge to somewhere that we're not going to get to because, unfortunately, this is the last Thin Lizzy record, their 12th and final album. But it might have potentially been the bridge to a brave new frontier without the passing of Phil Lynott just a couple years later.

Tim Durling: The music on *Thunder and Lightning* sounds completely different than anything else in the catalogue, but it's an album that I actually really enjoy nonetheless. One of the huge things that makes this album sound different is the addition of our young guitar hero freshman from Tygers of Pan Tang, John Sykes, the same John Sykes of Whitesnake and Blue Murder fame. The result is a much louder, heavier-sounding recording courtesy of producer Chris Tsangarides, not that it sounds anything like his other albums. It's a very thickly recorded album, and the way that the drums sound makes it bludgeoning. Lyrically, Phil is as philosophical as ever, but he's also getting into fights (laugh). But musically this is an album that you could slip on if you're in the middle of an old-school, early '80s metal fest. Nobody would bat an eye, whereas if you played *Jailbreak*, they'd be like, hey, this is good, but it doesn't sound like what we're listening to right now.

Martin: Yeah, it's funny. It's almost like a wilder or demo version of the Whitesnake self-titled album, both in the writing and in the production. Sean, what are your initial thoughts?

Sean Kelly: Well, man, I think that this is Phil's *Rocky* album. This is Phil up against the ropes, determined to go at it one more time. He's facing the onslaught of this new, commercial hard rock and heavy metal thing that's going to explode. The industry is coming out of punk and he's aware of what punk did. He's also aware that Lizzy could be perceived as a kind of a dinosaur band, and he wants to fight against that. Phil always wants to be current. He was a guy who wasn't going to be satisfied being on the nostalgia circuit, right? So, this is him taking on heavy metal, but, fortunately for us, he's unable to shake the inherent classiness of what Thin Lizzy is.

Martin: What's interesting is that he's already made arguably two records while the NWOBHM was happening, and now we get a third when that scene is in its sunset years.

Sean: Yeah, and he's aware of it and he realises he needs some firepower in the band. Snowy White was an incredible guitar player, obviously classy and bluesy, but Snowy is not the heavy metal guy, right? And Snowy actually left of his own accord. With Sykes coming in, you've got this energizing factor. And when I go back and listen, I realise, man, Sykes was ahead of his time. He had this ability to take the classic Gary Moore-type vibe and modernise it and energise it—he had the fire. He's playing way on top of the beat too, so he's this guy dragging the other guys with them into this brave new heavy metal frontier. Plus, he looked like a rock 'n' roll god.

Steven Reid: What's amusing is that this was Thin Lizzy's second highest charting album in the UK, at No.4. I think *Black Rose* got higher. There were influences writ large on this album, and the band were willing to pursue them. It's a confused old time, isn't it? You think Thin Lizzy and there are many things that you think. You think twin guitar sound. Absolutely, there are two guitars here. You think Brian Downey. Brian Downey's here. But past that, this album, to me, has always been a bizarre conglomeration of John Sykes and Darren Wharton. I've got a lot of time for both, but in the annals of Thin Lizzy, it's suddenly the wrong people who are driving the bus here. And that has always sat really uncomfortably with me concerning this record.

But there are lots of people—and probably not necessarily on this side of the Atlantic, me being in Scotland—that think that this is Thin Lizzy's moment. This is when it all clicks. I would guess that's more to do with the Whitesnake *1987* or self-titled thing, the John Sykes thing, that he's the messiah that can do no wrong. I like him—I do—and I admire everything that he's done. I still think it's an odd thing in this band.

Since Robbo's left, Gary's come and gone—hi, bye, back again, see you later again. We've had Midge Ure for a minute, which is just the weirdest thing. Actually, I saw Midge Ure do a solo thing a couple of weeks ago. It was great. He was in Thin Lizzy?! Makes no sense. We had Dave Flett. Who? We had Snowy White. I like Snowy White. I quite like those albums, but I can understand why people don't. Scott Gorham is the linchpin in all of that, really. He's the guy that seems to, you would imagine, keep it all together.

So, we get to *Thunder and Lightning* and he suddenly appears to take a step back, or is pushed a step back. Because it's clear to me that somebody somewhere has decided that we are at last going to play to the times. Let's be the band that everybody else is trying to be. But then overtly introduce keyboards into the game, and it's a strange old album, this. And a lot people love it. A lot of people think it's the best Lizzy album. I really like it. Not convinced it's a Lizzy album. Never have and I probably never will. But there are some great moments here. Don't get me wrong.

Martin: What are your thoughts on the album cover?

Sean: It's definitely saying, we're gonna try really hard to show how heavy metal we are. But not really inherently understanding what heavy metal is. It's pretty on-the-nose.

David: Yeah, it's very much like those books you get, *The Idiot's Guide to*. It's almost like something you flip through. So how can we really sell ourselves as heavy metal? We'll have some lightning on the cover. We'll have a fist coming out of the ground, and make sure it's a leather-bound fist. And we'll have a guitar in the ground. But as we know, it's a Fender bass isn't it? It's Phil's Fender bass that is stuck in the ground. But the whole composition looks very flat. It doesn't look 3D. It doesn't look like a foreground and background kind of thing. It's very two-dimensional. It may as well be a painting. It's one of those where it probably sounds killer to describe it rather than see it.

Tim: It doesn't even look like a Thin Lizzy album cover. It looks like a full-on New Wave of British Heavy Metal album cover, but on a small label or indie-released.

Steven: Agreed. It's a garbage cover. Who on earth signed off on an album cover that's black and grey with flashes of brown? Who thought that was a good idea? And like Sean says, it's so on-the-nose. We've got a guitar and a lightning bolt. I presume that we've got heavy metal thunder here. I love Saxon. I'm not gonna have a go at Saxon. I think Saxon would have been a bit embarrassed to put this on.

But then over and above that you give it the most corporate office font that you possibly could. Just nothing happens here. Then you turn it over and you've got a live band. Oh, they're a great live band. Nobody's looking at the camera. And I know it's heads down and getting on with it and all that, but it just looks like a band that are so far away removed from the incredible live outfit that they were. And then you open it up—over here, ours was a gatefold—and the most interesting thing about the whole package is that Phil's got an apple in his hand. That's the most interesting thing about the whole package that I could find. Scott looks like Scott, although he looks pretty unwell, to be fair. And Darren Wharton... I love Darren. He just looks lost. There's nothing about any part of this that is compelling.

Martin: That's true. Also, the title of the album is lower case, and it doesn't even line up with the band name. They thought the front cover was so good, let's just repeat it on the back. Also, I remember getting this and seeing the front and it looked like they were paving a road or something and one of the workers got submerged in tar.

Steven: It's basically gravel. The perspective's not even right. The gravel is still quite big way at the back where the guitar seems to be miles away. As you say the title has been moved up. But it's been moved up to avoid the clouds. It's not even a design choice. Somebody's not going, what would be interesting. If you put it a little bit off from the horribly written band name. It was genuinely probably lower than that, and somebody went, "You do realise it's in the clouds, right?" And the bass, it's rendered in such a way that you can't actually tell what it is. Yeah, it's just really shoddy. This is school assignment stuff. It's an art project and you're told the album is called *Thunder and Lightning*—go and design me an album cover. You would come back with this when you were in middle school.

Martin: For the record, Saxon actually would be stupid enough to use this as an album cover.

Steven: You may have a point. I love Saxon and but I'm not going to argue that point.

Martin: It's not far off *Power & the Glory*. Okay, we open with the title track.

Steven: Yes, everything about the album screams cheese until you put it on, because "Thunder and Lightning" is not cheesy—it's muscular. It's bristling, it's full of energy, but it's a million miles removed from that melody-based band that we were talking about. This is bludgeoning now, as a statement of intent. We are bloody well a hard rock band. We're not mucking about anymore. Or maybe we're a heavy metal band now, or as close as this band will ever be.

But to be fair, it works for Phil. He is able to embody any number of different personas. This one is more overtly aggressive, and it does kind of fit him. I lament how good Brian Downey is at just pummelling the drums, because I feel as if it's a bit of a waste. He's great at it. It really works. You listen and still think, man, that guy can play. But where's the subtlety? Where's his groove? Where are those little fills? Where's everything that made him what you wanted him to be?

And then you throw into the mix, right up front we've got a guitar god in play. We are going to rip up the fretboard. Fans who had been along for the journey were really tipping the whiskey jar to see if there was anything left inside, or had it all been drunk? This is a completely different band, and by 1983 standards, this is heavy metal. What they traded away in subtlety and atmosphere, they have gained in aggression and impact. It does still work. This is a really good song.

Lyrically, Phil is uncompromising. We all know that Phil had a reputation for being a bit handy, shall we say. He could look after himself. But this is pure glorification of the rumble, isn't it? And 40 years later, it's not very PC. I'm not convinced that people would swallow this and go, "Oh, what a great song about fighting this is." But don't get me wrong; the lyric conveys the mood of the song. They fit together really well. But for such a subtle writer, we're in a different ballgame entirely, really (laughs).

Sean: That title track, man, I put this on every time I want to get pumped up for a gig. I'm throwing this tune on. To me, it was an opening song by design. It sounds like a song that you would write if you were planning on a song to open your set with. It's got all the big riffs, the rapid-fire drums—you don't even know what's happening. And it's a song about a fistfight at a high school dance. Really?! And the funny thing is that if you've ever been in a fight in high school, this is exactly what it sounds like. You're just throwing punches and it's over so fast. This song is a great summary of that.

But in his heart, Phil's a romantic. It's like he's picturing the scene at the movies or the guy's fighting for the girl, but at the same time there's this heavy metal bomb going off. There's a keyboard solo, there's a shredding solo, and then another shredding solo. And when I talk about Gorham being an adaptable guitar player, I love hearing Scott. I think Scott takes that first guitar solo on the song. Scott's not a heavy metal guitar player, but he's throwing punches, man. He's picking fast and he's bending. He's doing whatever he can to emulate the aggression of '80s metal with '70s chops. And I think he's really effective that way because he's so innately melodic and he always plays for the song. And then Sykes just bulldozes through everything. I don't think playing for the song was in his vocabulary at that point just yet. But that's exciting too, right?

Martin: It sure is. And what's your take on the overall production situation?

Sean: It's interesting. Like, all of a sudden, all that beautiful, dynamic stuff we used to hear from Brian Downey, that's gone, because there are so many gates and compressors on the drums to make it sound au courant with like, I don't know, Def Leppard or whatever, right? You miss the subtleties. So, it's less dynamic but more aggressive, is probably what they were going for. It's definitely the outlier production-wise in the Thin Lizzy catalogue, but I like it. What I like about it though, is that there's a rawness. If you listen to the way that the solos tail off, for example, usually in the mix they'd kind of caress the end of it and blend it in. These just kind of start and end outta nowhere, and you hear the fingers flying off the strings. So, in that sense I think it's very effective because it creates this kind of raucous energy. But it's also very harsh.

Martin: To keep it in 1983, it's their AC/DC – *Flick of the Switch*. Or worse, their Black Sabbath – *Born Again*.

Sean: Yeah, it's pretty rough. I think they were trying to energise it with guitars. The guitars are blaring and loud. Plus, Phil's voice is starting to show the wear and tear of the drugs, right? That's why I mentioned *Rocky*. He's up against the ropes and you can hear the weariness. But he's trying, man; he's trying to get it out. He's trying to rise to the occasion.

Steven: The production is of its time, to be fair. We're saying badly recorded, but the drums are the main issue for me. Not because they're bad, but because it doesn't suit the guy that's playing them. He's playing really well, but it could be anybody. His distinct character's gone missing. You don't listen to Brian Downey on *Fighting* or *Black Rose* and go, you know what? That could be anybody playing these songs. No, absolutely not. Who else is playing those fills?

Martin: He's known as a guy with a light touch and is usually compared to Ian Paice and Mick Tucker.

Steven: Yeah, and a guy that absolutely builds groove and is so fluid. He's sometimes on the beat, he's sometimes in front of the beat, he can drop behind, and he does that in the same song sometimes. That's difficult stuff to do without losing everybody else in the band. Here, he's a metronome. It doesn't get any more regimented than that. It's great, it fits the album—it could be anybody.

Martin: All right, thoughts on "This Is the One?"

David: There's this bizarre kind of religious undertone to the whole album, even with the hackneyed resurrection scene on the cover, which has its own connotations. But in "This Is the One" and "The Sun Goes Down" and "The Holy War," there's all sorts of religious connotations, and not particularly positive, but quite dark, with doubt of religion and questioning the goodness of religion and how can a good God let children die? I like *Chinatown* a lot, but I think Phil is more in tune with himself here both lyrically and vocally. "This Is the One" is classic Phil, but on the music side, it has such a different kind of guitar duel approach than you would get with the classic lineup.

Sean: "This Is the One" is a pretty good, modern heavy metal track for the day. Like David says, it's dark and obscure, and then Phil's phrasing is unusual. He's not moving like a singer would move necessarily. But the production actually is the most single-ish, I think, of all the songs on the record. Like, I wonder if they recorded this early on when everyone was fresh, because this one actually feels a little more polished.

Steven: One of my favourite things about this song is Brian Downey's kind of metronomic cowbell. It really gives the song a regimented feel. The beat is rock-solid, locked in place. And the rest of the performance is much less in-your-face. We've taken the foot off the gas a little bit. It's still a rougher and tougher outlook, and the bass line is ultra-compact, but he's no longer kind of roaming the hills to see where the bass will take us—it's about tightness.

But this is where, for me, Thin Lizzy take a strange turn. We now have two guitarists that are gonna go, "Well, I wanna go that way." "No, no, we're going this way." And Scott Gorham seems to be left behind. He's still trying to play tasteful lines. He's trying to say, "You know what? Let's retain some subtlety here; we're not going to shove it all in your face. We'll let you work this out on your own." And John Sykes says, "No, no, no, I'm gonna tell you all right now. I'm going to leave you no questions or answers." There's nothing about this where you're going to walk away from and go, huh? What did he mean there? He meant to smack me over the head with his guitar solo. That's what he meant to do. And man, can he do it! I can't criticise anything about what he does. But to suddenly listen to two guitarists kind of talking a different language within the one song, I have always found that interesting but unsatisfactory, in many ways.

But credit to Phil, the lyrics are a self-examination—and he doesn't like what he sees. So, with all of this going on, he is still able to open his heart. This is the life of a rock god kind of sitting comfortably, but he's struggling to conquer his demons, and maybe even thinking about—if you read the song—doing something else. It sounds very much like he has thought long and hard about, "Do I want to be doing this? Can I do this? Is this right?" And you could almost feel the pressure of that aura and image and that bravado that has built around him. "Someday thy kingdom come/I can feel it in my bones." Tragedy is around the corner, isn't it? He knows what lies ahead. That's the scary thing. He ain't kidding anyone, including himself at that point.

But I listen to that duelling call-and-response guitar solo, and maybe this is overstatement, but a little part of me dies at that point, because you do really sense that for the first time somebody else has kind of put their stamp on the band. Prior to this, yes, there were fallings-out and fights and comings and goings, but you were listening to a gang that were together. And yeah, maybe somebody left the gang and somebody had come and taken their place. But you listened to lineups that even had like Gary Moore and Mark Nauseef—they're still a gang, they're still together, they're still in the fight, there was still shared purpose. But you get to *Thunder and Lightning* and you don't always feel that everybody is in it for the band. There's a guy on this album that's kind of going, "I could arrive if I play this right."

Martin: All right, next is the album's only ballad, and what a smart and unusual form of ballad it is.

Sean: Yeah, it's chilling listening to "The Sun Goes Down" because I think this is Phil essentially seeing the end. And he's singing in a lower register; he's really in his baritone and it comes off dark and almost sludgy. There are moments of light and some beautiful chord play that happens in kind of the pre-chorus, but then that chorus is coming back to deliver the downer every time.

Martin: And Darren Wharton avails himself well. So many well-reasoned sound and technology choices—on this album as well as on *Renegade*.

Sean: Yeah, absolutely. He fit in great. He's credited a little better on this album too. In fact, he's in on the writing of four songs. I feel like he was a guy who came in and really wanted this. He was really happy to have a big gig like this and really tried to make it work with the guys. I know Gorham was essentially checked-out by this point. He just didn't want to be there. He wanted to get healthy.

Steven: There's a kind of opening bass thrum and these gentle electric guitar chords that open up this song, then a bit of a throwback to the classic Lizzy sound. Next, Darren Wharton's underpinning keyboards kind of ensure that there's no doubt we've moved on from those days. There's a real willingness to say, "Yeah guys, that was then; we don't do that now."

As I've said, I liked Darren and his band Dare—I have all their albums. It's interesting because none of what he's doing in Dare, he does here. I've always wondered what this album would sound like if he hadn't been there. He co-writes nearly half the album. Not all the time, but his presence is way too much to the forefront on songs like this. The textures and the layers bring a different angle versus almost anything else, even on this album, to be fair.

But it's still a cool, slow-paced track that never kind of overplays its hand compared to the level of bombast that is going on elsewhere. It's a clever change of pace. It's maybe too one-note to fill up six minutes. It's not the most interesting six minutes that the band have ever put out.

And it's more of a vehicle for Phil than it wants to be. "There is a demon among us/Whose soul belongs in hell." We're referring to his demons—yeah, absolutely—but I think we're referring to the demons that he's placing within the band, shall we say. We're going to be talking about heroin and the kind of casual but vice-like grip that it seems to slowly but surely bring on the people unfortunate enough to use it. And it has an evil charm about it, in that sense too. It's quite revealing the way he's written those lyrics. I'm beginning to sound like I don't like this album, but I do (laughs). But when you break it down, it's a strange beast of a song.

Martin: Then comes "The Holy War," and just like that we're back to pounding drums and torrents of power chords.

Sean: I absolutely adore this song. I think it's super-effective. I love that they're kind of bucking against their religious upbringing here, sort of exposing the hypocrisy of religion. Lyrically he hits it on the head. I'm surprised it's a sole credit for Phil, because it feels like a song written by a guitarist, or even a drummer. I think it's an incredible showcase for Sykes. It's a good attempt at modern heavy metal and stands up. It still sounds powerful and heavy to me. But the drums are pretty stiff, and Brian Downey is not a stiff drummer. And that slap of the snare is almost distracting. It's actually pretty noisy overall.

David: It's almost a sort of upbeat dance tempo that we get with this song, which is a pretty odd choice for a song about the problems with religion, and not organised religion but the actual concept of religion as a whole. But you wouldn't know that from listening to the music.

Thunder and Lightning

So it's a wonderful juxtaposition. You've got John Sykes doing a solo that sounds like it's taken straight from *Slide It In*.

Yeah, for an album that's fairly NWOBHM, it's quite spooky in places. There's some wonderful production from Chris where he puts in this ethereal spoken female vocal when Phil is saying those Biblical verses. And then Phil uses his voice in a very gruff fashion to portray what's almost a Satanic part, in fact at times even literally. It's a different type of album, almost conceptual. One can pontificate that it maybe even started as a concept album, because it's sort of halfway there. It's as if there's half a concept album that's been created, and then the rest of it doesn't tie in at all.

Steven: Those '80s drums—man oh man. Wow. I don't think Brian Downey ever laid in his bed and dreamt he would ever have these horribly dated, kind of gated drums. It's so not him. And yet what a memorable chorus. It's Phil questioning blind religious faith. That's a theme he likes to play with—and understandably given his background. It's the contradictions that need to be answered by those that can live within those doctrines and, in my humble opinion, don't often manage to answer.

I love how it's surprisingly measured. In effect, the vocal is mostly spoken. It's an unusual delivery from him. He's really kind of trying to make his mark with it. That said, the production kind of drags it down. There's an actual narrated part midway through, with "The devil is in hell with the demons/This is The Holy War." It's got that horrible kind of heavy metal Satanic nonsense voice-over that just doesn't belong in it at all. It's not what Phil was about. "They'll lead us to our temptation/Lead us, take our souls/There is no evil in salvation/There is evil in us all." There could be real gravitas behind that but there really isn't. It's delivered like a horror movie. Again, they're trying to add to the band a kind of heavy metal mystique that not everyone is on board with.

Martin: Over to side two of the original vinyl, and we kick off with "Cold Sweat," which Megadeth most ably covered.

Sean: Yes they did. This is an absolutely driving Thin Lizzy riff as far as I'm concerned. Once again, we have Phil getting completely inside a character. When he sings "I put my money in the suitcase" he's got my attention; I totally believe him. I think this was the last one where he's like, hey man, I can write a tune that stands up with any of you young guys. And he nails it. If this is a Rocky fight and Rocky is going down, he at least knocks the young guy down once in the fight. And here Phil's knocked the guy down a couple of times.

Martin: And "Cold Sweat" is yet another song where you get the sense that the character in it is gonna have to leave town fast.

Sean: Yeah, that's so funny. I guess that's it. What do they say? You can't run away from your problems, right? People move out, but your core problems stay with you. He was always running. Yeah, when he gets the lyric right, like "Stone-cold sober and stone-cold sweat/ Running down the back of my neck," I'm right there—I feel it.

Steven: So if side one open with a blast of heavy metal riff-ola, wow, then side two begins with something that feels like a kind of hybrid between Judas Priest and early Ozzy. It's hardly what you might have expected, but it's pretty filling nonetheless. It's really good. I mean, Sykes, it's his show, isn't it? They've upped the ante in terms of guitar worship. We're tapping here on the solo. It's almost like he's trying to drag the band all by himself into something else. But he's been hired to do the job, so who knows? Lizzy's more subtle side has been replaced with utter bludgeon.

But Phil's bass playing is right at home. It doesn't sound out of place at all and his vocals, considering the stage of career he's at, are as good as ever on this song, as though he knew inside, he could just let this more aggressive side out completely. There's great vocal dynamics and phrasing. He's not a shouter, he's not a screamer, he's not a heavy metal singer, and yet he still makes something that is heavy metal really work.

You can't help but wonder, had some of these songs got the exposure that 1987 Whitesnake got, how the band might have fared. Okay, we're in a slightly different era and a slightly different sound and a slightly different scene. But Lizzy could have been taken over the top by this song, never mind, that album. This could have been their "Still of the Night." It would have been a strange legacy to have left if this had been the direction they would have gone from this point. Still, it's quite easy to draw those parallels, four years apart as they are. Sykes is trying to do the same thing here that he did for Whitesnake, Had the right songs got the right exposure at the right time, and despite them looking dowdy as hell in the gatefold of this album, they're a good-looking bunch of guys. There's no reason why they couldn't be making flash videos with the sexy lyrics, if that's what they wanted to do. Not that I'm suggesting that that's what they wanted to do, but that potential suddenly is here with this song, but not capitalised on.

Martin: As you describe it, the contours of the two catalogues might have wound up quite similar as well. You've got the traditional '70s band from the UK, and then you've got the flash '80s band from America, provided they got a big shot American producer and moved to Hollywood!

Steven: And you even have that kind of small build-up from those first few albums, including the initial UK success. Whitesnake didn't find their sound until maybe albums three or four. Lizzy didn't find their sound until maybe albums four or five, realistically. Yes, their journeys could have been similar. But it wasn't seen through.

Martin: Next is "Someday She Is Going to Hit Back," which I always considered sort of elliptical, fusion even.

David: Sure, first of all, John Sykes brings a completely different aesthetic to the band, even from the just-departed Snowy White. Midge Ure filled in a little bit as well and Gary Moore obviously was there in the late '70s. But Sykes is nothing like any of those players. Everything that he would go on to add to Whitesnake's mentality and take them forward into a brave new world, he very much does here as well. So, it's almost like Thin Lizzy and John Sykes, in a strange way, rather than being John Sykes in Thin Lizzy. There are parts of this where I could picture exactly where the classic melodic twin guitar sound would be, but instead you get shredding and tapping. And it's very odd if you're not used to that, in that Thin Lizzy context. If you're someone who's only used to, say, the classic lineup of Thin Lizzy with Robbo still in the band, then hearing Sykes doing his thing on top might not be your cup of tea, if you prefer the more melodic *Jailbreak* and *Johnny the Fox*.

Steven: I kind of view this as Lizzy's Survivor movement. It's got that kind of pace and commercial shape about it. There are hooks galore, it's melodic, there's still those kind of frantic guitar lines in there and it's notable for having a keyboard solo and it's a good keyboard solo. But it kind of goes against the grain, doesn't it? It belongs in the song—I'm not going to say that it doesn't—but it goes against the ethos of the band. I think lyrically Phil is commenting on himself about how far he's pushed the ladies in his life without ever really setting out to do so, I would suggest. Right straight-up, it's taking a woman that's having enough of the abuse that's been meted out. But ultimately, it's the man that loses out here. He's left alone, wondering how it happened. Or knowing how it happened, really, but unable to fix it. And that's definitely Phil at the time, unfortunately, it would appear.

Martin: Darren, I believe, was proud of this one, for the contribution of the jazzy chord sequence.

Steven: I think that when they did it prior, it's creating a narrative, it's part of the story, it's adding a bit of contradiction, edge. It's making what could be seen as reasonably straightforward rock songs, and just giving them that little bit of something that catches your ear. That's why we still listen to the band's classic songs. I'm not convinced that that's really what's happening on "Someday She Is Going to Hit Back." It's maybe an attempt to modernise that. And if that's what Darren was looking at, then I take my hat off to him. There's a great legacy. To me, it doesn't come across like that, personally.

Martin: Next, "Baby Please Don't Go" is the song I've blathered about all over the place as having one of my top three guitar solos of all-time, when I'm not railing on about how it's stupid to laud any handful of solos among hundreds of thousands. Sean, you and I even talked about doing a book about the top guitar solos together and I decided I was unqualified—but you can still do it!

Sean: That's right (laughs), I played this solo. We did a Thin Lizzy tribute at Jeff Healy's one year and I did this one. So, I learned this solo note for note. It's interesting because it starts off with this incredible, descending, rapidly-picked thing. And then what's really cool about it is the chordal stuff that happens, where it's like these dyadic chordal things that create all this tension and drama. To me it's the best of everything Sykes brings to the table, fast playing, aggressive vibrato, aggressive pick attack. And taking it right to the edge of the fretboard for the very last note. I don't know how much of it was composed. It sounds like something that was composed rather than like somebody who just absolutely went for it. Usually, my favourite solos are ones where there's some kind of theme. But then there's also the element that this could fall off the tracks at anytime.

Martin: And an odd trivia note to tack on, when people—me included—talk about the greatest riff of all time, "Still of the Night" usually comes up and that is Sykes as well.

Sean: Absolutely, oh, yeah, because he went to Whitesnake just after this. I think he learned a lot from Phil, and then went into Whitesnake with editing capabilities that he probably didn't have in Tygers of Pan Tang. Then again, the beauty of that riff is how it's the lengthiest, least-edited riff of all time (laughs). But no, I think he really admired and respected Phil and learned from him and listened to him and was able to harness all of that incredible natural dexterity and technique and aggression and then utilise it in his next band too.

Martin: But Sykes is a bit like Mutt Lange too, where he became an almost unworkable version of a perfectionist. Sykes gets this reputation for being difficult, and his output famously dwindles away.

Sean: Yeah, and it's funny, with difficult people, it's usually because they're hyper-focused on something. Mike Fraser told me that Sykes walks around with a little travel-sized guitar with the action this high off the neck. And he's constantly playing it, because it's difficult to do. This is so he can play more aggressively on an electric guitar. So it's almost like, yeah, he's so focused on his goal to do this thing. Maybe he doesn't see the whole picture sometimes. And I think with Mutt, it got to the point where he didn't see the whole picture. Like, "Hey, we've got to finish this record" or "We're running out a tape." You're actually gonna damage the whole thing because you keep overdubbing and overdubbing and overdubbing. Hyper-focus.

But yeah, "Baby Please Don't Go" is another one that is close to a Thin Lizzy classic for me. It's got the classic harmony thing at the beginning and Downey's personality with this sort of dark aggressive shuffle in there. Plus, I like the desperation in Phil's voice—I feel like he's lived this one.

David: "Baby Please Don't Go" is one of my favourites on the album because it's very much a song where you can hear the old Thin Lizzy. It could be a very standard Thin Lizzy song and then somebody lets

John Sykes go completely bonkers on the guitar and he delivers one of his all-time great solos. It's almost like you can hear a blues song or a bluesy song in there somewhere and then John says, "Eh, I'm not really a blues guy" and turns it into metal overtop the band. It's almost like "Baby Please Don't Go" is his audition for Whitesnake in one track. It's Sykes being unreal.

Steven: Yes, I think that's fair comment. I think that a lot of the guitar solos on this album are an exercise in exercise (laughs). It's really about dexterity. It's about the guitar god thing. We're almost heading into the days of shred, and Sykes is kind of seeing what's happening and fitting into the scene, to be fair. Lots of bands in the early '80s were trying to do that. Kiss is another great example, where they lose a guitarist and they go, "Oh, we gotta catch up. We gotta go and get this guy that can burn the frets." And you could argue that all of these albums work because lots of these albums are loved over the rest of the catalogue by people of a certain age or a certain era or a certain time. I love *Lick it Up*, but that's a separate discussion.

But on this album, I just feel like an awful lot of the guitar solos that John is playing are for John. This song is different. This song, he's playing for the song. And that's the biggest difference; he's actually put a solo in there that really listens to what is going on. There are lots of disparate pieces in this song that feel welded together. But at the same time, that's because the chorus and the verse seem to be at odds with each other. But the guitar solo helps to meld things together. It's almost like the contradiction to the rest of the song, where the solo does the job that the song doesn't necessarily do. Whereas in a lot of the other songs, the song's try to do the job that the guitar solo won't join in on.

And it's interesting; it's not one of my favourite songs on the album, and yet same again, there are parts here that are gold, absolute gold. And yet I think this is Sykes' shining moment. I'm not necessarily sold on the whole thing. I feel that Phil's lost in time. We've modernised the sound and this is the one song where you listen to his vocals and you go, oh, you're singing on an album from three or four years ago here. That aggression and that bite that's mostly through the rest the album isn't there. Doesn't make it a bad vocal, but it comes across as slightly confused to me.

Martin: Yeah, funny thing, just like I've always called "Warriors" the meat-and-potatoes or lunch-bucket version of "Emerald," I've always framed "Baby Please Don't Go" as the milder cousin to "Someday She Is Going to Hit Back." In both cases, the former is just a little more sober and rock 'n' rollsy. And these two songs here, they are about the same tempo, and they are more both chordal than riffy.

Steven: Yeah, that's a good point. Really, there's a good balance between riff and chords throughout the Lizzy catalogue. In that sense, they're a band that can sound cohesive from song to song without following the same blueprint. There are lots of songs on lots of albums where it's all about the riff. But the next one is all about the chords; it's all about the melody. And that's an interesting kind of process because you just buy into it. And I suppose with *Thunder and Lightning*, I'm gonna be buying into it slightly less.

Martin: Next is "Bad Habits," which our bar band in '84, '85, Torque, actually trotted out live, thinking somehow that we could make it a crowd favourite (laughs).

David: I get that! I love "Bad Habits." That should have been the single because it's got more of a radio-friendly vibe than anything else on the record. It'd been a long time since they'd had a hit single.

Sean: Punky kind of vibe to this one, even a bit of a skiffle mentality. Okay, not really skiffle, but maybe cheery old-time rock 'n' roll, like The Rolling Stones or Lemmy doing a boogie song.

Steven: Lyrically, "I know it gets in your brain/Sometimes it dribbles and goes in your veins/I'll tell you this, the boy's insane/This boy's got bad habits." It's tough going, isn't it? When you sit and just read these lyrics at this point, we're not dressing it up in any way. And he's not being particularly clever. We're not worried about that side of things now. He's more telling it like it is at this point.

Martin: And yet it's the only happy-time music on the whole album.

Steven: I was just gonna say that I love the groove. And it's not a word that I would use about this album. Groove's gone; groove is yesterday, man. But there's loads of groove in this song. And it does kind of harken back to the mid-'70s, but without compromising with the new ethos. The interplay between Scott and John is maybe more natural here than it is elsewhere. But that's perhaps because it's a less guitar-centric song. A lot of the songs on this album kind of go, "Cue the guitar solo!" And we don't get that here. That's one of the beautiful things about Lizzy at their best. They can give you great guitar solos and memorable licks and great melody lines, and they don't kind of go, "Here's the solo." And this song does that for me. Having said that, it doesn't stand out on the album. I don't know. It kind of tears away a little bit at this point. It's a good song and it's got great elements, but I don't think it's essential Lizzy. And as for the jauntiness, maybe I don't connect with that side of the band, particularly. Calling it disingenuous is maybe overplaying it, but it feels a bit manufactured, and I struggle with it.

Martin: All right, last song on the album—and last song of the entire catalogue—is "Heart Attack." How crazy is that?

Sean: Well, Phil was confessional. He was telling us right from a pretty young age where he was going. It turned out to be a self-fulfilling prophecy with him, unfortunately. But prophetic lyrics aside, musically, this sounds like a closing track on a heavy metal record to me.

Steven: Here's the thing: I love melodic rock. I have sitting behind me lots and lots and lots of keyboard-heavy music. But I struggle with the intro to this song. Plus, the chorus feels at odds with the heavy feel of the rest of the album. I don't necessarily think there's a bad song here, but the album starts with a bang, and then side two explodes even louder. And then as we come to the end of the album, it feels like they've lost their way. The guitar solos are cool—Sykes is firing on all six once more. "Heart Attack" hurtles along with real intent, but it's bluster. There's lots of bluster here, as opposed to real focus and drive. The bass work is holding it all together. It's Phil's trademark—I'll keep it all in line. But it's not as expansive as it used to be.

And while Phil is holding it down, Brian hammers it all in place. You wouldn't have said that about his playing on any other album. He's not inclined to hammer anything. You've just hired somebody else with a hammer (laughs). It's a really messy configuration of the band, and that's maybe why it doesn't connect with me in the same way. Taken in isolation, I like *Thunder and Lightning*. But when you actually think of it as a Thin Lizzy album, I think we're compromising all along the way.

But yeah, lyrically, you see this side of Phil right the way through the catalogue, these prophetic songs. "Heart Attack" is so on the money, isn't it? Phil knows what's coming before we do. That's painful. You're heartbroken knowing that at this stage, it almost feels inevitable, although we've still got a little bit of time. He's almost breaking up with himself here. This is a guy singing about himself, but he's almost singing about somebody else at this point. He's laid himself so bare that he's almost become disconnected to the guy he's singing about.

David: I think one of the reasons why we fans don't all love "Heart Attack" is it's too raw. To go out on a song where Phil is literally singing, "Mama, I'm dying," it's very hard to listen to sometimes if you're in a more thoughtful mood about Phil, the person, rather than just Thin Lizzy, the band. It's a hard lesson. You think about the relationship with his mother, Philomena, because there's not many rock stars who have said as much about their mothers as Phil has. So, it's not just singing about a mother; he's singing about a mother that we all know quite well. It's quite a difficult lesson.

As a side note, in the UK, the album didn't end with "Heart Attack." There was a limited bonus EP that came with the original version, and they made it a gatefold. It's got Snowy on guitar, from the Hammersmith in November of '81, and the songs are "Emerald," "Killer on the Loose," "The Boys Are Back in Town" and "Hollywood."

Martin: Nice one. Yeah, here in Canada we didn't get that, or the gatefold. All right, we're at the very end of our tale. Any final things that need to be said?

Steven: Hindsight is a great thing. We know what's going to come. This is not the album that I feel conveys that message. And that's the thing for me. There's so much melancholy throughout the Thin Lizzy catalogue. That's a word I've used a lot and I keep coming back to it. There is no melancholy on *Thunder and Lightning*, musically speaking. Nothing at all, They don't really, ever on this album, leave anything up to the listener. Nothing's behind the curtain. There's no magic and mystique; there's no mystery. This is what we're doing and we're doing it now! And that's what this album does.

But then you'll pay attention to most—not all—of the lyrics and Phil's telling a different story. I'm a great believer that not all sad songs have to be sad. I do like an upbeat song that's got a really touching lyric that when you read it, you think, wow, that's a different message entirely. But here, it's almost like words not connecting. The words don't really connect with the music in any way. I don't think that you can be as honest and as tired as much of this album sounds lyrically, whilst having a previously subtle drummer hammering everything home. It's a strange old place.

And yeah, I will go on record and say that I happily listen to this album and I do enjoy it. The first song on each side of this album—I've still got a nice old vinyl version of it here—yeah, great songs. I don't necessarily know that this makes a great album, for me. But I'm all too aware that there's an element of the Thin Lizzy fan base that would disagree with that to the utmost degree. This is Lizzy for them. And although I respect that, I strongly disagree.

David: Well, zooming forward, long after Phil's death in 1986, it's quite odd that John Sykes would be the one to attempt to instigate a revival of Thin Lizzy as a live band in the 2000s. In fact Sykes would be the most continual member despite the fact he comes in for a cup of tea at the end of the original run, pretty much. He's not really anything to do with it. In effect, the most work that John Sykes has done in the last 20 years is a revival of Thin Lizzy, which is quite bizarre to see. But as a direct post-mortem, the *Thunder and Lightning* album did very well. It was their best-selling album in quite a while in the UK. They'd pretty much written America off at this point. They'd just tried too many times and hadn't gone anywhere. Ironically John Sykes proved he could indeed make it in America.

Sean: I'll just add that in a general sense, *Thunder and Lightning* is not really heralded for great twin leads, really. And that might be because Phil only had one half of the equation firing on all cylinders. Scott brought what he could to the table but he was already checked-out. I think he wanted out of the whole situation. The album was more about heavy metal riffing and showcasing Sykes as an energiser that could compete.

Martin: I do love that story about how they talked about having Mutt Lange produce the album.

Sean: But Mutt tears songs apart looking for the hooks. It would have been interesting to see if Phil and Scott could have handled the discipline that goes along with that. Phil's a pretty headstrong guy. Like, I've talked to the Def Leppard guys and they have all said that they're basically vehicles for Mutt in a lot of ways. Like, Mutt's strength is that he sees the individual abilities of each person. But you've got to buy into the Mutt Lange concept. It's like, I'm going to push you because I trust in your ability. But you need to listen to me.

I remember reading an interview with Joe Elliott, where he talked about running into Phil at this time in a bar. Phil was sounding all defeated and going, "I can't compete with you" and Joe said, "Snap out of it, man. You're my hero. Like, don't do this." He was really disappointed that Phil was so down on himself. But it's tough. They were so close to really breaking in the States. That's something he wanted so desperately. Unfortunately there's a finite amount of time to achieve that in a rock performer's life before you're considered over the hill. I feel like in the end, Phil agreed with this all too well—he was too smart about music not to—and it's got to be a contributing factor in what ultimately killed him.

Honesty Is No Excuse: Thin Lizzy on Record

Contributor Biographies

John Alapick
John "The Music Nut" Alapick is an avid music fan and concert attendee who discusses music on several channels on YouTube. He resides in Monroe Township, Pennsylvania.

Brian Balich
Brian "Butch" Balich is a heavy metal vocalist from Pittsburgh, Pennsylvania. He's been singing in bands since he was 17, including Argus, Arduini/Balich, Penance, Molasses Barge and Kulvera. One of his fondest memories is spending an afternoon at the home of Philomena Lynott while on tour in Ireland in 2012. Never one to shy away from opining on all things music-related, Butch joined and has contributed to *The Contrarians* on YouTube. Lord help us all if he ever follows through with his threat of creating his own show in addition. Brian is a husband and proud father of four. He resides just outside of Pittsburgh with his beautiful, patient wife Erin, surrounded by dogs, cats and towering stacks of vinyl and CDs.

Andee Blacksugar
Andee is a Brooklyn-based musician, leader of "highly destructive electro-rock" initiative Black Sugar Transmission and guitarist for industrial rock kingpins KMFDM, with whom he has recorded four full-length albums. In 2021 he joined the ranks of Blondie, touring the US and UK together and contributing guitar and vocals to the NYC legends' most recent album sessions. He has also performed and collaborated with a diverse array of artists including Peter Murphy (Bauhaus), Vernon Reid (Living Colour), Jason Bieler (Saigon Kick) and members of King's X. Andee also possesses an English degree, wrote album reviews for Allmusic.com in the early 2000s and is a card-carrying Cure fanatic who has seen the band live six times and possesses an enviable collection of the band's recorded music, from proper releases to bootlegs, B-sides, rare videos and books.

Rich Davenport
Rich Davenport is a writer, musician and stand-up comedian from Bolton in the North West of England. He's written features and reviews for *Classic Rock*, *Record Collector* and *Rock Candy*, and sleeve notes for classic albums by Rory Gallagher and The Ruts. Rich also hosted a long-running radio show on *Total Rock*. As a musician, he's played with Atomkraft, Radio Stars, Martin Gordon (ex-Sparks), has fronted metal bands See Red and Black Sheets of Rain, and is currently playing with punk band Vicious Bishop and former Radio Stars/John's Children vocalist Andy Ellison. See richdavenport.com for more.

Tim Durling
Tim has worked in radio in various capacities, from on-air to commercial writing since 1993. His DJ career started back far enough to include spinning a few "gold" songs on actual 45s, then CDs, all the way up to digital, and he's played many a Thin Lizzy ditty. Tim is also the namesake of *Tim's Vinyl Confessions* on YouTube. Since 2014, he's talked passionately about the music he loves and collects. Speaking of collecting, Tim also has a peculiar habit of seeking out rare 8-track tapes from the later '80s, so much so that he wrote a book called *Unspooled: An Adventure in 8-Tracks*, on the subject. He's also been known to poke his head in on the author's *The Contrarians* YouTube channel from time to time.

John Gaffney
John Gaffney is a musician from Tampa, Florida. His past endeavours include the metal bands Sinister Realm and Majesty in Ruin. Currently he records dark electronic music with his project Chamber of Sorrows, who can be heard at chamberofsorrows.Bandcamp.com. John also has a YouTube channel called *Lair of the Alchemist* that discusses all things heavy metal and hard rock. Come see him over at YouTube.com/Lairofthealchemist.

David Gallagher
David was, like most musos, bitten at a young age and made a nuisance of himself long enough to work in a record store in Scotland through the 2000s. While he always maintained the passion, overly sharing his (sometimes) informed opinions via his YouTube channel *@flicksnpicks*, the pandemic gave him licence to unleash his almost impossibly lo-fi channel onto others.

Peter Jones
Peter has been in love with music his entire life. After starting on piano, Peter began drumming at age nine. Thanks to his two older sisters, he discovered popular music well before his time and spent hours and hours raiding their LP collections. He obtained his BA in music performance while drumming for the world class Millikin University Jazz Band where he toured the Bahamas, Aruba and recorded four albums. Peter has been in rock bands since the mid '70s. He has played in tribute bands to Queen, Cheap Trick, Deep Purple and AC/DC. He also has played with symphony orchestras, dinner theatre shows and local plays and musicals. Peter was also an audio buyer for Laserland back in the late '80s. A lover of all music, Peter's favourite rock bands are Deep Purple, Rush and Kiss.

Sean Kelly
Sean Kelly is a Canadian guitarist, educator, and author who has performed with Nelly Furtado, Lee Aaron, Coney Hatch, Alan Frew, Helix, Gilby Clarke, Honeymoon Suite, and Crash Kelly. He is the author of two books, *Metal on Ice: Tales from Canada's Hard Rock and Heavy Metal Heroes* (Dundurn Press) and *Don't Call It Hair Metal: Art in the Excess of '80s Rock* (ECW Press). In 2015 he performed in Twisted Sister frontman Dee Snider's *Rock N Roll Christmas Tale*, and is currently playing guitar in the Toronto production of the hit Broadway musical *Rock of Ages*. Sean is a Music Teacher with the Toronto Catholic District School Board.

Peter Kerr
Peter is a lifelong rock/pop music tragic case. Between trawling record stores in Sydney, Australia for that obscure album pressing or propping up the bar at various pubs and clubs in quest of the next killer live act, he runs the *Rock Daydream Nation* YouTube channel.

Reed Little
Reed began his love affair with music when he discovered Kiss in 1976. In the 1980s, MTV exposed him to new favourites such as David Bowie, The Cure and Iron Maiden. He took up playing guitar in the 1990s. Reed retired from a completely improbable career in law enforcement and is currently a part-time professor, a keen amateur luthier and the singer and guitar player in a cover band called Old Man Jam.

Steven Reid
Steven has been a staff writer with the *Sea of Tranquility* website for over a decade. His impenetrable Scottish twang can now be barely understood as a co-host on the site's *UK Connection* YouTube show and as a regular on *In the Prog Seat* and numerous other music discussion panels. Previously Steven spent over a decade as a writer for the *Fireworks* rock and metal UK print magazine and *Rocktopia* website, with the last four years of that tenure being as Assistant Editor. Steven has also contributed liner notes for albums by Robin George and numerous Eonian Records releases.

Honesty Is No Excuse: Thin Lizzy on Record

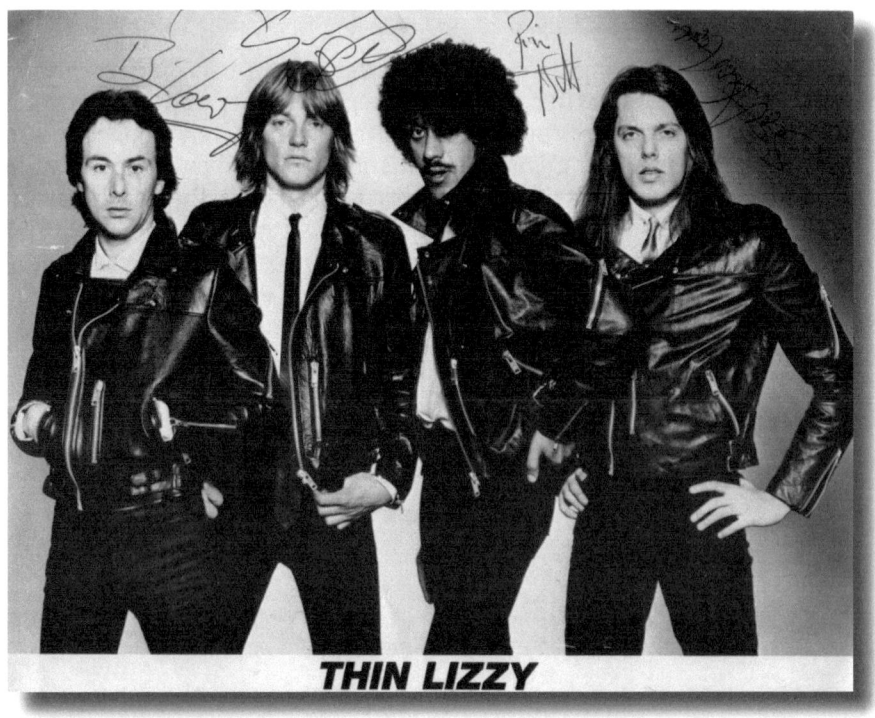

Special Thanks

A hearty appreciation goes out to Agustin Garcia de Paredes who applied his eagle eye to a copy edit of this book. Agustin is also one of the admins of the *History in Five Songs with Martin Popoff* podcast Facebook page plus a mean bass player, thumping the fat strings and providing backup vocals for his longtime band, Sinshine.

About the Author

At approximately 7900 (with over 7000 appearing in his books), Martin has unofficially written more record reviews than anybody in the history of music-writing across all genres. Additionally, Martin has penned approximately 120 books on hard rock, heavy metal, classic rock, prog, punk and record collecting. He was Editor-in-Chief of the now retired *Brave Words & Bloody Knuckles*, Canada's foremost heavy metal publication for 14 years, and has also contributed to *Revolver*, *Guitar World*, *Goldmine*, *Record Collector*, bravewords.com, lollipop.com and hardradio.com, with many record label band bios and liner notes to his credit as well.

Additionally, Martin has been a regular contractor to Banger Films, having worked for two years as researcher on the award-winning documentary *Rush: Beyond the Lighted Stage*, on the writing and research team for the 11-episode *Metal Evolution* and on the ten-episode *Rock Icons*, both for VH1 Classic. Additionally, Martin is the writer of the original metal genre chart used in *Metal: A Headbanger's Journey* and throughout the *Metal Evolution* episodes.

Then there's his audio podcast, *History in Five Songs with Martin Popoff* and the YouTube channel he runs with Marco D'Auria and Grant Arthur, *The Contrarians*. The community of guest analysts seen on *The Contrarians* has provided the pool of speakers used across the pages of this very book. Martin currently resides in Toronto and can be reached through martinp@inforamp.net or martinpopoff.com.

A Complete Martin Popoff Bibliography

2024: Honesty Is No Excuse: Thin Lizzy on Record, Pictures at Eleven: Robert Plant Album by Album, Perfect Water: The Rebel Imaginos

2023: Kiss at 50, Dominance and Submission: The Blue Öyster Cult Canon, The Who and Quadrophenia, Wild Mood Swings: Disintegrating The Cure Album by Album, AC/DC at 50

2022: Pink Floyd and The Dark Side of the Moon: 50 Years, Killing the Dragon: Dio in the '90s and 2000s, Feed My Frankenstein: Alice Cooper, the Solo Years, Easy Action: The Original Alice Cooper Band, Lively Arts: The Damned Deconstructed, Yes: A Visual Biography II: 1982 – 2022, Bowie @ 75, Dream Evil: Dio in the '80s, Judas Priest: A Visual Biography, UFO: A Visual Biography

2021: Hawkwind: A Visual Biography, Loud 'n' Proud: Fifty Years of Nazareth, Yes: A Visual Biography, Uriah Heep: A Visual Biography, Driven: Rush in the '90s and "In the End," Flaming Telepaths: Imaginos Expanded and Specified, Rebel Rouser: A Sweet User Manual

2020: The Fortune: On the Rocks with Angel, Van Halen: A Visual Biography, Limelight: Rush in the '80s, Thin Lizzy: A Visual Biography, Empire of the Clouds: Iron Maiden in the 2000s, Blue Öyster Cult: A Visual Biography, Anthem: Rush in the '70s, Denim and Leather: Saxon's First Ten Years, Black Funeral: Into the Coven with Mercyful Fate

2019: Satisfaction: 10 Albums That Changed My Life, Holy Smoke: Iron Maiden in the '90s, Sensitive to Light: The Rainbow Story, Where Eagles Dare: Iron Maiden in the '80s, Aces High: The Top 250 Heavy Metal Songs of the '80s, Judas Priest: Turbo 'til Now, Born Again! Black Sabbath in the Eighties and Nineties

2018: Riff Raff: The Top 250 Heavy Metal Songs of the '70s, Lettin' Go: UFO in the '80s and '90s, Queen: Album by Album, Unchained: A Van Halen User Manual, Iron Maiden: Album by Album, Sabotage! Black Sabbath in the Seventies, Welcome to My Nightmare: 50 Years of Alice Cooper, Judas Priest: Decade of Domination, Popoff Archive – 6: American Power Metal, Popoff Archive – 5: European Power Metal, The Clash: All the Albums, All the Songs

2017: Led Zeppelin: All the Albums, All the Songs, AC/DC: Album by Album, Lights Out: Surviving the '70s with UFO, Tornado of Souls: Thrash's Titanic Clash, Caught in a Mosh: The Golden Era of Thrash, Rush: Album by Album, Beer Drinkers and Hell Raisers: The Rise of Motörhead, Metal Collector: Gathered Tales from Headbangers, Hit the Lights: The Birth of Thrash, Popoff Archive – 4: Classic Rock, Popoff Archive – 3: Hair Metal

2016: Popoff Archive – 2: Progressive Rock, Popoff Archive – 1: Doom Metal, Rock the Nation: Montrose, Gamma and Ronnie Redefined, Punk Tees: The Punk Revolution in 125 T-Shirts, Metal Heart: Aiming High with Accept, Ramones at 40, Time and a Word: The Yes Story

2015: Kickstart My Heart: A Mötley Crüe Day-by-Day, This Means War: The Sunset Years of the NWOBHM, Wheels of Steel: The Explosive Early Years of the NWOBHM, Swords and Tequila: Riot's Classic First Decade, Who Invented Heavy Metal?, Sail Away: Whitesnake's Fantastic Voyage

2014: Live Magnetic Air: The Unlikely Saga of the Superlative Max Webster, Steal Away the Night: An Ozzy Osbourne Day-by-Day, The Big Book of Hair Metal, Sweating Bullets: The Deth and Rebirth of Megadeth, Smokin' Valves: A Headbanger's Guide to 900 NWOBHM Records

2013: The Art of Metal (co-edit with Malcolm Dome), 2 Minutes to Midnight: An Iron Maiden Day-by-Day, Metallica: The Complete Illustrated History, Rush: The Illustrated History, Ye Olde Metal: 1979, Scorpions: Top of the Bill - updated and reissued as Wind of Change: The Scorpions Story in 2016

2012: Epic Ted Nugent, Fade To Black: Hard Rock Cover Art of the Vinyl Age, It's Getting Dangerous: Thin Lizzy 81-12, We Will Be Strong: Thin Lizzy 76-81, Fighting My Way Back: Thin Lizzy 69-76, The Deep Purple Royal Family: Chain of Events '80 – '11, The Deep Purple Royal Family: Chain of Events Through '79 - reissued as The Deep Purple Family Year by Year books

2011: Black Sabbath FAQ, The Collector's Guide to Heavy Metal: Volume 4: The '00s (co-authored with David Perri)

2010: Goldmine Standard Catalog of American Records 1948 – 1991, 7th Edition

2009: Goldmine Record Album Price Guide, 6th Edition, Goldmine 45 RPM Price Guide, 7th Edition, A Castle Full of Rascals: Deep Purple '83 – '09, Worlds Away: Voivod and the Art of Michel Langevin, Ye Olde Metal: 1978

2008: Gettin' Tighter: Deep Purple '68 – '76, All Access: The Art of the Backstage Pass, Ye Olde Metal: 1977, Ye Olde Metal: 1976

2007: Judas Priest: Heavy Metal Painkillers, Ye Olde Metal: 1973 to 1975, The Collector's Guide to Heavy Metal: Volume 3: The Nineties, Ye Olde Metal: 1968 to 1972

2006: Run for Cover: The Art of Derek Riggs, Black Sabbath: Doom Let Loose, Dio: Light Beyond the Black

2005: The Collector's Guide to Heavy Metal: Volume 2: The Eighties, Rainbow: English Castle Magic, UFO: Shoot Out the Lights, The New Wave of British Heavy Metal Singles

2004: Blue Öyster Cult: Secrets Revealed! (updated and reissued in 2009 with the same title; updated and reissued as Agents of Fortune: The Blue Öyster Cult Story in 2016), Contents Under Pressure: 30 Years of Rush at Home & Away, The Top 500 Heavy Metal Albums of All Time

2003: The Collector's Guide to Heavy Metal: Volume 1: The Seventies, The Top 500 Heavy Metal Songs of All Time

2001: Southern Rock Review

2000: Heavy Metal: 20th Century Rock and Roll, The Goldmine Price Guide to Heavy Metal Records

1997: The Collector's Guide to Heavy Metal

1993: Riff Kills Man! 25 Years of Recorded Hard Rock & Heavy Metal

See martinpopoff.com for complete details and ordering information.